I AM LOVE

Yoga, Ayahuasca, A Course in Miracles & the Read Less Traveled Back to the Place We Never Left

Love, which created me, is what I am

* Artwork Courtesy of Maria Light

I Am Love

(& Here Only to Be Truly Helpful)

Because

Nothing Happened...

How Yoga, Ayahuasca & *A Course in Miracles*

Can Help Save Time On Your Journey Home

To the NoWhere We Never Truly Left

Dedication

AHOY THERE!

To You Who
I AM

This book is dedicated to anyone who ever truly wondered
who, or what, they truly are.

And so,
it is dedicated to all of us.

But moreso, to you who are now reading this,
for if you are, it is most likely because you are now truly
seeking the answer.

And also the answer to the related questions:

What Am I…
afraid of?
&
Who Am I…
to judge?

I AM HERE ONLY TO BE TRULY HELPFUL

This Is An Offering of Love from Love to Love,
And as such…

I am here only to be truly helpful.

I am here to represent the One who sent me.

*I do not have to worry about what to say or what to do,
Because the One Who sent me will direct me.*

*I am content to be wherever Spirit wishes,
Knowing Spirit goes there with me.*

I will be healed as I let Spirit teach me to heal.

~ A Course in Miracles[1]

---

1 From Chapter 2 of the Text, with slight edit by author.

*

My intention is for this present book offering to only be "truly helpful," bringing only peace and clarity to all those who read it – and maybe a little humor, too.

Thank you so much for listening – with & to your heart!

This is also dedicated to my blessed wife & baby,
Beata & Sonny, *dakujem!*

Namasté _/_ The One Spirit that is who I truly am knows & honors you as Itself for what we are: One Love.

Acknowledgments

There are so many who have helped in the process of writing this book, and here I will just mention a few names, with the acknowledgment that all errors in writing or judgment herein are my own.

First, I want to express gratitude to Ram Dass and Ken Wapnick (and the Hanuman Foundation and the Foundation for Inner Peace), who I consider to be two of my primary teachers and guiding lights for this book. I dedicated my first book to Ram Dass and Maharajji (Neem Karoli Baba – pictured below), and I see this book as a sequel to that first one.

I also want to greatly appreciate and thank Alexander George Ward again for his brilliant cover art, as well as allowing me to use some of his artwork in the book.

Finally, thank you to all who offered their help to get the book to this point, and thank you in advance for your feedback on the finished product. May this book be of some true help to you on your journey.

Table of Contents

Preluminaries 1

Nothing Real Can Be Threatened 30

Divining a De-Vine Mystery 157

Maya, Madhava & Moksha 268

Synthesis 360

Recommended Resources 415

Appendices 424

Love is the Strongest Medicine

Preluminaries

Preluminaries

Once upon a time... | Nothing Happened.

THE | END

The Beginning…
(…of the end of the beginning of the end of…)

Introduction: *Nothing Happened*

"Who in the world am I? Ah, that's the great puzzle."

~ Lewis Carroll

"The instant the idea of separation entered the mind of God's Son, in that same instant was God's Answer given. In time this happened very long ago. In reality it never happened at all."

~ A Course in Miracles[2]

The early working title of this book was "*Nothing Happened*," a title which I, at least, thought was pretty cool. "Nothing Happened" is a way of re-stating the "Atonement principle" of *A Course in Miracles*. The late pre-eminent teacher of ACIM, Ken Wapnick, used the phrase quite often in this regard. Ken coined it as a simple way of re-stating the idea that even though it seems as if we have entered a world of separation where the "unholy trinity of sin, guilt and fear" reign supreme, this is all just a dream we seemed to dream one afternoon long ago, and nothing ever *really* happened. We are all just dreaming of exile while still safely at home in God, the One Reality that can perhaps best be expressed simply as "Love." The acceptance of this idea is the "Atonement."

I liked the title, too, because in Ram Dass' story (presented below) about giving his guru a high dose of LSD, he also used this same phrase "nothing happened" to say that his guru did not appear to be affected whatsoever by the LSD (and come to think of it, Ken might have borrowed the phrase from Ram Dass :).

But then I got to thinking that not too many people would be interested in picking up a book called "Nothing Happened," and that more might be led to crack open a book called "I Am Love" – at least to

---

2   *A Course in Miracles*, Manual for Teachers, Section II.

look at all the colorful pictures! Others concurred with this brilliant line of thinking, which is why I ultimately changed the title. But because the idea that "nothing happened" is so precisely to the point of what is to be shared here, I will be harping on it quite a bit throughout.

One more thing: I like the title "I Am Love" because it's a very powerful answer to the title of my first book, "Who Am I?" But actually, that question pre-supposes that we are a "who," a person. A less presumptuous way of phrasing it, and one more in line with things as we will see, would have been "*What* Am I?"

Another very apropos title for this sequel might also be:
"*Who Am I…to Judge?*"

For to get at who I am, it appears that I must first let go of all my judgment, or at least be open to that possibility.

So let's together be open to that, and come to all of this with an open mind – not so open that your brain falls out, mind you. But if it does, you can just pick it right back up, wash it off, and put it right back in. And your brain will be washed!

Btw, here is how A Course in Miracles answers the "Who/What Am I?" question…

WHAT AM I?

*I am God's Son,
complete and healed and whole,
shining in the reflection of His Love.
In me is His creation sanctified
and guaranteed eternal life.
In me is love perfected,
fear impossible,
and joy established without opposite.
I am the holy home of God Himself.
I am the Heaven where His Love resides.
I am His holy Sinlessness Itself,
for in my purity abides His own.*

PRELUMINARIES

Okay, that was intense,
let's see if we can't rephrase that in a way
we mere seeming mortals can fathom...

So if God is truly One
& God is Love,
& I am not separate from God
(For in Perfect Love there can be no separation, no fear, no
duality/twoness, only Oneness)
then what I truly am
must also be Love, must also be One,
must just also be GodSelf...

& words are really only just words,
merely symbols,
but most of us still relate well to the
word "Love"
so let's just say that

I Am Love
&
both the "I" and the "Love"
include all of us!

(and the rest is commentary, *go and learn...*)

I Am Love

God is but Love
and therefore so am I

This is one of the most repeated phrases in the entire Course.
It is a reminder that our essence is one of innocence,
of perfect Love, and it is only that.
The "i" is the window to the soul.

Quotes to Read to Get *Read-y*
Notes on *"Nothing Happened"*

In 1967 when I first came to India, I brought with me a supply of LSD, hoping to find someone who might understand more about these substances than we did in the West.

When I had met Maharajji (Neem Karoli Baba), after some days the thought had crossed my mind that he would be a perfect person to ask. The next day after having that thought, I was called to him and he asked me immediately, "Do you have a question?"

Of course, being before him was such a powerful experience that I had completely forgotten the question I had had in my mind the night before. So I looked stupid and said, "No, Maharajji, I have no question." He appeared irritated and said, "Where is the medicine?"

I was confused but Bhagavan Dass suggested, " Maybe he means the LSD." I asked and Maharajji nodded. The bottle of LSD was in the car and I was sent to fetch it. When I returned I emptied the vial of pills into my hand. In addition to the LSD there were a number of other pills for this and that–diarrhea, fever, a sleeping pill, and so forth. He asked about each of these.

He asked if they gave powers. I didn't understand at the time and thought that by "powers" perhaps he meant physical strength. I said, "No." Later, of course, I came to understand that the word he had used, "siddhis," means psychic powers. Then he held out his hand for the LSD. I put one pill on his palm. Each of these pills was about three hundred micrograms of very pure LSD–a solid dose for an adult. He beckoned for more, so I put a second pill in his hand–six hundred micrograms. Again he beckoned and I added yet another, making the total dosage nine hundred micrograms–certainly not a dose for beginners. Then he threw all the pills into his mouth. My reaction was one of shock mixed with fascination of a social scientist eager to see what would happen.

He allowed me to stay for an hour–and **nothing happened.** Nothing whatsoever. He just laughed at me.

~ Ram Dass

"The reason Jesus was perfectly at peace and had absolutely no pain on the cross was that he knew he was not there. He knew he was not his body. Since he is part of the mind of the Sonship, he was aware of the dream. But he also knew he was part of God, and so he knew that this was only a dream and nothing was happening. Therefore for him, literally, **nothing happened**. A great deal seemed to happen in the eyes of the world, but nothing happening to him, because he knew he was not here."

~ Ken Wapnick

slok- ārdhena pravakshyāmi yad-uktam granthakotibhih |
brahma satyam jagan-mithyā jivo brahmaiva nāparah ||
'In half of a *sloka*I state what has been stated by millions of texts…

Brahman alone is real,
the world is mithyā
(not independently existent),
and the individual self
is nondifferent from Brahman.

~ Sri Adi Shankarcharya

"You have not yet gone back far enough, and that is why you become so fearful. As you approach the Beginning, you feel the fear of the destruction of your thought system upon you as if it were the fear of death. There is no death, but there is **a belief in death.** *"*

~ A Course in Miracles[3]

"This entire world is part of our imagination. It has no basis in reality. Keep in mind that when we mad the original judgment, we thought it was anything but a toy. We thought it was very, very serious. This was a judgment that said we turned against

---

3   ACIM T.3.VII.5:9,10,11.

God and stole from Him, that we destroyed God, Christ, and the unity of Heaven. That hardly seems like a toy! We are saying that our mind is extremely powerful. Look what it accomplished: the impossible. That is the original judgment, and it is expressed over and over again in everything that goes on in the world, without exception. Everything seems so heavy, so important, so real, so valuable, so vicious and destructive, and wonderful, etc. An all of it comes from the original judgment that I did a terrible thing to God. The other side is: "But isn't it wonderful? I now have my own individuality; I'm unique and self-important." And, of course, I stole all that from God, which means the underside of that sense of wonderment and joy is the terror. But the truth is that it is all a toy. Nothing happened. I only thought I stole from God. I only *thought* I destroyed Him. I only thought I destroyed Jesus on the cross.
Nothing happened.
The whole thing was made up.

~ Ken Wapnick

"Ramana Maharshi, Nisargadatta Maharaj and Nisargadatta's co-disciple, Ranjit Maharaj were all Indian teachers of Advaita Vedanta who were considered to be fully- realised beings. My partner once asked Ranjit Maharaj a question about *A Course in Miracles* ' teaching that God did not create the phenomenal universe and that ultimately it never happened at all. Ranjit responded that the Course's position was correct. I include this to show that this lineage's teaching, at the highest level, seems to correspond (in content at least) with the pure non-dualistic position of the Course."

"As the light comes nearer you will rush to darkness, shrinking from the truth, sometimes retreating to the lesser forms of fear, and sometimes to stark terror."

~ A Course in Miracles[4]

"I tried to think but nothing happened."

~ Curly Howard

"You may say I'm a dreamer, but I'm not the only one…"

~ John Lennon

---

[4] ACIM T.18.III.2:1.

Preliminaries

> Not one note in Heaven's song
> was missed...
> Love has forgotten no one.

**This is the Course's way of saying "*nothing happened*" –
Love is eternal and is our essential nature.
This has never changed.**

SNEAK PREVIEW
(Spoiler Alert: Excerpt from an Ayahuasca Journey Report)

A Momentary Glimpse Beyond the Veil

"Together we will disappear into the Presence beyond the veil, not to be lost but found; not to be seen but known."

~ A Course in Miracles[5]

There was a moment in the experience where suddenly it felt like all barriers to reality fell away and I was just sitting calmly observing the naked truth. It was like nothing had actually changed except that a fine film or veil that was obscuring the simple truth of existence had finally, at last, been lifted. And that last thin barrier was merely composed of all the last lingering fears in my consciousness that were obscuring this simple, unadorned truth of Being.

The Course says about enlightenment that it is "…but a recognition, not a change at all."[6] This made perfect sense now.

And so did all of the Course. It had all led up to this point. The Course was just what I needed on my journey to give me that last push over the edge, and the faith that the push would not end in death, but Life. And what was coming through was this: We are all so afraid to let go of our judgment, because we are afraid of losing our personal identity, which is intricately involved with our judgment. And with that judgment is our sense of personal specialness. Without our judgment and sense of specialness, the world that we think is so real, including our individual identity, would just dissolve and we would see what **is**, in fact, truly real.

---

5   T-19.IV-D.19:1.
6   ACIM Workbook Lesson 188.

Preluminaries

As Blake famously said: *"If the doors of perception were cleansed, things would appear as they truly are: Infinite."*

And this is what I saw. Suddenly, I was "above the battlefield," as the Course puts it, just calmly observing everything in me and as me (and I as It), without the filter of thought and judgment. A little later, yes, I slipped back out of that and, while still in that place of observation, I could feel something like a solid iceberg of fear and judgment mounting...

> The most important part of the pose is the purpose --
> What is it for?

The question being posed: What purpose is it serving?

Introduction

What Is It *For?*

(or: Oh, What's the Use?)

"In any situation in which you are uncertain, the first thing to consider, very simply, is ***"What do I want to come of this? What is it for?"*** *The clarification of the goal belongs at the beginning, for it is this which will determine the outcome."*

~ *A Course in Miracles*

*

"If you don't know where you're going, you might not get there."

~ *Yogi Berra*

*

My role in society, or any artist's or poet's role, is to try and express what we all feel.
Not to tell people how to feel. Not as a preacher, not as a leader, but as a reflection of us all.

~ *John Lennon*

PRELUMINARIES

First and foremost, this book is **for** *you*, for ***US***, and I thank you deeply for joining me on this journey. Our journey is one of seeking greater clarity and certainty about an often elusive subject: Spirituality, or the proverbial "spiritual quest." And the essential question to be asked in this regard is: *Who, or what, am I?* To that end, we will be looking closely at 3 primary sources – spiritual re*sources* with which I have taken the most recourse in my life and feel somewhat qualified to speak on: *A Course in Miracles*, yoga philosophy, and the mysterious Amazonian plant brew known as *ayahuasca*.

So that is what this book is for, but where this is all going, well, at this point, I really don't know! Or maybe I do! But it would be misleading to give you the impression that I have it all worked out ahead of time and could give you a summary of my findings right now and here at the start. This is why some writers write their introduction last, I understand, but I have chosen to do it first because I am here now setting my intentions for you to see, if only to highlight the importance of clarity of purpose and intention.

One thing I can very well tell you in advance is that this book will raise juicy, pointed questions for us to reflect on as we journey together and on our own. In a way, this will be similar to any relationship: My words will be a mirror for you on your own quest. And like any good piece of writing, I intend for this to bring up thoughts and issues that have been on y/our mind, if only in an unformed way, again for the purposes of greater clarity.

You will also learn a lot about the three specific resources that I mentioned, information that will hopefully help you to make a more informed decision about the direction you will subsequently take on your own journey. I have already explored two of these topics in a previous book ("***Who Am I: Yoga, Psychedelics & the Quest for Enlightenment***"). In that book – what I would call a "prerequisite prequel" to this one—I discussed how I went from the "right-hand path" of being a very disciplined yogi with a traditional guru, to the "left-handed" exploration of the often wild, jungle medicine, ayahuasca (primarily). The book concludes with my unexpectedly discovering *A Course in Miracles* and finding in it much needed guidance on my life's journey.

So again, this book is intended to be the sequel to that first book, where now we will really dig in to what this thing *A Course in Miracles* (or ACIM or "the Course" for short) is, and in the process, we will see how all of these 3 seemingly disparate elements (yoga, ayahuasca, and ACIM) fit together.

I am also writing this because I feel it's my calling, or to use a Sanskrit term, my **swadharma** (*swa* = one's own; *dharma* = duty, right livelihood, calling). Many have pointed to the interesting homonym "write" and "right", suggesting somehow that to *write* is to make *right*. Yes, and I feel that if I did not write, something would not be right! And if I am not doing what I am here to do, then I would be delaying my own righteous peace of mind. Or, as the Course puts it, I would not be in my "right mind"!

But I have no illusions that mere words can do much beyond pointing beyond themselves to an actual ***experience*** that will change your life. As the proverb goes, this is all just a finger pointing to the moon, or as I prefer to say, the "sun" → a finger pointing to the "point" of it all, to the Son, to the One, the place where it is all already undone, where "nothing happened." Or better yet, a finger pointing not outside of oneself at anything or anyone else, but back at oneself, with the message of the ages & the sages:

Know Thyself. All is within, the answer lies within, seek & ye shall find.

This book will especially help those of us who have been engaged with yoga, *A Course in Miracles*, or ayahuasca, and even moreso, 2 or more of these modalities. But it will also be of use and interest to any and all who are seeking a deeper and clearer understanding of the Meaning of Life (if Monty Python didn't get you there already ;), because the book is essentially a first person accounting of the mystic quest, with plenty of juicy/g(l)ory details to boot.

One thing I have seen within myself, and have heard enough from others by this point, is this tendency to backslide or fall away from the path. You know, you make progress for a while and even attain or catch a glimpse of some seemingly enlightened state, only to fall back down into the ego-depths once again. Why does this happen and how in hell does one keep it from happening? Well, there is a way to do so, for sure, and **there are short-cuts** or *time-saving methods to getting there*, contrary to common spiritual sentiment. The potentially troubling news, however, is that there is no getting around what needs to be faced, which is essentially our deep resistance to the potentially traumatic truth (which is only traumatic because we are unprepared for it). It's just a matter of whether this is confronted sooner, or later. It's just a matter of time.

Ultimately what needs to be understood, as the modalities dealt with here have intimated to me, is that our individual, separate existence is an illusion, meaning not ultimately real. Of course, this can be a horrifying proposition to the uninitiated, which is where a book like this could be helpful. Because it can be very comforting that there are others, seemingly separate from you, who are walking a similar path and who share your questions, agonies, spiritual crises and fears. In my case, I will also be offering my own decades of personal experience, revelations and reflections that will hopefully serve as a kind of mirror and "reality check" to those who are seeking guidance on the way.

So I invite you to sit back, buckle up, turn your cell phone off (unless you're reading this on your phone :), and enjoy what I feel is both the way coolest and hottest thing out there, which is the in-depth quest to understand who we truly are, and truly **Know**

That

I Am Love.

Ps. I want to also mention here at the outset that we will also be exploring the phenomenon of channeling, as several of the texts I will be referring to here are channeled writings. I am referring primarily to *A Course in Miracles* and *The Ayahuasca Manifesto*, but also the "sacred scriptures" of the yoga tradition. If you have any kind of issue with channeling, this might be a useful mirror for you to look at that. But also keep in mind that "scribing" or "writing through divine inspiration" may be more preferable designations.

> "I *Enlist* you
> to Be
> *Silent*
> &
> *Listen*
> to y/our Heart."
> **(But in the most gentle, undemanding way – please, take your time!)**
> (Ps. The pointed figure says, "Only One.. and the onus is on *you*.")

PRELIMINARIES

Quintessential Questions for Our Quest

Some of the main questions we will be inquiring about in this book…

Who wrote *A Course in Miracles*, and why has it become so popular?

Why/how is the Course similar to the non-dual teachings of eastern traditions like Hinduism and Buddhism, and how is it different?

More specifically, how is the Course similar to the philosophy of **Advaita Vedanta** (pure non-dualism), and what do the similarities tell us about the nature of reality?

Who, or what, created the Universe, or the world as we know it? And why does an answer to this question matter, or does it?

What is ayahuasca, where did it come from, and why/how has it so quickly become a worldwide phenomenon?

What do yoga philosophy, ACIM and ayahuasca have to teach us about "the ego," and how is this useful to us?

How important is direct experience of the nature of reality, as opposed to (or, in relation to) scriptural, textual or intellectual understandings?

What do yoga, ACIM and ayahuasca have to tell us about this thing called "enlightenment," or the possibility of totally freeing ourselves of fear, pain & suffering?

How might I work with these teachings in my everyday life in a chaotic world that often does not seem to be on the same page, let alone open to such wisdom?

Does it even matter, and why should I mind?

Who am I…to judge?
&
What am I… afraid of?

PRELUMINARIES

A Universal Theology is Impossible… Don't Let Your Questions Delay You

"All terms are potentially controversial, and those who seek controversy will find it. Yet those who seek clarification will find it as well. They must, however, be willing to overlook controversy, recognizing that it is a defense against truth in the form of a delaying maneuver. Theological considerations as such are necessarily controversial, since they depend on belief and can therefore be accepted or rejected. *A **universal theology** is impossible, but a **universal experience** is not only possible but necessary. It is this experience toward which the course is directed.* Here alone consistency becomes possible because here alone uncertainty ends…

"The ego will demand many answers that this course does not give. It does not recognize as questions the mere form of a question to which an answer is impossible. The ego may ask, "How did the impossible occur?", "To what did the impossible happen?", and may ask this in many forms. **Yet there is no answer; only an experience. Seek only this, and do not let theology delay you.**"

~ *A Course in Miracles* [7]

---

[7] Introduction to the "Clarification of Terms" in the Course's *Manual for Teachers*, paragraphs 2, 4. Italics added.

Pointed Questions for Course Corrections

[**NOTE:** The following are questions directly from *A Course in Miracles* and will make more sense as we proceed further along here...]

"Questioning illusions is the first step in undoing them."
***

> You are at home in God, dreaming of exile but perfectly capable of awakening to reality
>
> Is it your decision to do so?

"You are at home in God, dreaming of exile
but perfectly capable of awakening to reality.
Is it your decision to do so?".
***

Are you afraid to find a loss of self in finding God?
"Would you be hostage to the ego or host to God?"[8]

---
8   ACIM *(11.II.7:1-4)*

PRELUMINARIES

> Would you be hostage to the ego,
> or host to God?

***

"In any situation in which you are uncertain, the first thing to consider, very simply, is
"What do I want to come of this? What is it for?"

***

"Remember how many times you thought you knew all the 'facts' you needed for judgment, and how wrong you were!
Is there anyone who has not had this experience?
Would you know how many times you merely thought you were right, without ever realizing you were wrong?" [9]

***

"How long, O Son of God, will you maintain the game of sin?
Shall we not put away these sharp-edged children's toys?
How soon will you be ready to come home?
Perhaps today?
There is no sin. Creation is unchanged.

---
9   ACIM (M.10.4:1,2,3)

Would you still hold return to Heaven back?
How long, O holy Son of God, how long?"

***

"There is no problem in any situation that faith will not solve…
Is it not possible that all your problems have been solved,
but you have removed yourself from the solution?"[10]

***

"How willing are you to forgive your brother?
How much do you desire peace instead of endless strife and misery
and pain?
These questions are the same, in different form."[11]

***

"What if you recognized this world is an hallucination?"

***

"Your questions have no answer, being made to still God's Voice,
which asks of everyone one question only:
"Are you ready yet to help Me save the world?""[12]

***

Do you prefer that you be right or happy?"[13]

---

10   ACIM Text, p. 368.
11   Text chap 29, VI.
12   Clarification of Terms, The Ego – The Miracle
13   ACIM *(T-29.VII.1)*

PRELUMINARIES

> When you want only love,
> you will see nothing else.

Key Words: **Only** and **Nothing** (No Thing)

Are You Ready?

Are you open to hearing your heart's song?
Are you willing to put nothing else above?
Are you ready to stop thinking your part's wrong?
Are you ready?
Are you ready for Love?

Are you ready to let go of all your worry?
Are you ready to let go of all fear?
Are you ready to see no sense in hurry?
Are you ready to see it's already here already here

Are you ready to accept this invitation?
Are you ready to release control?
Are you ready to see no separation?
Are you ready to see your brother whole?
Are you ready
Ready for Love

And these words whisper in the wind and the sunshine
And this song sings softly in the heart
And this has all been deep on your troubled mind
And this is all secretly tearing, tearing you apart
Are you ready for Love?

…Just let go, and you will know
There was nothing to let go of

Just let be & you will see
There was only ever

Love

PRELUMINARIES

Nothing Happened: My Spiritual Journey (in one little page, more or less)

"You come from nothing you go back to nothing, what have you lost? Nothing!"

~Eric Idle, The Life of Brian

"Naked came I...naked I shall return."

~ Job

I am realizing now that I can write my spiritual journey in one page (or even less, really) because it's really pretty simple. And so the short, bittersweet & sour version is...

I was born the fourth son of four children in an upper middle class Jewish family in a suburb of Philadelphia (1970). I was a very happy and carefree boy who was an avid reader and loved music, sports, reading and creative writing.

When I was eleven, my parents separated and I went to live with my mother and maternal grandmother (who had helped raise me from my birth). This whole period was very traumatic for me, partly due to my parents' ongoing domestic war of attrition, and this would affect me and my entire family for years to come. In that year I also noted the onset of puberty and took up the guitar.

I subsequently turned into a teen who was very shy, awkward, antisocial, introverted and thoughtful. I did fairly well in school, but was still tormented by the difference between the carefree world of childhood and the comparably caustic world of adolescence. I took up long distance running which became a great outlet and medicine for me, and I approached it religiously. Running was my first spiritual practice; I found that it really helped clear the mind.

Yet I teetered on the verge of insanity until I was 19, when I fell/rose blissfully in love for the first time, a love that was yet unrequited. Despite this, the experience of being in love showed me that unconditional love and true joy was possible. Once the blessed experience wore off (months later!), I sought to recapture it again somehow. I became the proverbial "seeker."

My seeking led me to the academic study of religion and spirituality, both in the States and Israel, and ultimately to yoga (age 26). Indeed, it was a deep encounter with the Yoga tradition that brought me closest to what I had been seeking. Later, however, I grew somewhat disillusioned with yoga because I found it challenging to fully surrender to a guru and to follow a more traditional path. Today I understand what was happening to me then as a kind of dark night of the soul. This eventually led me to explore plant medicine (particularly ayahuasca) and receive its "teaching," and this in turn brought me to *A Course In Miracles*, which I currently feel to be the one spiritual path that makes sense of it all for me.

In this whole process, I have become more and more myself, my true self, meaning I've been more and more able to get the ego/false self out of the way. And that's why I called this little segment "nothing happened," because all that I feel is happening is that I'm shedding the "something" that wasn't really me to begin with.

And if you already get that, then feel free to stop now and see ya on the flipside.

But if you want the juicy details of how the shedding happens in real time, plus ways and means to do so that might be of assistance to you in your own journey, then please read on...

[You might also check out my first book, *Who Am I? Yoga, Psychedelics and the Quest for Enlightenment* (available on Amazon), for a fuller version of my spiritual memoir, too.]

Nothing Real Can Be Threatened

An Introduction To
A Course In Miracles

Intro To The Intro: Why A Course in Miracles Needs An Introduction

A Course in Miracles requires an introduction or "way in" to it because it is just so challenging to read and understand on its own. Many have picked it up and attempted to plow through it, only to put it back on the shelf, often just to gather dust. Mark Twain once said that a classic is a book that everybody has on their bookshelf and wants to read, but nobody actually does. Just over 5 decades old, the Course is definitely on its way to becoming something like that. It's the *Moby Dick* of the spiritual world, up there with the *Urantia Book*, Madame Blavatsky's writings, and the *Zohar*.

So an introduction that helps explain why the Course is so important and potentially useful, as well as to elucidate some of its challenging language and concepts, can be very helpful. The thing is, every introduction to the Course is its own interpretation of sorts, including the one you are about to read. So in the end, the Course really is best approached on its own terms. And yet, again, those terms are just so elusive to most of us!

In what follows, I attempt to get out of the way and point you toward those that I feel really are tried, true and trustworthy guides and resources for the spiritual masterpiece that is *A Course in Miracles*, thank you for listening… with and to your heart.

From the Course's own Introduction…

> Nothing real can be threatened.
> Nothing unreal exists.
> Herein lies the peace of God.

This is Jesus' summation of his entire Course.
Anything within us that can be threatened is not real and is in the way of our return to God (Love, Oneness, Wholeness, etc.).
In other words, the ego is not real – it's nothing, never happened.

Questions That Everyone Has About ACIM

(and which we will attempt to get some clarity on…)

- *Who is the author of ACIM? Jesus? Really? How can we know this is so?*
- *How is the Course similar to and how does it differ from traditional Christianity?*
- *What is the ego and where did the ego come from? Is it a thing?*
- *The Course says that God did not create the world. Well, if not, who the hell did? In other words, how did the whole shebang come to be?*
- *I find it hard to believe/accept that this world with all of its majestic beauty is an illusion, besides the fact that it all feels so real. Please help me with this!*
- *I'm scared of letting go of my ego, I don't feel ready to wake up just yet. It's so hard to forgive some things. Should I continue on this path?*
- *How do I know if I'm making progress with ACIM? Sometimes it feels like things are getting worse, not better!*
- *The Course says that it is pointing to an experience of Perfect Love (Oneness) beyond all symbols. Do we know if anyone has ever had this experience? If so, where are they, I need to talk to them!*
- *There are so many teachers of ACIM, and I'm discovering that not all of them agree with one another. How do I know which one to follow, if any?*
- *How do I distinguish between the voice of the ego and the voice of Spirit (or, the Holy Spirit)?*
- *How do I practically apply the Course to my daily life, especially considering that the Course says nothing specific about what to do/ how to live?*
- *Can it all really be as simple as the Course suggests?*

A Course in Miracles in One Page

(more or less)

"This course does not aim at teaching the meaning of love, for that is beyond what can be taught. It does aim, however, at removing the blocks to the awareness of love's presence, which is your natural inheritance... Your task is not to seek for love, but merely to seek and find all of the barriers within yourself that you have built against it. It is not necessary to seek for what is true, but it is necessary to seek for what is false."[14]

To distill the message of ACIM in just one or a couple of pages is kind of ridiculous as the Course calls to be read and studied and practiced on its own terms and on one's own. That said, perhaps someone who reads this will feel inspired to actually pick up the darn tome and be willing to wade through its difficult language in order to reap the benefits of working with it. For clearly it is the case that many who are, in fact, interested in ACIM do not get very far due to being hung up on the words and wordiness of it all. So! *Without further ado...*

The Course presents us with what Jesus was really wanting to get at 2,000 years ago, if only his followers could have understood the profound mystic basis of his teaching. They couldn't, of course, because he was teaching at such a high level, and as its said, "it takes one to know one."

But essentially, Jesus' message was/is very simple, and because it is so simple, clear and direct, it has the unique ability to save you a lot of time in your life and on the path of awakening.

---

14   *A Course in Miracles,* Introduction and T-16.IV.6:1-2.

And the simple message is to recognize that we are in each moment doing either one of two things: Living from fear, or from love. Otherwise put, we are always either choosing to follow the ego, or choosing Spirit as our teacher. The problem is that we are generally not conscious that we even have this choice moment to moment, because we are already so deeply identified with the ego that we have allowed much of our decision-making to be unconscious. Because of this, we think that the world is somehow being done to us (victim-consciousness), rather than that we are fully responsible for our life and liberation.

And because we are so identified with the ego, we don't even realize that we have chosen to identify so deeply with our body and personhood because the ego has as its mission to convince us that we are limited, that we are not what we truly are. And it uses every means necessary (variations on the themes of sin, guilt and fear) to keep us asleep so that we will never wake up to the reality that the ego is actually *nothing* but a false idea about who we are that we have accepted, and that we are really still safe at home in God (Perfect Love, Absolute Oneness).

Now, the most important tactical weapon in the ego's psychic arsenal is "projection." Projection works through seemingly *projecting* outside of the mind what is actually within it. So ultimately, the whole universe of time and space is actually a projection of the mind, but on the level most of us are at right now, we can see how projection works if we begin to recognize how invested we are in continually seeing the "problem" *out there*, rather than *in here* (though in truth, as the Course says, there is nothing truly outside of ourselves).

Which is where forgiveness comes in. Forgiveness means recognizing that there is nothing being done to you by anyone, and it is actually up to you to choose to make the unconscious conscious and realize that you always have a choice to see peace and innocence and perfection and unity everywhere, or not. And as you learn – slowly, slowly and with gentleness and patient perseverance – to lay aside judgment and see everyone and everything this way, not only will you become happier and more at peace, but at some point along the way, you will have an experience (and perhaps more than one) of what it feels like to be Home again. And like the road less traveled, such revelatory experiences will make all of the difference.

But you gotta do the work. It's up to you. *You* are the one you've been waiting for, *you* are the only one that needs to wake up, and both the problem and the solution lie inside of *you*.

And the truth is that this is all so mind-blowingly elegantly simple, yet not so easy. Which is why so few ever go all the way with this process of "undoing the ego" and unwinding the mind back to God. In fact, there has only been one who has ever fully done this.

Maybe you will be the One? ;)

Introducing A Course In Miracles

"This is a course in miracles. It is a required course. Only the time you take it is voluntary. Free will does not mean that you can establish the curriculum. It means only that you can elect what you want to take at a given time. The course does not aim at teaching the meaning of love, for that is beyond what can be taught. It does aim, however, at removing the blocks to the awareness of love's presence, which is your natural inheritance. The opposite of love is fear, but what is all-encompassing can have no opposite."

This **Course** can therefore be summed up very simply in this way:

"Nothing real can be threatened. Nothing unreal exists. Herein lies the peace of God."

And here is a beautiful "prayer" from the Course that I would like to once again share with you here at the outset, especially as it highlights my role as both a teacher AND student, as well as your role as student AND teacher…

I am here only to be truly helpful.

I am here to represent Him who sent me.

I do not have to worry about what to say or what to do,
Because He Who sent me will direct me.

I am content to be wherever he Wishes,
Knowing He goes there with me.

I will be healed as I let him teach me to heal

*

> I am here only to be truly helpful.
>
> I am here to represent Him Who sent me.
>
> I do not have to worry about what to say or what to do, because He Who sent me will direct me.
>
> I am content to be wherever He wishes, knowing He goes there with me.
>
> I will be healed as I let him teach me to heal.
>
> *A Course in Miracles*

"Every good teacher hopes to give his students so much of his own learning that they will no longer need him.
This is the one true goal of the teacher."

~ *A Course in Miracles* [15]

The intention behind this presentation is to provide a contemporary, up-to-date introduction to the phenomenon that is A Course in Miracles (aka "ACIM" and/or "the Course"), one that brings together the most helpful information about the Course from the Web and other resources. This is primarily intended for those who are new to ACIM, but it could also very well prove helpful to those who are already somewhat familiar with it or even "seasoned." Keeping with the Course's own emphasis on simplicity,

---

15   ACIM, *T 4.I. 5:1-2.*

every attempt will be made to keep this as simple and clear as possible, as well as fair and balanced. Because of this, feedback on this presentation is most certainly welcome.

So let's begin…

Finding Another Way, A Better Way

"Tolerance for pain may be high, but it is not without limit.
Eventually everyone begins to recognize, however dimly,
that there must be a better way.
As this recognition becomes more firmly established,
it becomes a turning point.
This ultimately reawakens spiritual vision, simultaneously
weakening the investment in physical sight.
The alternating investment in the two levels of perception is usually
experienced as conflict, which can become very acute.
But the outcome is as certain as God."

- A Course in Miracles [16]

---

16   ACIM, T2.III.3.5-10.

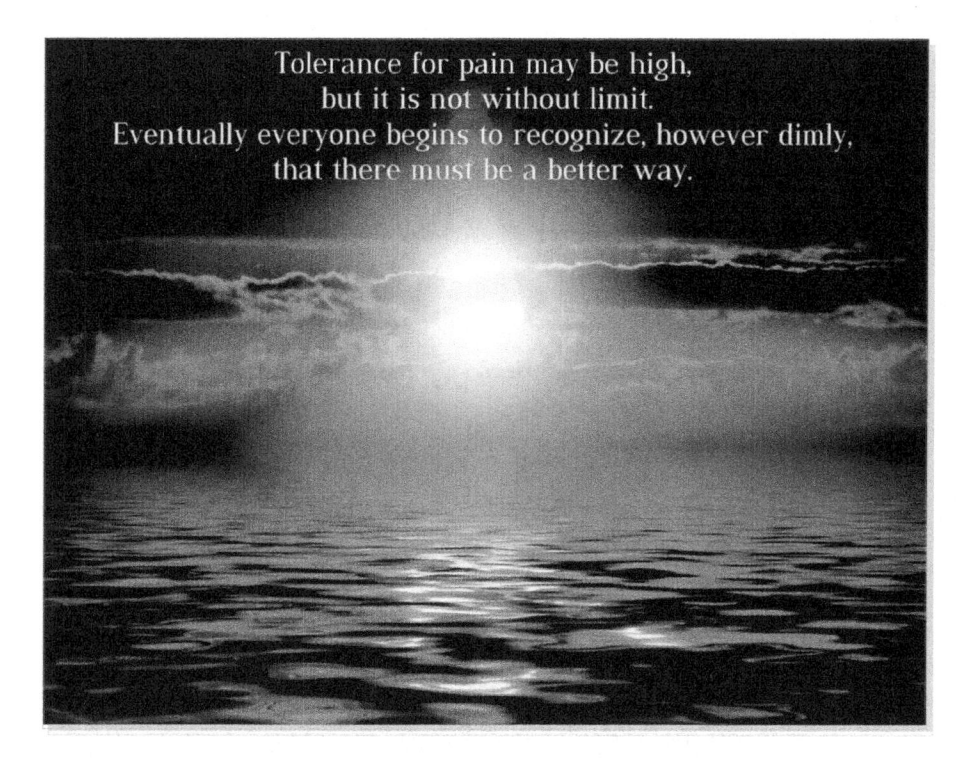

> Tolerance for pain may be high,
> but it is not without limit.
> Eventually everyone begins to recognize, however dimly,
> that there must be a better way.

The writing of the Course actually began with the decision of two people (Helen Schucman and William Thetford, research psychologists at Columbia University from the '50s onward) to find "another way" to communicate and be with each other harmoniously as opposed to their usual antagonistic encounters. Perhaps you are now coming to the Course because you, too, are seeking "another way" in your life. Well, you should know that although the Course was ostensibly a way to help Helen and Bill to find peace in their relationship with each other, it is really meant for all of us, as the Course teaches that at essence we all have a ***shared interest*** in peace, love and understanding, and in finding our true self (Self). To help better understand this point, here are some of the issues that might have led you here (i.e., reading this book), see if one or more of these applies to your life:

- *A failed or troubled relationship, whether with a spouse or significant other, parent, sibling, or friend.*
- *Achievement of worldly success, only to find that you are still not happy.*
- *Or conversely, failure to achieve success in life, leaving you feeling hopeless.*
- *A sense that there must be more to life than this.*
- *Fear about dying, or anxiety/panic about the future, for you or someone close to you.*
- *A sense of deep regret and/or guilt about your past actions.*
- *Confusion about spirituality and religion and how to know what the truth is regarding them.*
- *A falling out with your birth religion, or religion in general.*
- *A deep sense of loneliness and despair, or otherwise depression.*
- *An unshakeable feeling that you are a fraud, a phony and/or that you really don't like yourself, or worse.*
- *Putting your trust in someone or something, only to be betrayed.*
- *A perfectionism that leaves you paralyzed.*
- *Recognizing that nothing is bringing you the happiness (love, peace, etc.) you truly seek.*
- *A spiritual experience that left you with questions as to its meaning, one that you cannot seem to find in the world of traditional religion.*

And so on...

Now, if any of these applied to you, then the Course might just be for you. And in fact, the Course really is for **every body**, and isn't it the case that everybody experiences one or more of those things that were just listed? The thing is that not everybody is ready yet for the Course because it either might not be the right spiritual path for them, or they might not be at the point where they are ready to seek its guidance.

This idea can be summed up in a very simple statement:

*"The Course is for everybody,
but not everybody is for the Course."*

(Or: The Course is for everyone who thinks they're a body – more on this soon…)

The Course itself says:

*" 'Many are called but few are chosen' should be,
'All are called but few choose to listen.'"*

I sense that your being here right now means that you have in some sense heard the "call" and are in a place to really listen to and consider what the Course says and has to offer you. Given this, let's get waste no time to get into the thick of it…

"Portal" by Alexander George Ward.

Go To The Source

First off, as the Course itself advises us in various ways, it's generally a good idea to "**consider the source**" and start with the original source material (though on a deeper level, "consider the source" would mean the ***Source***, aka God, Spirit, the Ground of Being, Love, etc.), and for that you might want to purchase the following comprehensive edition of the Course put out by the **Foundation for A Course in Miracles**, click HERE. This is the most reliable version of the Course available, and it's also the "standard" edition in the sense that most people citing chapter and verse are referring to this edition.

The entire Course can also be read for free online **HERE**.

For a summary background on how the Course came to be written and what it says, I recommend starting with the following:

Introduction to A Course in Miracles by ACIM.org...

"*A Course in Miracles* is a complete self-study spiritual thought system. As a three-volume curriculum consisting of a Text, Workbook for Students, and Manual for Teachers, it teaches that the way to universal love and peace—or remembering God—is by undoing guilt through forgiving others. The Course thus focuses on the healing of relationships and making them holy. *A Course in Miracles* also emphasizes that it is but one version of the universal curriculum, of which there are "many thousands." Consequently, even though the language of the Course is that of traditional Christianity, it expresses a non-sectarian, non-denominational spirituality. *A Course in Miracles* therefore is a universal spiritual teaching, not a religion."

> "*There is a course for every teacher of God. The form of the course varies greatly. So do the particular teaching aids involved.... This is a manual for a special curriculum, intended*

for teachers of a special form of the universal course. There are many thousands of other forms, all with the same outcome."

~ A Course in Miracles[17]

The Introduction to the Course by Jesus and Helen Schucman ("How It Came," "What It Is," and "What It Says" – found in the Foundation's printed edition of the Course).

After you read these, I would also highly recommend watching at least the first part of the following film (free on Youtube) that goes into more detail about how the Course came into existence: **The Story of A Course in Miracles** . It's a very beautiful film and had my eyes welling up the first time I watched it. It is also available for sale from the Foundation for Inner Peace.

Secondary Sources – Books About The Course

Ironically, most people don't get into the Course by actually reading it first, however, because it is initially so challenging to understand; rather, people generally get into it through secondary sources such as books that have been written about the Course. The potential pitfall and caution with secondary sources is that they are only as good as the author themselves understand the Course (every "translation" is an interpretation). So with that cautionary word to the wise, here are a few of the most popular of these books about ACIM, and please keep in mind there are many other very helpful ones, these are just a few of the bestsellers:

Love Is Letting Go of Fear, Gerald G. Jampolsky

A Return to Love, Marianne Williamson

The Disappearance of the Universe, Gary Renard

A Course in Miracles Made Easy, Alan Cohen

---

17   *Manual for Teachers 1.3:1,2, 4:1,2.*

Of these, it appears that **Gary Renard**'s book has been the most helpful on a mass level in serving as a kind of "primer" or preparation for the Course. Not only has the "**D.U.**" (as it's been called) brought many new students to the Course, but it has also brought back many "lapsed" Course students and/or those who had difficulty understanding its message. So of the 3 books above, I would recommend that you read Renard's book to help get started with ACIM, yet with the following caveat …

There has been one big issue with Renard's book, and it is this: While it purports to be a dialogue between the author and two ascended masters (Arten and Pursah) who teach him all about the Course in a series of meetings over the course of a decade, some have cast doubt upon this claim. Renard's detractors, some of whom are also long-time students of the Course and Renard's peers, argue that D.U. draws heavily upon the teachings of Ken Wapnick, the first teacher of the Course and one of its earliest editors.

Without saying more about this controversy here, I would just like to acknowledge that if it weren't for Renard's book, many people, myself included, might never have gotten interested in the Course. So whether Gary's book is based on a true story or not, it definitely served its purpose for me, and many others as well. This is why I do recommend it for those who would like to get a kind of overview of the Course before they actually dive into the Course itself. [Note: Two contemporaries of mine who also got into the Course through Gary Renard's book deserve mentioning here: Kenneth Bok, creator a popular ACIM video series on YouTube; and Alexander Marchand, author of *The Universe is a Dream*. The latter is a particularly helpful and fun way to explore the teachings of ACIM.]

Ken Wapnick As A Portal

That said, let's entertain for a moment the possibility that Renard did draw primarily on the work on Ken Wapnick, in a sense popularizing Wapnick for the layperson. Then it would be a question of: 1) Did Renard accurately re/present Wapnick's work; and 2) Is Wapnick's own work true to the Course? These are very important questions to answer for oneself because it is VERY helpful, perhaps even essential, to have a guide for the Course, a kind of interpreter who can put the Course's sometimes challenging language and concepts into more accessible terms. After all, not a few people have put the Course down due to its seeming incomprehensibility.

Once again, I answer a definitive "Yes" to both of these questions. Yes, Renard's book does fairly accurately represent Wapnick's work (again, assuming for a moment that he might have borrowed from it), and yes, Wapnick (who just passed in 2013) did have a very trustworthy understanding of ACIM, perhaps better than anyone has ever had. And well he should have, because after all, Wapnick was both the first teacher of the Course and also the original editor of it who worked closely with Helen and Bill from 1972 onward. He even was present with Helen for some of the scribing of the Course, when she was receiving dictation from Jesus. Apparently he even helped to explain some difficult passages to Helen herself(!), though as Wapnick himself has expressed, Helen knew the Course better than anyone (even if she chose not to practice it – Ken has suggested she didn't need to). Wapnick also oversaw the Course's translation into 20+ foreign languages, etc.

Yes, one might ask, but perhaps Wapnick still misunderstood the Course, and what other evidence do I have to support my claim? How do I know that Wapnick is/was a very trustworthy interpreter of the Course, especially when not everyone (such as "The Circle of Atonement" group – more on this later) agrees? Yes, believe it or not, there have been those who sometimes radically disagree with Wapnick's interpretation of the Course (including other channels for Jesus, apparently), which is one reason why I feel it important to bring all of this up here. Because as a new Course student, you will no doubt be exposed to many opinions about the

Course, and depending on who you read first, you might be led to greater confusion about what the Course says than not.

My answer to all of this is that after reading and practicing the Course myself – and not only that, but directly *experiencing* what the Course is leading us to – I feel that Ken Wapnick had the most comprehensive, clear and deep understanding of the Course's essential message than anyone I have seen. And I do believe that he did his very best to be a true messenger for the radical message of the Course, without letting his ego unduly influence that message (to my mind, he did not unduly mess with nor massage the message!). Others apparently see it differently, and that is really all good, I just feel the need to weigh in with my own two cents and six sense here. Not to mention, again, my own direct experience, which confirms to me that Ken was teaching from his own experiential glimpses of the One Reality beyond all duality, without which it seems impossible the Course can be fully understood.

And in any case, I feel that it will be "truly helpful" to, at the very least, start with Wapnick as a guide, or read Renard's book as a primer for both Wapnick and the Course. Starting with D.U. is not a bad idea as Wapnick is a little less accessible than Renard, whose book could be seen, again, as an attempt to present ACIM to the layperson. (Note: Two other really useful starting books are D. Patrick Miller's **Understanding A Course in Miracles** and **Living with Miracles**.)

So with all of that said, I definitely highly recommend you explore Wapnick's work, starting with the very valuable information found on the Foundation for a Course in Miracles website (**facim.org,** and its sister website, **acim.org**), and Wapnick's numerous YouTube videos, plus his books, CDs, etc. I think that anyone with an eye to see will understand that Wapnick was a master of the material and saw himself as simply there to assist us all in better understanding what is often a challenging message to grasp (let alone practice!). Also highly recommended is Wapnick's biography of Helen Schucman, *Absence of Felicity*, which goes into great detail about how the Course came to be written, as well as Wapnick's book *The Message of A Course in Miracles*.

And **YET**, all other agendas aside, I do believe and trust that Spirit will guide you to just the right way to get into the Course, including the books you read, websites, etc. Perhaps it was by leading you to this book...?

The Read Less Traveled…

> Both read the same book day and night
>
> But you read BLACK and I read WHITE

This quote by British visionary artist and poet William Blake gets at Jesus' emphasis on the "spirit" rather than the "letter," or as the Course puts it, "content" vs. "form." The Course is more poetic and metaphoric than not, and while it can be taken literally, reading it "between the lines," so to speak, will give access to its deepest message. This is "the read less traveled."

Embracing Content Over Form

"**Content Over Form**" is a central theme of the Course and one that Ken Wapnick often highlighted. To help make this more understandable for us, I will use Ken himself as an example, and please do note the tongue-in-cheek nature of this!

So when you look at Ken and hear him talk (in the many videos on Youtube, or elsewhere), at least at first look he might give the impression of a skinny, nebishy guy with a thick Long Island accent and a kind of harsh quality to his voice that makes him sound maybe a bit even snobby at times, not to mention the speech impediment that made him occasionally stutter.

"Help me see this brother through the eyes of truth and not of judgment."

But when you go beyond that superficial appearance (that is, the "Form"), you begin to see both the depth of his understanding, and his commitment to the message of the Course and helping others to understand it (that is, the "Content"), not to mention the gleam in his kind eyes. So, too, the Course asks us to look beyond appearances to see the underlying sameness of all people, that **at heart we are all just seeking but one thing**, and we can call that thing **Love**, which is a word that, thank God, it seems is not so off-putting! And we get to Love through the practice of forgiveness, which involves looking at all the ways in which we are blocking our own awareness of Love. So let's talk about this core Course message, which beyond all of the verbiage is very simple: It's all about love and forgiveness; or, the practice of forgiveness as a way to return to Love, our true nature.

[Note: For a really nice Ken Wapnick tribute video, please see Jon Mundy's Youtube video, click **HERE**. I highly recommend this video for helping to understand Ken better, as well as for an introduction to Jon Mundy himself. Mundy is also one of the great teachers of the Course, and I also highly recommend his own introduction to the Course, which starts **HERE**. And for more about Ken Wapnick: http://www.miraclestudies.net/KenWapnick.html]

The Forgotten Song

"Listen-perhaps you catch a hint of an ancient state not quite forgotten; dim, perhaps, and yet not altogether unfamiliar, like a song whose name is long forgotten; and the circumstances in which you heard completely unremembered. Not the whole song has stayed with you, but just a little wisp of melody, attached not to a person or a place or anything particular. But you remember, from just this little part, how lovely was the song, how wonderful the setting where you heard it,

"The notes are nothing. Yet you have kept them with you, not for themselves, but as a soft reminder of what would make you weep if you remembered how dear it was to you. You could remember, yet you are afraid, believing you would lose the world you learned since then. And yet you know that nothing in the world you learned is half so dear as this. Listen, and see if you remember an ancient song you knew so long ago and held more dear than any melody you taught yourself to cherish since." [18]

---

18 A Course in Miracles From Chapter 21, "Reason and Perception."

The Notes Are Nothing

This is Jesus' way of saying that the "notes" of the Course (or the *form*), is really ultimately not the thing itself, they are only pointing to something beyond them. They are but a "soft reminder" of our real essential nature, beyond all words, beyond all worlds.
And in learning the Course, we are learning to read/hear (and play) the spaces between the notes, the silence behind the music.

Simple, But Not Easy

"Love and forgiveness is not for the faint-hearted."

~ Meher Baba

Okay, so thus far I've thrown a lot of words at you and you might be wondering why it took this long to get to this **simple message of love and forgiveness**? Well, look at the Course itself! It's over 1200 pages of material with half a million words, most of it quite intimidating to the new reader (again, think in terms of Form & Content here). Everyone asks at some point or another this question: If it really is all just about releasing the barriers to Love's presence, why so many darn words, and why did it have to be written in such a freakin' convoluted, Christian/biblical/King Jamesian, and male-chauvinistic way? The Course says it is simple, but so why not just say: "Love thy neighbor as thyself... because at essence they are Thy Self!" and be done with it? Isn't that the bottom line of all of this?

The simple answer to this question is that the Course is so seemingly long and complicated because we ourselves are so complicated with so many "complexes," most of which are veils for a profound guilt and self-hatred. We're not ready for the simple truth, because it's TOO simple. We feel, for one thing, that the spiritual quest somehow requires some great sacrifice and achievement to be won. And we're not ready to let go of all of our conditioned beliefs and attitudes (our "story") that quickly, we really have to warm to that idea, and hear it repeated over and over again until it really sinks in. As the saying goes:

"The truth is simple, but it ain't easy!"

The Course itself says:

"Nothing is so alien to you as the simple truth, and nothing are you less inclined to listen to."

And now consider the following passage from one of the Course's workbook lessons (189)…

"Simply do this: Be still, and lay aside all thoughts of what you are and what God is; all concepts you have learned about the world; all images you hold about yourself. Empty your mind of everything it thinks is either true or false, or good or bad, of every thought it judges worthy, and all the ideas of which it is ashamed. Hold onto nothing. Do not bring with you one thought the past has taught, nor one belief you ever learned before from anything. Forget this world, forget this course, and come with wholly empty hands unto your God."

I do believe that when Jesus says "simply" here he is half kidding... as if it's that easy!

Waking up is hard to do

It's not just hard, but as we will see, it's the hardest thing.

But when it comes down to it, the way home *is* as simple as seeing everyone and everything as yourself, with the recognition that as you treat anything that seems to be outside of you is how you treat yourself, and vice versa. So when we judge, blame or condemn others, it is only because we have already done that to ourselves. And when we see others as who they truly are, which is totally blameless, without any sin or needing any judgment or condemnation or fixing, then we also simultaneously remember who we truly are, which is totally innocent. And this is all as simple as a change of mind, just a little shift of perception! But to do this requires that we first truly take the Course seriously, and so that's the next idea/theme we will turn to…

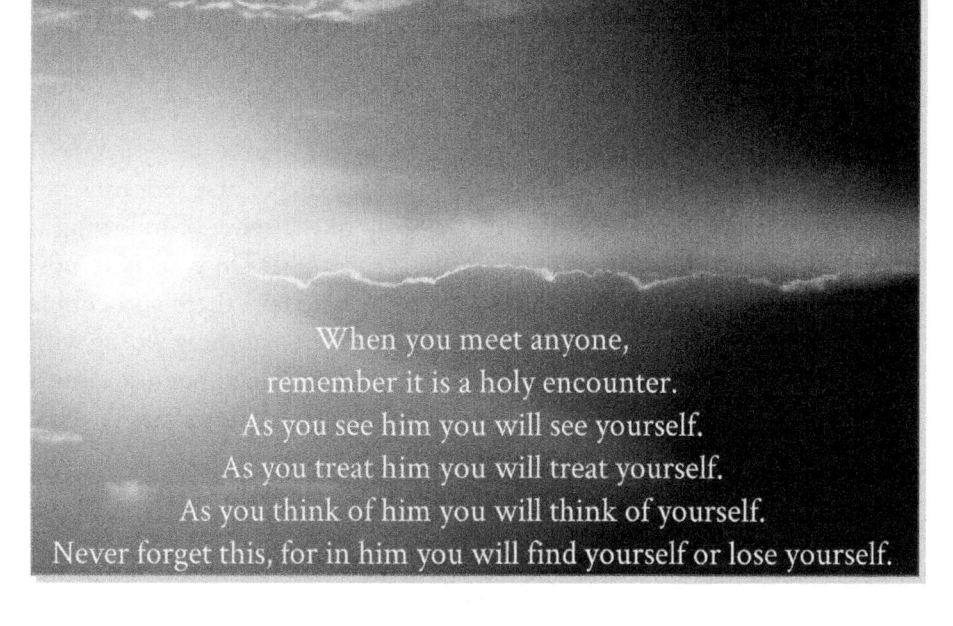

When you meet anyone,
Remember it is a holy encounter.
As you see him you will see yourself.
As you treat him you will treat yourself.
As you think of him you will think of yourself.
Never forget this, for in him you find yourself or lose yourself.

Seeing It All The Way Through

"Think this through with me
Let me know your mind
Oh Oh what I want to know is…
Are you kind?"

~ Robert Hunter/The Grateful Dead

First, let me say that this is not just about taking the Course seriously, but about taking any true spiritual path seriously in the sense of following it all the way through to the end. Who does that, right? Do you? No, most of us seem to take little bits and pieces from here and there and cobble together a spirituality that works for us. While there's nothing wrong with this in theory, it doesn't generally work over the long haul because almost inevitably the ego gets in the way. As the Course says in so many words (so many! – and I paraphrase…), we end up bringing the Truth to the illusion, rather than our illusions to the Truth. In other words, we end up making our illusory self and world real, making spirituality just another thing we do to feel better about our self (small "self") and our life in the world, and find it hard to go beyond that. And if anyone (like the Course) suggests we do consider the flimsiness of the world and our own self-concept, we heavily, and sometimes *very* heavily, resist it.

[Resistance, by the way, is a Freudian psychoanalytic concept that the Course uses (reinterprets) to explain how the ego attempts to distract us from the process of awakening to who we truly are. It's very helpful to think about how resistance might be at work in our approach to the Course and what we find problematic in it – and also to the book you presently hold in your hands.]

"Begin at the beginning," the King said, very gravely, "and go on till you come to the end: then stop."

~ ***Alice in Wonderland***

So the point I want to make here is this: If you really want to understand the Course, please give it your full attention and read it *on its own terms* as best as you can. Here's my suggestion (and do keep in mind that we all have our own pace to get to the peace, so this is a very general statement!): Go through the *Text*, the *Workbook*, and the *Manual for Teachers* sequentially as best you can for a full year, doing just a section and a lesson a day (please see appendix for a full year calendar of readings). It will make a world of difference in helping to understand the Course. Believe me, if you have trouble with the language, such as the King Jamesian-ness of it all, or all the masculine pronouns, or even the term God or Holy Spirit, by the end of a year all of that will (in theory, at least!) drop away because you will have understood the underlying **CONTENT** (that is, intention, message) and overlooked the **FORM**. And that's exactly what the Course is asking us to do about everything! Go beyond the appearance to the underlying essence, and then you shall truly see!

And perhaps most importantly: Don't make your study of the Course into an idol by making it such a serious thing. Remember to forgive yourself for judging yourself (and judging yourself for not forgiving yourself, etc.), especially when you fail to study and practice the Course. As Ken Wapnick put it so eloquently, "a good Course student is a bad Course student who forgives themselves."

> You need to hear the truth about yourself as frequently as possible, because your mind is so pre-occuppied with false images.

This is one reason why the Course is so long and repetitive. We seem to need constant, but gentle reminders to keep bringing us back to the elegant simplicity of it all.

God Is In The Details…Or Is It The Devil?

One other little point I would like to make here is that even though the Course does basically say the same damn thing over and over and over again throughout its 1200+ pages (Jesus is Johnny One Note), it's not that there aren't a lot of nuances and subtleties that we are requested to take note of. Ken Wapnick likened the Course to a symphony in which a certain theme or motif is introduced, then dropped, only to return again later to be further expanded with variations. Numerous examples of this could be noted, but just dig in and read it and you'll see how that all works. I will just add that this is why a close reading of the Course will make a difference in your understanding and practice, simply because of those nuances and new perspectives on the same one thing. This very well reflects the saying that *"God is in the details."*

And yet there is also the converse idea that *"the devil is in the details,"* and you will also recall Shakespeare's famous quote that even the devil can quote scripture. This is a caution to not get so caught up in the details that you miss the forest for the trees and get bogged down in sectarian theological disputes, something that the Course itself cautions again in several places.

> *"A universal theology is impossible, but a universal experience is not only possible but necessary.*
>
> *It is this experience toward which the course is directed"*
> *(C.in.2:5,6)*

On that note, there is a great story that shows the humor and wisdom of Helen Schucman's co-scribe and colleague, Bill Thetford…

One day two Course students were heatedly arguing about the meaning of a passage in the Course. Bill came in and they asked him which one of them was right? Without missing a beat, Bill said to them: *"Oh, just tear that page out."*

You get it? There are actually a number of places in the Course where Jesus says that it's not about the Course – "the notes are nothing," he says, and "forget this Course" – cautioning us not to get too caught up in the words (again, the FORM), but *do* understand the spirit of it all (the CONTENT) which is to get in touch with the perfect love that resides in your heart. Like a musician, learn your notes and scales by going through the Course carefully, but once you've done that, do not be afraid to tap into your own intuitive, improvisational brilliance, ever guided by Spirit, of course. All rules are ultimately mean to be broken, after all, all except one: The Golden Rule. And even that one will not be necessary in the end.

The Little Problem Of Faith

Okay, so we've gotten a little ahead of ourselves here and we might want to go back to one of the most fundamental problems with understanding the Course, and again it does have to do with resistance, but it also is a simple matter of **faith**, as well as **reason**. And the essential question is: **WHY** should we take the Course seriously? I mean, what proof do we have that this is all really the "Word" of Jesus? Maybe Helen and/or Bill made it all up? Maybe Helen really did channel the words of the Course, but they were given to her by a discarnate entity that had some secret agenda of its own to delude humanity? (I heard this argument from a seasoned yogi whose opinion I respect.) Or maybe Satan himself somehow orchestrated all of this in his mass plan to lead us like lambs to the slaughter? Or how about this one: It's all a CIA-hatched plot to control the minds of the many – A Course in Miracles as the opiate of the masses! (See further on for my take on all of this.)

Obviously you must know my answer to these questions, because otherwise I wouldn't be here enthusiastically introducing the Course if I had such grave doubts about it (and you wouldn't be here to keenly listen if you weren't at least a little open to all of this). But the truth is that, yes, even I have some lingering doubts about all of this because of one simple fact: *I just don't know*, and how could I? How can any*body*? And this is a key point that the Course makes: Only the ego asks questions and doubts, and so to the extent that we are still identified with the ego (and nearly everyone here is), we will be confused about all of this. But the Course does not ask for or require perfect certainty, only, as it says, a "little willingness" to look at the contents of our mind in the light of perfect love and forgiveness. So perfect faith is not required, nor even better-than-average faith!

Another way of saying this is: Have you experienced the gracious miracle of unconditional love or perfect peace in your life? Well, if yes, then it doesn't matter where the Course came from, because its purpose is to help us to return that perfect, unconditional love or peace that we have already experienced, if only fleetingly.

That said, I will still, briefly, attempt to answer some of those initial concerns that I mentioned…

So firstly, how do we know the Course really expresses the thoughts of Jesus? Well, we don't know, but many who have engaged with it, including myself, feel that it is the most loving, beautiful, wise and true expression of spirituality they have ever encountered. So if Jesus is perfect love (and as the Course says, he does symbolize that) then we can say that, yes, these are the words of Jesus. And interestingly, the Course does not insist that you use the term "Jesus," because all those who have attained the state of perfect love are ONE, and so call IT by any name you choose, because a rose is a rose is a rose. Love by any other name is still Love.

Ok! So I realize that answer will not be satisfying for a lot of people; namely, the response that it doesn't matter Who dictated the Course to Helen, because it's freakin' brilliant and it seems to be helping a lot of people, so who cares? Well, YOU might care. And don't look at me, but *I* still care about this question.

Remember I mentioned that someone close to me, a veteran yogi whose opinion I respect, gave me a very forceful argument of why the Course is potentially dangerous if its source is a discarnate spirit seeking to delude humanity (or at the very least ACIM students!)? While I did and do take this kind of issue with the Course very seriously, this is the very kind of controversial issue that the Course is wanting to tell us we will never truly be able to answer. And thus it becomes a "delaying maneuver" on the part of the ego to keep us from actually practicing its teachings on forgiveness and watching the ego be "undone." (Oh yes, by the way, I forgot to mention that the Course's practice of forgiveness does this: It undoes the ego, it dissolves it back to the no-thing it truly is. It's actually a gradual, gentle process for most of us that requires quite a bit of patience and forgiveness… mainly for our own lack of patience and forgiveness!)

And yes, I realize that this, too, might not be the convincing argument to do the Course. It seems to smack a little bit of cultish reasoning: Don't ask questions because they can't be answered, just do what we tell you to do and no one gets hurt! Some people have actually called the Course a form of brainwashing, yet you can see from the very introduction where it says that while this is a required Course (namely, the return to Spirit will happen for all of us at some point), the time you take it is voluntary. Not too many cults with brainwashing agendas will say that! And the Course points out that any attempt at coercion of any kind will not work, that all spiritual work must be voluntary to really bear fruit. So in other words: No one's telling you to do anything, you're here in this now moment considering all of this because you are truly seeking "another/ better way" and are open to hearing how the Course might be of help to you. Comprende? Verdad?

So at this point, let me talk about my own experience a bit more, because I feel it might help…

> You have no idea of the tremendous release and deep peace that comes from meeting yourself and your brothers totally without judgment.

Key Word: **Totally**.

My Yoke/Yoga Is Easy

"When you are tempted by the wrong voice, call on me to remind you how to heal by sharing my decision and making it stronger. As we share this goal, we increase its power to attract the whole Sonship, and to bring it back into the oneness in which it was created. Remember that 'yoke' means 'join together' and 'burden' means 'message'. Let us restate 'My yoke is easy and my burden light' in this way; 'Let us join together, for my message is light.'" (ACIM T:5:II:11)

Wait, this section is perhaps better titled: "**OF COURSE!**" Which is also a good title for this whole presentation. Because all of that heady stuff aside, what the Course did for me (and many of us, it seems) was appeal to the truth that I have always known. It was like what happened when I discovered yoga (or/and it discovered me), my thought was: "EUREKA! This is what I've been looking for all these years, it really exists!"

"This world you seem to live in is not home to you. And somewhere in your mind you know that this is true."[19]

And in fact, my current understanding is that we're all doing the Course, we just don't know it yet, and we might even consciously resist it. So it doesn't matter who its author was, whether Jesus or not, whoever it was is/was freaking brilliant.

I had this experience when I was 19 years old that I consider perhaps the most important one of my whole life: One night as I lay in bed thinking about a young woman friend, I felt an energy surge up my body up to my heart, and suddenly, I was in bliss. The next morning, it (the bliss) was still there. Like many teens, I had had a very hard time coming of age and was dealing with a very heavy load of guilt, anger, and self-judgment to the point of extreme self-loathing. And in one night, with one fell stroke, it was all gone! Imagine that! And please note that it didn't require accepting Jesus Christ as my Lord and Savior to happen! (I had actually tried that a couple of years earlier in dread response to a fire and brimstone preacher and…got nothing :) This experience lasted for months, long enough to

---
19 *A Course in Miracles*, Workbook Lesson 182.

really make me realize that, yes, it was really happening, and that THIS, not my old neurotic self, was my true nature, this state of unconditional love, joy, peace. And then it was gone, and thus began a soulful search to bring it back... and so it is for so many spiritual seekers, yes? You, too?

And so I looked everywhere for the Beloved, and finally found "Her" again... in the yoga tradition. (Mind you, this is making a very long story very short!) And then I got into plant medicine, particularly ayahuasca, which ultimately led me to the Course, because there were things that were being revealed to me by the plants that were truly shocking... you know, little things like ego-death and tours of various hellish realms, strange meetings with demons of varying shapes and surprises. And the Course helped me make sense of those experiences, to see them in a more universal, less personal way. For example, with its help, I could begin to finally accept that there's really nothing special about me, neither the abject misery that I've experienced, nor the transcendent bliss, neither the agony nor the ecstasy, the self-loathing or the megalomaniacal delusions of grandeur. All of that is part of the one ego-mind that we all share, it's nothing personal, really. I am not, as I formerly thought (when I was clinging to my "specialness") the *only lonely* one" out there... no, there are, in the words of that old Police song, "a hundred million [other] castaways looking for a home." Or 7+ billion, but who's counting?

In other words, we're all in the same boat with the call to now row it gently down the stream; or, as the Course would put it: We're all equal and integral parts of the one "Son*ship*."

And here's another thing to note here, and this also goes back to the "Of Course!" theme I've been playing on: **The Golden Rule**. Why is the Golden Rule what it is? Why should we, as the Hebrew Bible (Torah) commands, love our neighbor as ourselves? Deep down, we all know why, right? It's because at our core essence we are part of the same One Self. And so to even think for a moment otherwise is to deny the truth of what we are. So imagine what it would feel like to walk this earth and literally not have a second thought other than pure appreciation, compassion and forgiveness for everybody and everything? Imagine that? Well, that's the "mind training" that the Course is leading us to, and though we might never get it "perfect," it will be far sight/cry better than what we've got going on right now! Even a little more peace is not a little gift.

The Course As A "Christian Vedanta"

Bill Thetford was Helen Schucman's partner in crime in all of this, and far from being just Helen's scribal helper, Bill also had a deep understanding of the message of the Course. At one point, Bill referred to the Course as a "Christian Vedanta," and this is something that has since been repeated often enough for me to bother repeating it here.

Bill was pretty accurate in his assessment, though what he says does require some clarification.

Let's take the "Christian" part first: The Course is not actually Christian in the sense of following Church orthodoxy and dogma, but rather it is Christian in that it is Christ-centered. In fact, in the Course Jesus says that as he foretold, his disciples did not fully understand what he was saying 2000 years ago, so the Course is a way of correcting the errors of Christianity that crept in over time by revealing the deeper, inner meaning of the gospel accounts.

Did you know there is actually a gospel that was never included in the New Testament canon, but which some scholars believe actually predated Mark, Matthew, Luke, and John? It's called the Gospel of Thomas and it really just a collection of sayings of Jesus without any storyline except for brief contextual clues. The reason some scholars believe that the Gospel of Thomas (GOT) is older than the canonical gospels is because the gospel writers used sayings from the GOT in their accounts and pick up those little contextual clues in the GOT and create a story around them.

Now, if this is true, it's quite ground-breaking to say the least – "earth-shattering" might be a better descriptive. Because what Jesus says in the GOT is considerably more mystical than what we find in the canonical gospels. Consider the following saying from the GOT:

"When you make the two into one, and when you make the inner like the outer and the outer like the inner, and the upper like the lower, and when you make male and female into a single one, so the male will not be male and the female will not be female...then you will enter the Kingdom."

And also this one:
The disciples said to him, "When will the Kingdom come?" He said, "It will not come by watching for it. It will not be said, 'Behold here,' or 'Behold there.' Rather, the Kingdom of the Father is spread out upon the earth, and people do not see it."

What I am getting at by bringing in the Gospel of Thomas and these passages is that Jesus appeared to have been teaching about "oneness," or "non-duality," something that is not so clearly evident in the canonical gospel accounts. These are the teachings that, in reality, there is only One reality, and we can call it God, or Source, or Spirit, or Love, or Home, or OM, or IT, or you name it, but it's something pointing beyond the world of opposites and multiplicity that we currently seem to inhabit. Now, the word "non-duality" is an exact translation of the Sanskrit word "***advaita***" (literally "not two"), and this word generally goes hand-in-hand with another Sanskrit word: **Vedanta**. Vedanta is actually one of 6 philosophical systems found in the Hindu tradition. It is based primarily in the teachings of the Upanishads, and it is the essential teachings of the Vedas (literally, it translates as "the end of the Vedas"). Both of these collections of writings are widely considered to be the most sacred writings of Mother India.

Advaita Vedanta, the ancient Hindu philosophy of non-dualism, is actually becoming more and more well-known these days, partly due to teachers like Gangaji, Mooji, Ekhart Tolle, Craig Hamilton and Adyashanti who have been in a sense popularizing/translating this for a Western audience (they are sometimes called "neo-advaitins"). This is actually the world that I inhabited for years before getting into the Course, and it was the *Advaita* philosophy that always seemed the highest and most profound for me. So when I discovered the Course, to go back to the issue of doubt and skepticism about its message, I can't tell you what a confirmation it was to see how very similar the Course is to Advaita Vedanta. I mean, it's uncanny. It's like, c'mon, how could this possibly be?

Now, even though these two traditions are so similar, and even though I was so grounded in the Advaita Vedanta tradition, currently the Course speaks to me more and it has helped me as much as *Advaita* has, if not more. It might well be that this is so just because it's all so new to me, but it could also be that I've finally found the one thing to lead me home, which is what it feels like. I also sense that the Course will be easier for westerners to grasp, not to mention gentler, plus it's all in one book, so I've found it useful to use it as an aid in the teaching of yoga, and non-duality in particular.

The thing about the Course is that there's a bit of a learning curve involved, and it has to do with its language – again, the FORM in which its author chose to present the material. Essentially, to use another term from the yoga tradition, the Course is presenting us with a form of **Jnana Yoga**. What is *Jnana Yoga*? Jnana Yoga is actually one of 7-8 major paths to God found in the yoga tradition. Some of the other paths are: **Karma Yoga** (the path of selfless action), **Raja Yoga** (the meditative path), **Bhakti Yoga** (the devotional path), **Tantra Yoga** (the path of sacred ritual), and **Hatha Yoga** (the path of transcendence through the body). Today in the West, it is really Hatha Yoga that has really caught on with the general population, but the other paths of yoga have also taken root, though to a far lesser extent. For example, the Hare Krishna movement has brought more of the Bhakti element to the fore, Bhakti being the devotional path of the heart. And Transcendental Meditation (TM) has brought more of the Raja Yoga path, Raja being the meditative path. Krishnamurti liked to talk shop and thus introduced many to the path of Jnana Yoga, etc.

So Jnana Yoga is often called the path for the thinkers, those who are more philosophically oriented. After scribing the Course, Helen apparently said something to the effect, "*Finally, there's something for the thinkers!*" Yes, Helen was proud of the Course and even somewhat protective of it, even though she herself ostensibly chose not to practice it and even said some things contrary to it toward the end of her life. Another interesting thing she said at one point was: "*I know it's all true, I just don't believe it!*" I feel Ken Wapnick was correct in saying that Helen didn't need to practice the Course, it wasn't necessary for her to do so. She had fulfilled her purpose in her lifetime by getting her ego out of the way and being a pure channel for the Course's message, and that was enough.

Helen also apparently didn't feel the radical message of the Course was for everyone, just really for a small group of people who were truly ready for it. This may very well be the case, yet it is true that as I said before, the Course is also for *every body* (everyone who still thinks they are a body), and everyone can be helped by its message, even if they don't accept all of its terms and conditions and go all the way with it. My understanding is that the Course is saying that we all wake up to what the Course is pointing to on our own eventually anyway, with or without the help of the Course – in fact, it's already happened, we just missed the memo and are currently in the process of remembering that accomplished fact. And when we wake up, we all paradoxically wake up together – "together or not at all."

Just to give you an idea of how we are all in this process, willy nilly (whether we know it or not), even my dad was doing the Course in the end. One thing dad started to say in his last years (he just passed this last April) is *"you can make yourself happy, or you can make yourself sad."* Well, that's the Course's essential message right there – it's all our choice, suffering is optional. And my dad also started to say: *"Would you rather be right or happy?"* Which is one of the Course's brilliant lines that has really caught on. My dad must have heard that somewhere because he didn't even know what *A Course in Miracles* is, nor do I think he would have outwardly cared much for it if he did. But my point is that we either come to these things on our own (and then if we do pick up the Course, again, it's often a eureka moment like: "Of Course!"), or we learn them from the Course itself, or from the many popularizations and spin-offs on the Course (and other perennial wisdom) that are out there these days. And of course, we learn them from each other, too – my dad learned that in a way from me when I stopped judging him so much and learned to see he was just doing the best he knew how.

In any case, it's the Jnana Yogis who I feel can appreciate the Course the most, because the Course is a completely worked-out and consistent "thought system," a whole philosophy. It's very logical and it also points out the extent to which we can go with intellectual reasoning. I personally was drawn to the Course because of this element, but not just that – it has an authority about it that I still have not found any way to dismiss. I want to add that my early training was in philosophy and psychology, and Plato/ Socrates were my greatest inspirations early on.

Jnana Yoga is also the path of discerning between the real and unreal in each and every moment. Simply put for our purposes, this means making choices out of Love, not out of fear. The ego and all that spawns from its thought system of sin, guilt and fear is "unreal" according to the Course, and God, who is also Love in the sense of Absolute Oneness, is the one and only reality. So our return to God must be through a process of searching our mind and separating out our incorrect and misguided thinking, choosing to think only as God thinks (so to speak), aligning our will with God's Will. Again, though, in this process we are not adding anything, only removing what is not true.

"The first step toward freedom involves a sorting out of the false from the true."

Besides Jnana Yoga, the Course does contain elements of the other yogas, too, particularly **Bhakti Yoga**. In Bhakti Yoga we find the elements of trust, surrender, humility, faith and devotion. Essentially, the Course is asking that we listen to its message, and follow it to a "t" (get it?), but gently and in our own time. Surrender is not a word found anywhere in the Course. Everything is voluntary, there is no coercion here, no fear of punishment. Jesus, the symbol of the Perfect Love within all of us, is saying to us: You will have to do this sooner or later, my dear, so why not now? So the Bhakti element here would be the extent to which we can let go and accept its perfect message of love and forgiveness. May we all have Godspeed with this, and we will!

I will accept Atonement for myself.

Here is the end of choice.
For here we come to a decision to accept ourselves
as God created us.
And what is choice except uncertainty of what we are?
There is no doubt that is not rooted here.
There is no question but reflects this one.
There is no conflict that does not entail the single, simple question,
"What am I?"
This does Atonement teach, and demonstrates the Oneness of
God's Son is unassailed by his belief he knows not what he is.
Today accept Atonement, not to change reality,
but merely to accept the truth about yourself,
and go your way rejoicing
in the endless Love of God.
It is but this that we are asked to do.
It is but this that we will do today.
I will accept Atonement for myself,
For I remain as God created me.

~ **A Course in Miracles**[20]

---

20 ACIM Workbook Lesson 139. Bold mine.

Who wrote the Book of Love?

In my book
you can do no wrong,
just open up and find this song…
And when you do, Love,
you know it won't be long
that you'll be back where you belong.

And though the winds of change
may blow and rage,
still we are gonna be
on the very same page –
Taking it slow,
taking our time,
moving forward
to the end of the line…

(Well I wonder wonder who?)

Who Wrote The Book Of Love?

(Or: *Who wrote A Course in Miracles?*)

Before we go into this, let's again ask: *Who wants to know?* And what purpose will it serve in getting an answer to this question? In other words, what's at stake for you here? Because your investment in whether the Course comes from Jesus (just a symbol for perfect Love) or not will determine what you see. In other words, I could give you all the most persuasive reasons why the Course could not have been merely the work of a brilliant human mind (Helen Schucman), but if you don't want to believe that, or don't feel ready to accept it, you will find reasons not to and will try to justify it. It will fall on deaf ears. "Believing is seeing."

I could tell you, for example, that Mrs. Schucman was a self-professed atheist with a longstanding argument with God, not always an outwardly forgiving person by any stretch of the imagination. And furthermore, she was openly resistant to writing down the messages she was receiving from a voice that she understood to be Jesus, just as she was later resistant to practicing the Course. Her colleague, Bill Thetford, was a witness to all of this (and not, as some have recently proposed, the author of the Course), at least so the story goes. Was Helen just a really good actor, or did they both agree to concoct a whole story to dupe the masses? If so, why wouldn't either of them agree to put their names on the Course, and gain fame and fortune from it? What motive did they have in the whole process except for what seems to me the only plausible reason: Somehow they felt it was their responsibility to publish the Course because they knew the world needed its message – or at least, their own return to Source somehow depended on their sharing the message.

As I have already noted, Helen once famously replied to someone's asking whether she felt the Course was the truth: *"I know it's all true, I just don't believe it!"* I used to think this was funny and a sign of how resistant Helen was to the Course (as we all are), but I've lately begun to feel how honest and real Helen was. Because if we really consider what the Course is saying, it flies in the face of everything we've been taught to believe in a world that appears to be very real. To begin with, nearly everyone with any religious background believes that God created the world; or if you're an agnostic or atheist, you doubt or outright deny that there is a God who created our world. Most of us can't wrap our minds around a God who exists (and in fact, is *the only thing that really exists – or better, just IS*), but does not have any awareness of this world of duality, of separation.

The other thing that seems so apparent once you start looking deeper into the Course is its unique, authoritative voice and internal coherency and consistency. While it is true that on the surface it seems to contradict itself in many places, yet this is due to its being more of an artistic-poetic-holographic presentation than a strictly logical, literal and linear one. In one rare extant video interview, Helen says that she would never have written something like this, and many have wondered (including myself) whether any human could. Other channeled writings speak with similar authority and clarity about elusive spiritual subjects, for example Jane Roberts' Seth material. And this all leads to the next big question, *if* you can accept that channeling is a real phenomenon…

Assuming this is a channeled writing – "scribed" is actually the word that is used, as Helen was completely conscious when dictating the message – and not the product of a genius human mind, then who are the alleged "spirits" who speak through their human mouthpiece? And are they "good," or "bad"? Do they have our best interests in mind, or do they have some hidden agenda to confuse and distract us? And the question that everyone wants to know: How do we know that the apparent entity (id-entity) that told Helen it was Jesus really was Jesus?

Ego or Evil, God or Devil, Christ or Anti-Christ

"A universal theology is impossible,
but a universal experience is not only possible but necessary.
It is this experience toward which the course is directed"

~ A Course in Miracles[21]

***

This brings us to one of the biggest issues weighing on my mind when I read the Course, namely the question of its provenance, its source. Because I fully believe in the phenomenon of channeling, and that Helen channeled (really "scribed") the Course, it is hard for me to deny that there is *something* going on. The issue is this: just what that *something going on* is, as with everything in this world, is open to debate. Some traditional Christians have been quick to dispense with ACIM by citing passages such as Matthew 24:4ff that *'many will come in my name, saying, "I am the Christ," and they will lead many astray…For false messiahs and false prophets will appear and perform greats signs and wonders to deceive, if possible, even the elect. See, I have told you ahead of time.'*

These words do give me pause, and yet, on second thought, that seems a too easy way to eliminate the competition!

But let's take a step back: It's difficult to be a critical person today and not have doubts or at least questions about the authorship of the New Testament itself (let's leave the Hebrew Bible out of this for now, but that, too), because it is well-known that gospel writers lived decades after the events which they depicted. So even if we consider the possibility that the gospel writers were themselves channeling (or "divinely inspired"), or that God somehow ordained the New Testament to take exactly its current form (and what would that be exactly?), we still have the same basic epistemological question that we have with ACIM: How do we know? Who is the S/source?

---

21 *(C.in.2:5,6)*

Clearly there's no easy answer to this question, and I would question anyone who claims to have a definitive one. I can only tell you how I resolved this issue for myself…

First, I will point again to the dubious claim to being the one true Word of God that Christians have made for the New Testament, for the very reasons already mentioned, including late authorship, internal contradictions in the gospel accounts, Paul's theological innovations, etc. etc. Personally, it was quite challenging, given all of my reading and training in philosophy, to take the New Testament as more than a document of some of what Jesus said and did – and what that exactly was seemed very open to debate!

And yet, even with my skepticism about details, I couldn't deny that the figure of Jesus that the gospels present was inspiring to me, not to mention highly quotable. When I discovered ACIM, I wondered: Why not? How can we limit Jesus' gospel to just one writing? And why wouldn't I believe just as much in a gospel coming through a reluctant atheist Jewish professor as anywhere else? Especially when that gospel was a far more mystical, gnostic gospel that was more in line with the wisdom of the East – wisdom that I had already been deeply engaged with for years?

Now, I can certainly understand why traditional Christians would feel disturbed by the Course, because at least on the surface, it seems antithetical to their belief system. For the sake of clarity here, I feel it will be helpful to lay out 10 basic points of difference between traditional Christianity and the teachings of Jesus in the Course. Please keep in mind that I am here doing my best to present this to you in as non-judgmental and non-confrontational a way as possible, and I can be forgiven if I err on either side of things here. I also do not feel that the differences are ultimately all that great! This is something we will discuss, but in the meantime…

10 Ways ACIM Departs from Traditional Christianity

1. God is both transcendent and immanent. God is transcendent in the sense of not partaking at all in the world of duality. And God is immanent in the sense of being within you and everything as "the Holy Spirit." You are God, though that "you" is not the small *you* that you currently take yourself to be.

2. God did not create the world, a "tiny, mad idea" of separation did (though this is a poetic metaphor). In other words, the world is a manifestation of the desire (or possibility) to have a life apart from God. It comes from the mind's seeming choice to take on a "mistaken identity."

3. You are the messiah, the Christ, as much as Jesus is. The only difference is that Jesus fully realized this. Others who have fully realized this like Jesus, even if they are not "Christians" per se, are also one with the "Christ," or are "Christ Conscious." In other words, there is only one begotten Son of God, and we're all it. Those who get there only get there a little sooner (in the illusion of space-time), that is all; and we will all get there, for we are already there.

4. There is and can be more than one Bible, or revealed scripture, just as there can be many paths or ways to God, for the simple reason that Spirit meets us where we are. It is ever seeking our return and uses any and all means available/necessary to do so.

5. We are not inherently sinful; rather, we are inherently sinless, innocent. The more we focus on our guilt and sinfulness, the more we make real what is not truly real.

6. Satan is not any more ultimately real than the ego is, both are merely part of the illusion/dream of separation; and again, the more reality/belief we give to them (and to sin, guilt, and fear), the more real they are for us. Likewise, eternal damnation (or

burning in hell for eternity) is not possible, except in dreams/illusions, because our God-essence is fundamental.

7. Accepting Jesus as our savior is not enough; we must seek also what he sought, using him as our guide. We must return our minds to God, being ever-vigilant in sifting fear from Love, ego from Spirit, illusion from Truth. We must eventually listen only to Spirit, not the ego, just as Jesus did, to finally realize our unity with Christ and God.

8. Only through direct experience of Perfect Love (what Jesus and any true master is) can we truly have knowledge of what it is; dogma and indirect experience are not sufficient.

9. Real forgiveness is not found by holding anything against our brother, but to recognize our oneness with him (her, or it), and that we both are in our deepest core-essence not guilty, but innocent.

10. The "Second Coming of Christ" is a shift in perception that occurs in your mind when you accept y/our reality as God's one and only Son. Christ has already come – again and again. He can't stop coming! Can't keep a good man down!

I want to especially note and reiterate that all of these apparent differences don't really make any real difference in the end, because there is a path for everyone. So this is not to say that the Course is right and traditional Christian theology is wrong (or even that one is more right than the other); it's rather to highlight that these are two separate, but valid ways to get back Home. And also, the divide might not be so great as was just expressed!

In The Cosmic Game

In the Cosmic Game,
The Score is as it's always been,
still the same:

Fear is 0
&
Love is 1

Or,
Fear Nothing, Love Won

All is already all right
& there is nothing left to do
except *accept*

(the work is already undone)

& have fun
Dear One

> Perfect love casts out fear.
> If fear exists,
> Then there is not perfect love.
>
> But:
>
> Only perfect love exists.
> If there is fear,
> It produces a state that does not exist.

This is what is known in the field of philosophy as a "syllogism." Jesus uses these in several places in the Course to communicate his message. Apparently, Helen was very logical and these were partly used for her benefit. The above syllogisms are just variations on the original in the introduction: If nothing real can be threatened, and nothing unreal exists, then only the real exists and, as such, cannot be threatened.

10 Reasons Why It's Challenging to Understand *A Course in Miracles* (and how to better understand it)

IT'S CHALLENGING TO UNDERSTAND A COURSE IN MIRACLES BECAUSE...

1) Text & Context

It's helpful to begin at the beginning of the Text, not skip around. The problem with skipping around is that, even though the Course is very much a holographic presentation (as we'll talk about), it also presents things in a linear way, too. For instance, there are terms and ideas that are clarified in the first several chapters, and if you haven't read them carefully, you will not fully appreciate what is being said later on. For example, Jesus explains the difference between "knowledge" and "perception" early on and then basically assumes that you know what the distinction is whenever he discusses these terms later. There are numerous occasions in the text where Jesus says "I said before," and he generally is not just expounding the same idea again, he is expanding upon it.

2) Jesus Is the Narrator

Jesus is presenting the teaching throughout the entire Course — Jesus is the sole narrator of the Course (this includes the Text, Workbook, Manual for Teachers, and the supplements). So when someone says, "The Course says..." what's really meant is "Jesus says..." This makes all of the difference in understanding what is happening, especially when you recognize that not only does Jesus quote the Bible quite often, but he puts a new spin on it, and that spin is almost always a complete 180-degree reversal of what the Bible says. Jesus is essentially saying: "You know, I told the apostles 2000 years ago that they weren't going to understand everything I taught them, and they didn't. They got a lot of it wrong, they got it twisted. They ended up bringing truth to the illusion, instead of illusion to truth. So I'm back, baby! And I'm going to set the record straight, here we go..."

(You must forgive my cavalier attempts at humor here – truly you must ;)

3) Symbol & Metaphor

It's also challenging to understand the Course if you don't realize that much of what Jesus is saying is symbolic and metaphorical in order to help us relate to the content more easily. For instance, when he says that God or the Holy Spirit does this or that, that God is lonely or sad, that the Holy Spirit calls you, etc., these are all just metaphors to help us grasp the situation a little better, and also to motivate us and inspire us to do the work. If you don't understand this point, you are going to see seeming contradictions and inconsistencies in the text. For if God is perfect Oneness and does not even know about the separation (because it is not real), then how can God know about us, be lonely, be sad, and so on? So it's essential to recognize that Jesus is putting things in ways that we can understand, given that we are currently so identified with the ego to the point that we can't even think about God without a body, or without human qualities (the anthropomorphization of God). Even saying that God is Light or Love is also just using symbols that we can understand, for God is even beyond what we currently understand by these words, too, and can only be experienced, not intellectually understood.

4) Thought Reversal

Connected to the last point, many of the Christian-sounding terms used are the complete opposite of what the Bible and Christianity means by it. Take the word "miracle," for example. The Course is not by any means talking about a miracle as a supernatural event that a holy person does, such as to magically heal the sick or resurrect the dead. Nor is it talking about even "minor miracles" like finding your long lost keys, or something like that. For the Course, a miracle does not have anything to do with changing anything in the external world or our behavior in regard to it, but rather it has to do with changing our mind about the world. That involves joining with the Holy Spirit or Jesus *in your mind* for help in seeing things in the light of true forgiveness, which is to accept the Atonement principle that "nothing happened," there was never a separation from God, and so anything we see which is creating a disturbance is of the ego and is nothing to be disturbed about.

So forgiveness is also not forgiveness as the world has come to think about it, where I forgive you even though you hurt me and I feel you were wrong for what you did; forgiveness, for the Course, is recognizing that you didn't do what I think you did, because in fact, there is no "you" or "me," this is all a projection of the Mind due to the original supposed separation from God, a separation which, again, never really happened. Which brings us to the next point…

5) Theory & Practice
It's difficult to grasp the deeper intention and practice of the Course without understanding the underlying metaphysics of the Course, which helps clarify WHY, for example, Jesus emphasizes forgiveness, and WHY we don't truly forgive until we forgive totally. The Course is actually presenting a unique metaphysics that really cannot be combined with other systems of thought, such as New Age thinking. Take the idea of the original apparent separation from God (apparent separation – it didn't really happen), which led to the Big Bang and apparent creation of the universe as we know it…Other systems will say that God created the world and that the world is essentially good, being a creation of God. To this, the Course says that not only did God not create the world, but God could not create the world, because God did not even recognize that a separation from God ever occurred or could occur. But if the separation never occurred, and God did not create the world, who created it and where does that leave us? Right, the ego created it and so we got nothing! But then the Holy Spirit comes along and gently tells us that the world now is solely there for us to learn our lessons in forgiveness and go home again. So Jesus is gently, patiently leading us to this recognition, and because it's so scary to us, and Jesus is so kind, he uses just the right mixture of literalness and metaphor to awaken us from our long slumber gently. This brings us to the next point…

6) Threatening to *I*-dentity & "Level Confusion"
Perhaps the main reason we don't understand the Course is because what it's saying is too threatening to the ego. "When the student is ready, the teaching appears" means that we will only understand things when we

are ready, willing, and able to understand them. Which is why we can read the same book several times over the course of our lifetime and get that much more from it each time we read it. We will understand it on a much deeper level as we deepen and mature – or rather, as we slowly *slowly* remove the barriers to Love.

So with ACIM, the more we are invested in the ego, the less we will understand the finer points of Jesus' presentation. Jesus is ultimately leading us to the understanding that the "individual" we take to be so real, what it calls the "hero of the dream" (me!) is a complete fiction. Who wants to hear that? We'd rather at least hear that God really did create us and loves us and will re-connect us with our loved ones when we die, etc. But the Course is gently bringing us to the realization that ultimately only Perfect Love remains, and as "perfect love casts out all fear," and fear is of the ego, no individual identity can remain intact and fully return to God. Everything must go! We can be okay with this intellectually, but when push comes to shove? Very scary. At least to the ego.

…On that note, Ken Wapnick was the first to propose that the Course is written on two levels. The first level is the level of Absolute Truth which is that only God is real and nothing else is real. This is the radical non-dual idea which we've been talking about and which, as we'll see, we also find in the Hindu scriptures, the idea that God is "one without a second." This is where we're going and this is what Jesus in the Course more rarely brings up, saying things like the world is not real, there is no reality outside of God, etc.

But since this is too intense and scary for most of us, the second level on which the Course is written, and which actually comprises the largest portion of the material, is to meet us where most of us think we are at, which is in a body and a dualistic universe. Jesus suggests that we not deny this, but to see how powerful the mind is that it could produce such a powerful illusion. And in the meantime, we gradually and gently awaken from the dream/illusion by doing our forgiveness practice. Most of us would have it no other way because going more quickly would be terrifying and traumatizing. As we will see, this is exactly why psychedelics like ayahuasca are not for everyone.

7) The Language Barrier.

One of the biggest reasons we don't understand ACIM is because we can't figure out the language of the Course, or find it unappealing. On the surface, the Course is decidedly not cool, nor very fun — pretty dry, far from juicy (even though Jesus does occasionally make some pretty funny word plays). This connects with some of the other points already made about language. At first blush, the Course looks very biblical, "old school" (but also New Age), patriarchal and patronizing, hierarchical, elitist, etc. This initially turns many off to it. If you can get past this initial superficial reading of it, though, you will be greatly rewarded. It's been suggested that Jesus purposely chose to express things as he did in order to help us understand the symbolic nature of language, and also to help us to transcend the "form" of things, and to see only the "content." And the content, again, is the perfect love that inspired the Course, which is beyond language, beyond all symbols, beyond all form.

8) More Holographic than Linear.

Even though as noted, Jesus' presentation of the material of the Course is linear and methodical, it is also holographic. This means that each individual part of the presentation includes the whole message. How can that be? Well, for one reason, because the message of the Course is so simple: Only God is real, the separation from God never occurred, forgiveness is the way back Home... so get with *de*-program! Jesus is "Johnny One Note" – it's the same essential message over and over and over again, expressed in so many various ways to make it all more understandable, and more importantly, to motivate you to take it all seriously. And for it all to begin to really sink in.

Now, this also means that if you don't understand any part of the Course, or are in disagreement with any part, you don't understand any of it, because the message is a very coherent and unified message. This is a complete and internally consistent "thought system" (Jesus actually calls it that), and as such, you either take all of it, or you get none of it. Similarly, Jesus says you either forgive totally, or not at all. You either identify totally with God, or you identify with ego. Jesus says a number of times there can be "no compromise" in this, even though, again, we are told from the outset that we do have free will (ultimately an illusion) to decide how fast or slow we want to take this whole process, especially if we don't feel ready for it, or parts of it, yet. But ultimately, we're going to realize there can be no compromise when it comes to truth.

9) Intellect & Heart

It's difficult to understand the Course if you approach it only with the intellect, and not also with the heart. This is a confusion of Form and Content, a theme that is played on greatly throughout the Course. On the level of *form*, the Course is like a Textbook you read in school, and it indeed all looks very heady. Yet on the level of *content*, which is the deeper level at which we are to read it, the Course is a manifestation of Perfect Love to awaken that same love within you. It is actually meant to appeal to both head and heart, because most of us are so caught up in thinking, and are conditioned to favor linear, rational thought. So Jesus uses thinking/thought to gently, gradually lead us beyond thinking. Looked at this way, there's a sense in which we could feel very devotional and in our heart even reading the most intellectual-sounding passages from the Course. Yet there are also such beautifully poetic passages all throughout the Course, too! Here is but one:

All Your Past Except Its Beauty is Gone

> "*How can you who are so holy suffer?* ***All your past except its beauty is gone****, and nothing is left but a blessing. I have saved all your kindnesses and every loving thought you ever had. I have purified them of the errors that hid their light, and kept them for you in their own perfect radiance. They are beyond destruction and beyond guilt. They came from the Holy Spirit within you, and we know what God creates is eternal*" (T.5.IV.8:1,2,3,4,5,6).

I want to also mention here that in the Hindu scriptures, it is often said that God resides in the heart – not the physical heart, mind you, but in the spiritual heart, "the cave of the heart." But let us not get too caught up in symbols. Whether we say "mind" or "heart" doesn't matter in the end, it's the wording that works for *you* that matters.

10) It's Helpful to Have a Good Interpreter/Translator

And finally, we are challenged to understand the Course because we rely too much on our own powers of understanding when there are some who have devoted their lives to studying, practicing, experiencing and teaching the Course whose perspectives could save us a lot of time and agony, if we would just let them help us. For me, the two most important guides in this respect are Gary Renard and Ken Wapnick, though more the latter than anyone. I have said elsewhere that Ken Wapnick is my "go to" guy for help in understanding the Course. In fact, much of what I have written here is influenced by his writings and talks. I highly recommend to everyone wanting to understand what the Course is saying to check out Ken's videos (Youtube) his writings (many of them on the Foundation for a Course in Miracles website facim.org), and his books.

One final point here is Gary Renard's emphatic position that "there is only one correct interpretation of A Course in Miracles," and that is the Ken Wapnick school's interpretation, which Gary follows. This is obviously a very controversial point. Much has been made of the fact that Ken Wapnick's understanding of the Course changed over time, and that he later corrected things he had said in earlier years. To this I would suggest that this is no different than a great artist maturing and doing his or her best work in their later years. But even more to the point: As I said before, I highly doubt anyone can understand A Course in Miracles without having the revelatory experience at which the Course is pointing. Once even getting a glimpse of that, the radical non-dual essence (what Ken termed "Level 1") makes much more sense, if not perfect sense. Without it, good luck.

I do believe that Ken was privy to this experience (or perhaps it all "dawned on him" in a more gradual unfoldment), which is why his teachings changed over the years. This does not negate the usefulness of his earlier writings and talks, but certainly his later, mature teachings are the ones to which we would be wise to pay most careful attention. A strong case could also be made that Ken knew it all from the start (even if he did made some mistakes), which is why he chose to be chosen to take on the role that he did.

Summary Of Study Tips For Those New To ACIM

1. Instead of skipping around, consider reading the Text and doing the Workbook a little bit each day for an entire year, or more if you need it. (Please see the ACIM calendar in the appendix for how to do this.)

2. It will be helpful to make use of the Foundation for Inner Peace's quality resources as your guide for interpretation, particularly the work of Ken and Gloria Wapnick. These can be found at facim.org. Their Q & A "Master Index" archive is also a very useful aid, I contains answers to thousands of questions from Course students around the world.

3. Gary Renard's book, *The Disappearance of the Universe,* might be helpful as a primer for the Course. It has already helped many to get a clearer understanding of the message and general thrust of ACIM. But there are other equally useful "ways in" to the Course, and none at all also works.

4. The Course asks us to accept it on ITS terms and conditions, which means not to bring to the study and practice of it ideas from other spiritual paths, however seemingly helpful they might be. This is where really engaging with the Course and only the Course for a good year can be extremely helpful. Otherwise, we will tend to interpret it in terms of other systems, which may or may not be in accord with its message. That said, however one approaches the Course, it will still no doubt be helpful.

5. On that note, perhaps the closest other "system" to A Course in Miracles is the philosophy of radical non-dualism that we find in Advaita Vedanta, a philosophy we will be exploring later in this book.

Ok, so here's what I was NOT saying in this presentation…

What ACIM Is & Is Not

It's Not...

Easy
A religion
Traditional Christianity
A cult (though perhaps *diffi*-cult)
A form of brainwashing or CIA project
Complex, though it might be challenging
a New Age philosophy
Satanic
A Church
Elitist

It Is...

Simple
Universal
One path of many
Unique
A fully worked out philosophy/thought system,
similar to Gnosticism and Jnana Yoga
A practical guide to your True Self
Meant to be practiced by the individual

I Am Love

> The lion and the lamb lying down together
> symbolize that strength and innocence are not in conflict,
> but naturally live in peace.
>
> ~ A Course in Miracles

Gandhi: "Only the strong can forgive."
(Artwork by Berushka.)

11 Great Teachings of *A Course in Miracles*

1) "Nothing real can be threatened, nothing unreal exists. Herein lies the peace of God."

The whole Course is summed up in this one simple statement. Yes, it is really all this simple and if you truly get this one statement, the rest of the Course is not necessary. But also, if you really think you get this, you might be deluding yourself. Or in other words, your identification with the ego (the thought system of separation), which is the only thing that can be threatened, is preventing you from seeing how "scared of the sacred" you really are.

2) "It is not our task to seek for love, but to remove the barriers to love's presence."

Continuing from #1 above, the "barriers" here are all those things that feel threatened within ourselves, all of our fears (and everything that is of "Fear"). In other words, we don't know what Love is (or we do, but it's hidden most of the time), and the only way back to Love, to our true nature, is to very patiently and forgivingly begin to look at the things in our mind that are blocking the awareness of Love's presence. Simply put, we get to what we truly are by removing *what we are not*. Btw, this quote has been mistakenly attributed to Rumi.

3) "Love holds no grievances" & *"There is no order of difficulty in miracles."*

Emphasis here on "no" grievances. And *grievances* include all grief for there is "no order of difficulty in miracles" and "no hierarchy of illusions." Can we imagine what it would be to not grieve, to never despair or shed tears of sorrow every again? Can we understand what it would feel like to live completely without judgment, just as "a little child"? Can we imagine a state in which instead of automatically judging, we automatically forgive?

> "Love brings up everything unlike itself for the purpose of healing and release."
>
> ~A Course in Miracles

4) *"Seek not to change the world, seek only to change your mind about the world."*

This goes hand-in-hand with #2, removing the barriers to love's presence. Now we seek truly **Cosmic** change, not **cosmetic** change, and we do that by going to the root cause of our suffering. This is the meaning of the word "radical," and this is a *course* in **radical** change through **radical forgiveness**. In fact, Jesus tells us that the world will not end until the ego's thought system has been completely reversed. But keep in mind that this doesn't mean that we need to change anything "out there" necessarily (though this might be called for), we just need to be ever-vigilant about the contents of our own consciousness. We need to "mind the gap" and recognize when and where we are falling in the temptation to see ourselves or others as wrong or sinful, or even as bodies and personalities. Reversing the ego's thought system (and thus dissolving the ego) happens gradually as we merely witness the machinations of the ego for what they are: Nothing. They have no effect on our true, essential nature, and we only prolong our suffering and homecoming when we identify with the ego.

> "The journey to God is merely the reawakening
> of the knowledge of where you are always,
> and what you are forever.
> It is a journey without distance
> to a goal that has never changed.
> Truth can only be experienced.
> It cannot be described and it cannot be explained.
> I can make you aware of the conditions of truth,
> but the experience is of God.
> Together we can meet its conditions,
> but truth will dawn upon you of itself."
>
> ~ A Course in Miracles

5) *Through learning to see our brother (each and every "other") as completely blameless, without any sin or guilt, we gradually make our way back Home to God. This is the true meaning of forgiveness.*

Again, this is radical forgiveness. One of the final things to go apparently is divisiveness in regards to spiritual matters. This includes all argument and debate about how to understand God, because there will never be one way of approaching God that satisfies everybody. "Seek only the experience [of God] and do not let theology delay you." Don't seek controversy, seek only clarification. There are many valid paths to the same One Reality, and the truly wise allow *"to each his own."* Also, the Course teaches that the way to remember our original innocence is not to see "sins" to be punished, but merely "mistakes" that can be corrected.

6) *We are all each other's teachers and students, and we are always teaching and always learning either of two thought systems, that of the ego or that of the Holy Spirit.*

We are all in the same boat here, we who think we're really here! And herein lies the problem of the ego. We've identified with the ego and we have a deep investment in separation. The only way out is to slowly "undo" this identification by choosing to see everyone and everything the same, that everyone has the same "shared interest" as we do, which is the return to Love. So we seek "another/better way" together with everyone we meet by choosing to see them as they truly are, which is no different than God, Love, the same in essence as ourselves.

7) *We always do one of two things: we either extend love, or we call for it.*

In essence, if someone is being "mean" toward you in any way, it is possible to see that negativity as a call for Love, not a call to war, attack, or reaction. Even the most atrocious acts can be seen as this, for again, in addition to there being "no order of difficulty in miracles," there is also no "hierarchy of illusions." Ultimately, what Hitler did can be seen as no different than the pettiest of crimes, for both stem from the same misguided egoic mindset, the same deluded thought system. This is VERY challenging for us to even consider, let alone actually see things this way, but that is what we are being asked to do.

8) "Would you rather be right, or happy?"

The Course tells us that the ego's agenda is to keep us feeling alone and divided, which means that to the extent that we identify with the ego, we will be invested in feeling special and separate from others. This shows up, for one, in how we are constantly engaged in seeing ourselves as "right" or "righteous," and others as being not so much. Like everything, this happens in both gross and subtle forms, but remember, one is no different than the other according to the Course's methodology.

9) Salvation is actually very simple as we can always very simply "Choose Again"; that is, we can choose to see things how the Holy Spirit sees them, not how the ego sees them.

Think about the profundity of this: it's all as simple as choosing to change our minds about what we're seeing, to choose to see them with the eyes of Love and not judgment. Whoa, mama! Is it really that simple? Yes, Jesus tells us, it really and truly is – but not always so easy!

*10) **Our true nature is only Love, and Love already won (one). All we need do is learn to accept this, or at least be willing to allow this is true. This is what the Course calls "the Atonement Principle."***

Jesus at one point makes the startling statement that "there is no world," and in another place he tells us: "This world waHJs over long ago." In other words, God/Love has always been there, the impossible never happened, we just didn't get the memo, the "Note to Self" – or maybe we did, but we weren't ready to see it yet. And now we are, at least to more of an extent than previously. We are no longer in complete denial!

Btw, the Course tells us that the ego does not need to be destroyed, it just needs to be "undone." And the way to undo it ultimately is to finally accept that it already has been done, there's absolutely nothing we can do to find God, for God has never changed. God is infinite and in infinite patience awaits our return. *"Now it is for you to learn that only infinite patience brings immediate results."*

11) God Is.

No words could ever describe what God is. We can say Perfect Peace, Perfect Love, Perfect Oneness, but these are just symbols for what lies beyond them. We cannot conceive of what God is from where we are now. We can also say what God is NOT (God doesn't change, has no darkness, no impurity, etc), but the experience will only come when there is no more subject-object split. In other words – and this is the "threatening" part – there will be no more little "me" left, there will only be "we" – God. We can't conceive of this, and we're actually very afraid to even think about it. And yet, when we finally get there, we'll see that our fear was completely unfounded; in fact, it truly was nothing!

God Is

*"Oneness is simply the idea God is.
And in His Being, He encompasses all things.
No mind holds anything but Him.
We say "God is," and then we cease to speak,
for in that knowledge words are meaningless.
There are no lips to speak them,
and no part of mind sufficiently distinct to feel
that it is now aware of something not itself.
It has united with its Source.
And like its Source Itself,
it merely is.*

*We cannot speak nor write nor even think of this at all.
It comes to every mind when total recognition
that its will is God's has been completely given
and received completely.
It returns the mind into the endless present,
where the past and future cannot be conceived.
It lies beyond salvation; past all thought of time, forgiveness and
the holy face of Christ.
The Son of God has merely disappeared into his Father,
as his Father has in him.
The world has never been at all.
Eternity remains a constant state."*

~ **A Course in Miracles**[22]

---

[22] Excerpted from Workbook Lesson 169 of *A Course in Miracles*.

Acim Antecedents

Please Note: The following scriptures and personages point to the self-same vision as ACIM, though they might not quite have been on exactly the same page. In other words, these great figures and holy writings might have touched part of the whole truth, but not gone far enough, and thus ended up presenting a "mixed bag" of sorts. Or, they might have presented a different path to the same goal.

The fact is that the Course is truly a unique thought system, and while it does share much of the same ideas and wisdom with some of the great poets and philosophers of the past, its message and presentation are *sui generis;* that is, it is one of a kind. It is also wholly consistent in its message, which cannot be said for too many other thinkers or holy books. This does not mean that it is "better" or "best" – it itself says that it is but one of thousands of valid paths – just that it has an expression and internal logic all its own.

So below are just a few select, representative quotes of the historical figures who figure most prominently in all of this, having figured a good piece of the God puzzle before the Course emerged in our 3D awareness. Please also keep in mind the possibility that time is an illusion, and that these great spirits all succeeded in tapping into the truth beyond the boundaries of time and space.

The Torah/Hebrew Bible

Be still and know, I am God.

Love thy neighbor as thyself.

Hear, O Israel, the Lord thy God, the Lord is One.

*And thou shalt love the Lord thy God
with all thy heart,
with all thy soul,
and with all thy might.*

Vanity of vanities, all is vanity.

The Lord is my shepherd, I shall not fear.

God answers all who call God truly.

Trust the Lord with all your might and lean not on your own understanding.

…And after the fire – a still, small voice.

*Behold, I have set before you a blessing and a curse…
Choose Life.*

The Bhagavad Gita & Upanishads

*The one who sees me in everything
and everything within me
will not be lost to me, nor
will I ever be lost to him.*

*The one who is rooted in oneness
realizes that I am
in every being; wherever
that one goes, they remains in me.*

*When one sees all being as equal
in suffering or in joy
because they are like oneself,
that one has grown perfect in yoga.*

*The wise grieve neither for the living nor for the dead.
There was never a time when you and I and all the kings gathered here have
not existed and nor will there be a time when we will cease to exist.*

*They alone see truly who see the Lord the same in every creature, who see the
deathless in the hearts of all that die. Seeing the same Lord everywhere, they
do not harm themselves or others. Thus they attain the supreme goal.*

*They live in wisdom who see themselves in all and all in them, who have
renounced every selfish desire and sense-craving tormenting the heart.*

*One who sees all beings in the self alone, and the self of all beings,
feels no hatred by virtue of that understanding.
For the seer of oneness, who knows all beings to be the self,
where is delusion and sorrow?*

Gautama Buddha

Hatred is never appeased by hatred in this world.
By non-hatred alone is hatred appeased. This is an eternal law.

Holding on to anger is like grasping a hot coal with the intent of throwing it at someone else; you are the one who gets burned.

We are what we think. All that we are arises with our thoughts.
With our thoughts, we make the world.

No one saves us but ourselves. No one can and no one may.
We ourselves must walk the path. Buddhas merely teach the way.

Work out your own salvation. Do not depend on others.

Any kind of material form whatever, whether past, future, or present, internal or external, gross or subtle, inferior or superior, far or near, all material form should be seen as it actually is with proper wisdom thus: "This is not mine, this I am not, this is not my self."

Those who are free of resentful thoughts surely find peace.

You will not be punished for your anger, you will be punished by your anger.

Peace comes from within. Do not seek it without.

Question everything.

The Tao Te Ching

*The Tao that can be told
is not the eternal Tao.
The name that can be named
is not the eternal Name.*

*To attain knowledge, add things every day.
To attain wisdom, remove things every day.*

*We mold clay into a pot,
but it is the emptiness inside
that makes the vessel useful.*

*All creatures in the universe
return to the point where they began.
Returning to the source is tranquility
meaning submitting to what is and what is to be."*

*The Tao is called the Great Mother:
empty yet inexhaustible,
it gives birth to infinite worlds.*

*Without going out the door,
Know the world.
Without looking out the window,
See the Way of Heaven.*

*Be content with what you have;
rejoice in the way things are.
When you realize there is nothing lacking,
the whole world belongs to you.*

NOTHING REAL CAN BE THREATENED

A journey of a thousand miles begins with a single step.

> BE KIND.
> FOR EVERYONE YOU MEET IS FIGHTING A BATTLE YOU KNOW NOTHING ABOUT.

Plato (Socrates)

Be kind, for everyone you meet is fighting a hard battle you know nothing about..

We can easily forgive a child who is afraid of the dark; the real tragedy of life is when men are afraid of the light.

All true learning is remembering.

An unexamined life is not worth living.

True knowledge exists in knowing that you know nothing.

To find yourself, think for yourself.

I cannot teach anybody anything, I can only make them think.

On the walls of the cave, only the shadows are the truth.

Ignorance, the root and stem of all evil.

Let him that would move the world first move himself.

Jesus Christ/The Gospels

The Kingdom of Heaven is within you.

Seek first the Kingdom of God, and all else shall be added unto you.

My Kingdom is not of this world.

I and my father are one.

Forgive them, for they know not what they do.

Blessed are the pure in heart, for they shall see God.

A house divided against itself cannot stand.

You cannot serve two masters.

Judge not lest ye be judged.

Behold, I stand at the door, and knock.

Know the truth, and the truth shall set you free.

And know that I am with you always; yes, to the end of time.

The Gospel of Thomas

When you make the two into one, and when you make the inner like the outer and the outer like the inner, and the upper like the lower, and when you make male and female into a single one, so the male will not be male and the female will not be female...then you will enter the Kingdom.

Jesus said, "Congratulations to the person who has forgiven and has found life."

Look to the living One as long as you live.
Otherwise, when you die and then try to see the living One,
you will be unable to see.

I am the one who comes from what is whole.
I was given from the things of my Father.
Therefore, I say that if one is whole, one will be filled with light,
but if one is divided, one will be filled with darkness.

Whoever has come to understand this world has found merely a corpse,
and whoever has discovered the corpse,
of that one the world is no longer worthy.

I said, "Come to me, for my yoke is comfortable and my lordship is gentle, and you will find rest for yourselves."

Be Passerby.

Plotinus

Withdraw into yourself and look.

We must enter deep into ourselves,
and leaving behind the objects of corporeal sight,
no longer look back after any of the accustomed spectacles of sense.

Life is the flight of the alone to the alone.

When we look outside of that on which we depend we ignore our unity;
looking outward we see many faces;
look inward and all is one head.
If a man could but be turned about,
he would see at once God and himself and the All.

This All is universal power, of infinite extent and infinite in potency, a god so great that all his parts are infinite. Name any place, and he is already there.

Self-knowledge reveals to the soul that its natural motion is not, if uninterrupted, in a straight line, but circular, as around some inner object, about a center, the point to which it owes its origin.

Those who believe that the world of being is governed by luck or chance and that it depends upon material causes are far removed from the divine and from the notion of the One.

All teems with symbol;
the wise man is the man who in any one thing can read another.

"It is in virtue of unity that beings are beings."

Shankara

When our false perception is corrected, misery ends also.

Like the appearance of silver in mother of pearl, the world seems real until the Self, the underlying reality, is realized.

Knowing that I am different from the body, I need not neglect the body. It is a vehicle that I use to transact with the world. It is the temple which houses the Pure Self within.

When your last breath arrives, Grammar can do nothing.

There is sorrow in finitude. The Self is beyond time, space and objects. It is infinite and hence of the nature of absolute happiness.

What is enquiry into the Truth? It is the firm conviction that the Self is real, and all, other than That, is unreal.

From a clear knowledge of the Bhagavad-gita all the goals of human existence become fulfilled. Bhagavad-gita is the manifest quintessence of all the teachings of the Vedic scriptures.

Just as the fire is the direct cause for cooking, so without Knowledge no emancipation can be had. Compared with all other forms of discipline Knowledge of the Self is the one direct means for liberation.

The Soul appears to be finite because of ignorance. When ignorance is destroyed the Self which does not admit of any multiplicity truly reveals itself by itself: like the Sun when the clouds pass away.

The Kabbalah

There is no place where God is not.

*Truth undermines the self to which we so desperately cling.
The truth is not hidden from us. We are hiding from it.
Who can imagine a world that is not filled by the Creator?*

We do see things as they are, we see things as we are.

THE ESSENCE of divinity is found in every single thing—nothing but it exists. Since it causes every thing to be, no thing can live by anything else. It enlivens them; its existence exists in each existent. Do not attribute duality to God. Let God be solely God.

Arouse thyself, arouse thyself, for thy light is come: arise, shine; awake, awake; give forth a song; the glory of the Lord is revealed upon thee.

God is wherever you let God in.

The Gnostics

What you seek after (is) within you.

Beware that no one lead you astray, saying 'Lo here!' or 'Lo there!'
For the Son of Man is within you. Follow after him!
Those who seek him will find him.

He who has known himself has...
already achieved knowledge about the depth of all.

Abandon the search for God and the creation and other matters of a similar sort. Look for him by taking yourself as the starting point. Learn who it is within you who makes everything his own and says, "My God, my mind, my thought, my soul, my body." Learn the sources of sorrow:, joy, love, hate . . . If you carefully investigate these matters you will find him in yourself.

Those who have come to know themselves will enjoy their possessions.

Each person recognizes the Lord in his own way, not all alike.

I am not your master. Because you have drunk, you have become drunk from the bubbling stream which I have measured out. ... He who will drink from the bubbling stream which I have measured out.... He who will drink from my mouth will become as I am: I myself shall become he, and the things that are hidden will be revealed to him.

Having entered into the empty territory of fears, he (Jesus) passed before those who were stripped by forgetfulness, being both knowledge and perfection, proclaiming the things that are in the heart of the Father, so that he became the wisdom of those who have received instruction.

NOTHING REAL CAN BE THREATENED

The wound is the place where the Light enters you.

~ Rumi

Rumi

*Out beyond ideas of wrongdoing and rightdoing there is a field.
I'll meet you there.
When the soul lies down in that grass the world is too full to talk about.*

Why do you stay in prison when the door is so wide open?

*If you wish to shine like day, burn up the night of self-existence.
Dissolve in the Being who is everything.*

Silence is the language of God, all else is poor translation.

*The miracle of Jesus is himself, not what he said or did about the future.
Forget the future.
I'd worship someone who could do that.*

*This is love: to fly toward a secret sky,
to cause a hundred veils to fall each moment.
First to let go of life.
Finally, to take a step without feet.*

*There are a thousand ways to kneel and kiss the ground; there are a thousand
ways to go home again.*

*Everything that is made beautiful and fair and lovely
is made for the eye of one who sees.*

That which is false troubles the heart, but truth brings joyous tranquility.

William Shakespeare

*To thine own self be true, and it must follow, as the night the day,
thou canst not then be false to any man.*

There is nothing either good or bad, but thinking makes it so.

*Love looks not with the eyes, but with the mind;
and therefore is winged Cupid painted blind.*

Life ... is a tale Told by an idiot, full of sound and fury, Signifying nothing.

*There are more things in heaven and earth
than can be dreamed of in your philosophy.*

The devil can cite Scripture for his purpose.

*Love is not love that alters when it alteration finds.
God has given you one face, and you make yourself another.*

I say there is no darkness but ignorance.

*What's in a name?
That which we call a rose by any other name
would smell as sweet.*

*We are such stuff as dreams are made on;
and our little life is rounded with a sleep.*

St Teresa of Avila

*Let nothing perturb you, nothing frighten you. All things pass.
God does not change. Patience achieves everything.*

The closer one approaches to God, the simpler one becomes.

*We need no wings to go in search of Him,
but have only to look upon Him present within us.*

Pain is never permanent.

It is love alone that gives worth to all things.

*It is foolish to think that we will enter heaven
without entering into ourselves.*

Trust God that you are exactly where you are meant to be.

*In light of heaven, the worst suffering on earth will be seen to be no more
serious than one night in an inconvenient hotel.*

Meister Eckhart

God is at home, it's we who have gone out for a walk.

Only the hand that erases can write the true thing.

To be full of things is to be empty of God.
To be empty of things is to be full of God.

He who would be serene and pure needs but one thing, detachment.

Truly, it is in darkness that one finds the light, so when we are in sorrow, then this light is nearest of all to us.

The eye with which I see God is the same eye with which God sees me.

When you are thwarted, it is your own attitude that is out of order.

There exists only the present instant... a Now which always and without end is itself new. There is no yesterday nor any tomorrow, but only Now, as it was a thousand years ago and as it will be a thousand years hence.

The knower and the known are one. Simple people imagine that they should see God as if he stood there and they here. This is not so. God and I, we are one in knowledge.

I Am Love

XXVII
I'm nobody! Who are you?
Are you nobody, too?
Then there's a pair of us — don't tell!
They'd banish us, you know.

How dreary to be somebody!
How public, like a frog
To tell your name the livelong day
To an admiring bog!

Emily Dickinson
1830-1886

"I'm nobody! Who are you?"

Emily Dickinson

Forever is composed of nows.

Beauty is not caused. It is.

Tell the truth, but tell it slant.

I dwell in possibility.

*Not knowing when the dawn will come
I open every door.*

*Dogs are better than human beings
Because they know but don't tell.*

*Who has not found the Heaven — below —
Will fail of it above —*

*I'm nobody! who are you?
Are you nobody, too?*

Where thou art, that is home.

Ralph Waldo Emerson

What lies behind us and what lies before us are tiny matters compared to what lies within us.

To be yourself in a world that is constantly trying to make you something else is the greatest accomplishment.

Once you make a decision, the universe conspires to make it happen.

For every minute you remain angry, you give up sixty seconds of peace of mind.

He who is not every day conquering some fear has not learned the secret of life.

Always do what you are afraid to do.

Make your own Bible. Select and collect all the words and sentences that in all your readings have been to you like the blast of a trumpet.

Adopt the pace of nature: her secret is patience.

To have friends, you must be a friend.

Nobody can bring you peace but yourself.

William Blake

Don't believe the lie.

*Both read the Bible day and night,
but you read black
and I read white.*

I myself do nothing. The Holy Spirit accomplishes all through me.

If a thing loves, it is infinite.

*To see a world in a grain of sand and heaven in a wild flower
Hold infinity in the palm of your hand and eternity in an hour.*

*If the doors of perception were cleansed
everything would appear to man as it is, infinite.*

The glory of Christianity is to conquer by forgiveness.

Do what you will, this world's a fiction and is made up of contradiction.

*He who binds to himself a joy Does the winged life destroy;
But he who kisses the joy as it flies, lives in eternity's sun rise.*

I am in you and you in me, mutual in divine love.

Nietzsche

*He who fights with monsters might take care
lest he thereby become a monster.
And if you gaze for long into an abyss,
the abyss gazes also into you.*

*You have your way. I have my way.
As for the right way, the correct way, and the only way,
it does not exist.*

There are no facts, only interpretations.

*There exists in the world a single path
along which no one can go except you:
Whither does it lead? Do not ask, go along it.*

We believe that we know something about things themselves when we speak of trees, colors, snow, and flowers; and yet we possess nothing but metaphors for things — metaphors which correspond in no way to the original entities.

Amor fati: let that be my love henceforth! I do not want to wage war against what is ugly. I do not want to accuse; I do not even want to accuse those who accuse. Looking away shall be my only negation. And all in all and on the whole: someday I wish to be only a Yes-sayer.

Whenever I climb, I am followed by a dog called "Ego."

*And those who were seen dancing were thought to be insane
by those who could not hear the music.*

Lewis Carroll

*"Begin at the beginning," the King said, very gravely,
"and go on till you come to the end: then stop."*

*'But I don't want to go among mad people,' said Alice.
'Oh, you can't help that,' said the cat. 'We're all mad here.'*

Who in the world am I? Ah, that's the great puzzle.

The rule is, jam tomorrow and jam yesterday - but never jam today.

*That's the reason they're called lessons,
because they lesson from day to day.*

Take care of the sense and the sounds will take care of themselves.

There comes a pause, for human strength will not endure to dance without cessation; and everyone must reach the point at length of absolute prostration.

*'Tis a secret: none knows how it comes, how it goes:
But the name of the secret is Love!*

Sigmund Freud

Being entirely honest with oneself is a good exercise.

*One day, in retrospect, the years of struggle
will strike you as the most beautiful.*

Psychoanalysis is in essence a cure through love.

*The psychic development of the individual is a short repetition of the course
of development of the race.*

*The mind is like an iceberg,
it floats with one-seventh of its bulk above water.*

*The voice of the intellect is a soft one,
but it does not rest until it has gained a hearing.*

*Unexpressed emotions will never die.
They are buried alive and will come forth later in uglier ways.*

*We choose not randomly each other.
We meet only those who already exists in our subconscious.*

*I became aware of my destiny:
To belong to the critical minority as opposed to the unquestioning majority.*

The purpose of Psychoanalysis is to make the unconscious conscious.

Addendum

Some Freudian Terms Applicable To Acim

Freud wrote in German, so most of these terms actually were his translator's words.

ANXIETY

ASSOCIATION & DISSOCIATION?

DEFENSE MECHANISM

DENIAL & REPRESSION

DREAM OF CONVENIENCE
(Dream to avoid having to wake up, because you wish to sleep.)

EGO

IDENTIFICATION

MANIFEST & LATENT CONTENT

MOTIVATION

PROJECTION
(Experiencing someone emotionally in the present in terms of someone in your past.)

REACTION FORMATION
(Freud said the goal of psychoanalysis is to make the unconscious conscious.)

REGRESSION

RESISTANCE

SUBLIMATION

UNCONSCIOUS

WISH FULFILLMENT

WORLD'S DREAM and SECRET DREAM

Carl Jung

*Your vision will become clear only when you can look into your own heart.
Who looks outside, dreams; who looks inside, awakes.*

*Everything that irritates us about others
can lead us to an understanding of ourselves.*

*There is no coming to consciousness without pain.
Knowing your own darkness is the best method
for dealing with the darknesses of other people.*

In all chaos there is a cosmos, in all disorder a secret order.

*We cannot change anything until we accept it.
Condemnation does not liberate, it oppresses.*

When an inner situation is not made conscious, it appears outside as fate.

*Christianity really arose from the spirit of Gnosticism, but came into conflict
with it later, because the Gnostics threatened to dissolve Christianity with
their philosophical speculations.*

*No tree, it is said, can grow to Heaven unless its roots reach down to hell.
Christianity, like every closed system of religion, has an undoubted tendency
to suppress the unconscious in the individual as much as possible, thus
paralyzing his fantasy activity.*

Mahatma Gandhi

*The weak can never forgive.
Forgiveness is an attribute of the strong.*

In a gentle way, you can shake the world.

Be the change you wish to see in the world.

Nobody can hurt me without my permission.

*Happiness is when what you think, what you say,
and what you do are in harmony.*

An ounce of practice is worth a thousand words.

Where there is love there is life.

Those who know how to think need no teachers.

*Truth is by nature self-evident.
As soon as you remove the cobwebs of ignorance that surround it,
it shines clear.*

*If one reaches the heart of their own religion,
he has reached the heart of the others, too.
There is only one God, and there are many paths to him.*

*First they ignore you, then they laugh at you, then they fight you,
then you win.*

My life is my message.

Albert Einstein

The only source of knowledge is experience.

We can't solve problems by using the same kind of thinking we used when we created them.

Reality is merely an illusion, albeit a very persistent one.

I do not believe in a personal God and I have never denied this but have expressed it clearly.

The idea of a personal God is an anthropological concept which I am unable to take seriously.

When the solution is simple, God is answering.

*The intuitive mind is a sacred gift
and the rational mind is a faithful servant.
We have created a society that honors the servant
and has forgotten the gift.*

A human being is a part of the whole, called by us Universe, a part limited in time and space. He experiences himself, his thoughts and feelings as something separated from the rest-a kind of optical delusion of his consciousness. This delusion is a kind of prison, restricting us to our personal desires and to affection for a few persons nearest to us. Our task must be to free from this prison by widening our circle of compassion to embrace all living creatures and the whole nature in its beauty.

"A HUMAN BEING IS PART OF A WHOLE, CALLED BY US THE "UNIVERSE," A PART LIMITED IN TIME AND SPACE. HE EXPERIENCES HIMSELF, HIS THOUGHTS AND FEELINGS, AS SOMETHING SEPARATED FROM THE REST – A KIND OF OPTICAL DELUSION OF HIS CONSCIOUSNESS. THIS DELUSION IS A KIND OF PRISON FOR US, RESTRICTING US TO OUR PERSONAL DESIRES AND TO AFFECTION FOR A FEW PERSONS NEAREST US. OUR TASK MUST BE TO FREE OURSELVES FROM THIS PRISON BY WIDENING OUR CIRCLES OF COMPASSION TO EMBRACE ALL LIVING CREATURES AND THE WHOLE OF NATURE IN ITS BEAUTY." – ALBERT EINSTEIN

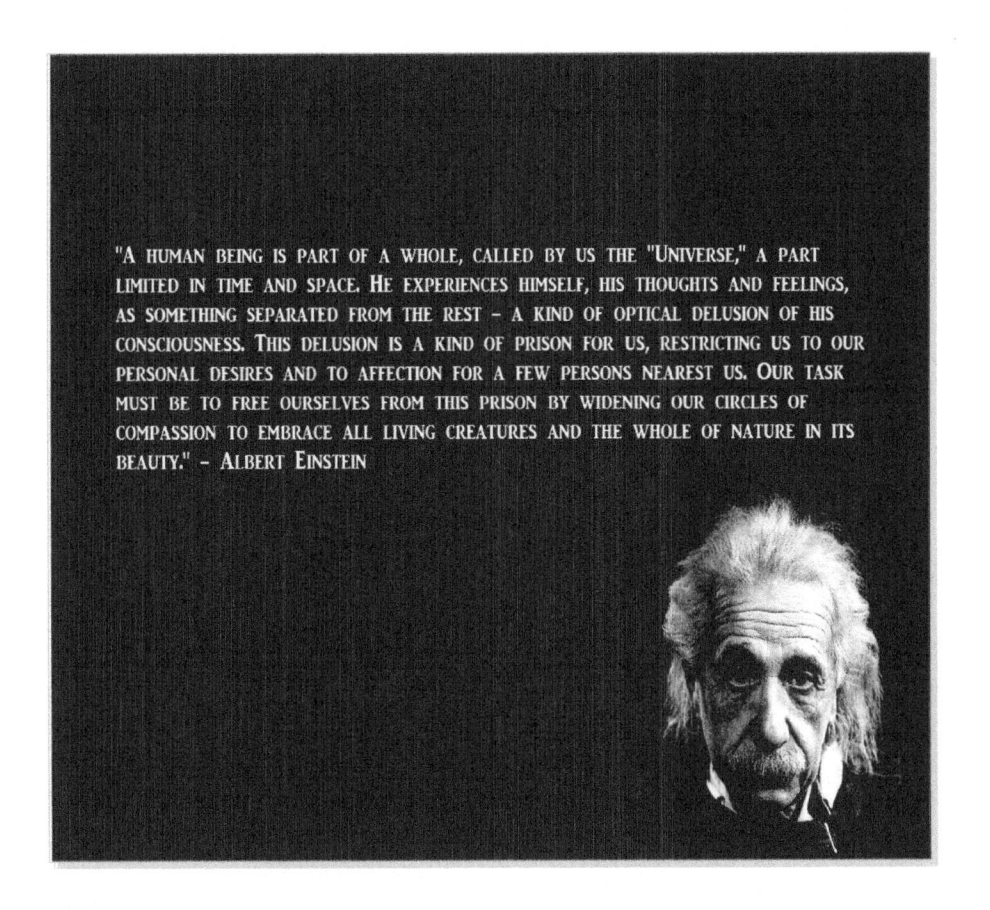

Separation is an "optical delusion."

Meher Baba

God and love are identical, and one who has divine love has received God.

God has to be temporarily cruel in order to be permanently kind.

Who says God has created this world?
We have created it by our own imagination.

There is no higher or lower goal. There is only one goal, Self-Realization.

God alone is real, and all else is illusion.

Truth is simple, but Illusion makes it infinitely intricate.
The person is rare who possesses an insatiable longing for Truth;
the rest allow Illusion to bind them ever more and more.

Love and forgiveness is not for the faint-hearted.

Love can attain what the intellect cannot fathom.

Why is it so difficult to find God?
Because you're looking for something you've never lost.

Seek a reality deeper than the changing forms.

All illusion comes and goes, but the soul remains unchanged.

God cannot be explained... God can only be lived.

I Am Love

> If there is a God, we're all it.
>
> *John Lennon*

John Lennon

There are two basic motivating forces: fear and love. When we are afraid, we pull back from life. When we are in love, we open to all that life has to offer with passion, excitement, and acceptance.

Part of me suspects that I'm a loser, and the other part of me thinks I'm God Almighty.

It seems to me that the only true Christians were the Gnostics, who believed in self-knowledge, i.e. becoming Christ themselves, reaching the Christ within, the light is the truth. Turn on the light. All the better to see you with, my dear.

You're just left with yourself all the time, whatever you do anyway. You've got to get down to your own God in your own temple. It's all down to you, mate.

Jesus was all right, but his disciples were thick and ordinary. It's them twisting it that ruins it for me.

Everything will be okay in the end. If it's not okay, it's not the end.

Whatever gets you through the night, is alright, is alright.

If someone thinks that love and peace is a cliché that must have been left behind in the Sixties, that's his problem. Love and peace are eternal.

The more real you get, the more unreal the world gets.

If there is a God, we're all it.

War is over ... If you want it.

All you need is Love.

I Am Love

"I would like my life to be a statement of love and compassion—
and where it isn't, that's where my work lies."
~ Ram Dass

Ram Dass

We're all just walking each other home.

Your problem is you're... too busy holding onto your unworthiness.

Only that in you which is me can hear what I'm saying.

Treat everyone you meet as if they are God in drag.

I would like my life to be a statement of love and compassion and where it isn't, that's where my work lies.

We're here to awaken from the illusion of separateness

The spiritual journey is individual, highly personal. It can't be organized or regulated. It isn't true that everyone should follow one path. Listen to your own truth.

Everything changes once we identify with being the witness to the story, instead of the actor in it.

A feeling of aversion or attachment toward something is your clue that there's work to be done.

The game is not about becoming somebody, it's about becoming nobody... But you've got to be somebody before you can be nobody.

Be Here Now.

Own Your Projections

In light of the Course's teachings delineating what ego is, we can now more readily become aware of our egoic projections and "own" them rather than to keep denying responsibility for the world we see. As we do this, we will come more and more into our "own."

And Now, to Give Some Brief Answers to Some of Our Initial Questions…

Who is the author of ACIM? Jesus? Really? How can we know this is so?

Yes, the scribe of A Course in Miracles, Helen Schucman, understood that the message was coming from Jesus. Even she had a hard time with that at first. I don't feel that anyone on this side of the veil can 100% know this is the truth. One must begin by accepting the Course as a path and being open to the possibility that it's true (having "a little willingness," as the Course says), and sooner or later whether it is true or not will reveal itself to you.

That said, ultimately, like everything in this world, Jesus is also an illusion, a fiction. So we could say that what Helen really received was the message of Perfect Love (the content), using the person of Jesus (the form) because that is what Helen, and so many who would later read the Course, could understand and would find inspiring. Perhaps if the Course had come through a professor in China, it would have been Lao Tzu or Buddha who was revealing the message. In the end, it doesn't matter who it was, because the ultimate message is that names and forms only matter to those of us who have yet to go beyond names and forms.

How is the Course similar to and how does it differ from traditional Christianity?

I have already given some answer to this in my intro to the Course above. Clearly, ACIM refers to the Bible (both Old and New Testaments) quite often, and it does so generally as a correction, meaning that Jesus is wanting to express what was really meant, what *he* really meant. And what he really meant is generally a more mystical/gnostic/non-dual approach. Simply put, it's the Golden Rule taken to its mystical conclusion – *do unto others as you would have them do to you*, because they **are** you. But it's not so much about what you **do** that is ultimate; rather, Jesus takes it all back to the mind, to looking at the ego in our mind and seeing how identifying with it leads to divisiveness and suffering.

Without going into every little difference and similarity here, we can also just note that because of this emphasis on seeing our "brother' as we would want to be seen, Jesus in the Course wants to show how the concepts of sin, hell, guilt, etc, are ones that we do not want to give power to. They are all just mistaken ideas of the ego, they are not God's Thought. In fact, perhaps the biggest difference between ACIM and Christianity (as well as most other world religions) is that ACIM posits that **God** merely **IS** and was not and could not be the author of the world we see. Which brings us to the next question…

What is the ego and where did the ego come from? Is it a thing?

No, ultimately the ego is not a thing, it is *no-thing*. But Jesus does have a lot to say about it, so much that we might be led to think it is a real entity, except that there are passages where Jesus assures us that the ego does not really exist – nor do we, as a personality, in a body, in a world.

Then again, because of our identification with the ego, which is based in the "tiny, mad idea" of separation (what would it be like to be separate from God?), we very much think the ego is a real thing, just as we think the world and our ego personality is ultimately real.

And therein lies the crux of the biscuit: We feel we need the ego as a way to protect ourselves, yet what are we really protecting? We are protecting ourselves from waking up, because due to identification with the ego, we have so much invested in the "reality" to which we have become very much habituated. We are in fact scared of letting go. That fear is due to our uneasy alliance with the ego, which has as its mission to keep the illusion going for as long as possible. But as the Course says, all we need to have is a "little willingness" to look at the ego with the lamp of

Spirit, and the ego will be dispelled – it will dissolve into the nothingness from which it came and which it is.

> A sense of separation from God is the only lack you really need correct.

The Course says that God did not create the world. Well, if not, who the hell did? In other words, how did the whole shebang come to be?

God is. That's all we can really say about this question, and the Course does not attempt to really answer it, except to talk about the "tiny, mad idea at which the Son of God remembered not to laugh" (that is, forgot to laugh). Now the problem was not that there was this idea in the mind of God of what would it be like to be separate from God, to have a life apart from God – obviously, this is an impossibility, in fact an absurdity (which is what the ego is). The problem was that the idea was taken seriously by the Son of God (please remember this is all metaphorical/ poetic), which spun out a whole series of serious ramifications, and those ramifications included an entire universe of duality (separation), plus the near impossibility that it would ever be remembered how it got to be that way. Namely, it was simply a choice in the mind. And now, all that is needed is the choice to choose against the original choice. And what that looks like is a gentle smile and laughter at the absurdity of it all; in other words, not taking the ego and all its "problems" seriously.

The Course also says that it is only the ego that asks questions like this, because it is only the ego that could need the answer. Only thing is, the ego doesn't really want the answer! If it did, it would not be the ego. That is why the Course does not try to answer such questions, but is rather pointing to an *experience* that lies far beyond such questions, and counsels that we not be delayed by theological or philosophical considerations. The experience itself will answer every question – that is, at least, until the experience is over. Then you might return to doubt, but it won't be the same degree of doubt as before. *Two steps forward, one step back,* as they say.

I find it hard to believe/accept that this world with all of its majestic beauty is an illusion, besides the fact that it all feels so real. Please help me with this!

Again, all that Jesus in the Course is requiring is a "little willingness" to consider that we made all of this up, and that the world is actually an "attack on God." We've become so habituated to our new habitat that we can hardly remember how flimsy it all is, and that there was a time when we knew the truth.

That said, early on in the Course, Jesus does make a point to say that it is not helpful to be in denial. That is, if we really think we are here, in a body and in a world, separate from others, etc., then don't deny this, but *do* be open to looking at what Jesus is trying to teach. And this means that if we do love the beauty that we see in our life or in nature, it's not necessarily bad to enjoy this; in fact, it could be very helpful. But at the same time, keep that "little willingness." And it is indeed usually "little" because Jesus knows how hard this is!

I'm scared of letting go of my ego, I don't feel ready to wake up just yet. Should I continue on this path?

Don't forget that the Course can still be helpful even if taken in very little bites. To go beyond all fear is no little task, which is why Jesus says at the outset that you can take your time with this – take all the time you need, in fact. Because ultimately you will see that time is illusory, too, and the eternal now is truly the only time there is.

But the truth is that while the Course is for everybody (who thinks they're a body), not everybody is for the Course. Perhaps another path or paths would be of better service to you. This is something only you can decide. Just don't forget to forgive yourself and the Course and whoever/whatever else you feel you need to release judgment around.

How do I know if I'm making progress with ACIM? Sometimes it feels like things are getting worse, not better!

It is true that many who first encounter the Course and begin to work with it actually experience that things seem to be getting worse, not better ("sometimes things get worse before they get better"). It is very likely that they are now just more aware of the shadows of the unconscious that had heretofore been kept from conscious awareness. And the reason they had been kept from awareness was because those dark thoughts are not comfortable to hold in awareness. Which is why some do not continue with the Course, and this applies to other valid spiritual paths, as well. It is important to keep in mind that our resistance to what is a very challenging message plays a big part in all of this, and the work and the challenge is to stop putting the problem outside of yourself.

How do we know we're making progress? This is difficult to know for sure, but in general we can say that if the time it takes from when you get upset at something to when you are able to feel peace of mind begins to diminish over time, then you are making progress. For example, if you used to feel great anger and frustration towards a family member, and that lasted for months or even years, and now it's only a few weeks, then you're making progress. And there may come a time when it might just be days, or even just an hour or a minute that you get upset. And eventually, if you really practice and apply these principles, you might find you are able to let things go immediately. You will automatically forgive, where before you automatically got agitated.

We could also say that we are making progress when we stop taking things so seriously, including and perhaps especially *A Course in Miracles* itself.

The Course says that it is pointing to an experience of Perfect Love (Oneness) beyond all symbols. Do we know if anyone has ever had this experience? If so, where are they, I need to talk to them!

You have already had the experience (in fact, it is what you are), you just don't remember yet. Those who have had the experience don't need to talk about it. If they needed to talk about it, they wouldn't have had the experience. It seems to come only to those who can keep the secret. Of course, it's not really secret, but it's just something that really can't be talked about, words generally only get in the way. And anyway, who would listen, who would believe it? And why would you need to tell anyone anyway? You've woken up to realize there's no one really out there. Who is there even out there to impress?

That said, there is no reason why someone who has woken up from the dream (even for just a moment) should not talk about their experience, especially if to do so might be helpful to others (and again, the other is oneself). Such a person might be careful of making claims for themselves, however, such as being enlightened, being a guru, avatar, etc. Actually, if they truly are at that level, they don't need to make any claims, their level of attainment will show in their very being. "By their fruits ye shall know them." As the Course says, a true teacher of God teaches in many ways, but above all by example, by demonstrating that Christ did not die, but lives in them. The Course also says that those who are at the same place as you will recognize you for who you are; and those who aren't will also recognize you, too.

There are so many teachers of ACIM, and I'm discovering that not all of them agree with one another. How do I know which teacher to follow?

Remember that ultimately there really is only one teacher, and that teacher is You – the You that is the U, the Universe, the one song singing itself for all eternity. All external teachers are only there to point you to this simple truth.

Just keep following the voice inside of you that tells you that everything is already all right, and that Love has already won. Resist the temptation to give in to fear or worry about anything. If you can do this, there is no need for a teacher. Keep it simple!

That said, I have noted here that I have found the teachings of Ken Wapnick to be most helpful. I would suggest he be the person you go to first for educating yourself about the Course. What I also love about Ken is that he didn't allow himself to get into conflicts or arguments about what the Course means. Not that he didn't make general statements to make his stance clear as a caution to those who he felt were misunderstanding the Course, he just didn't go there when he was basically being egged into conflict. He knew better.

How do I distinguish between the voice of the ego and the voice of Spirit (or, the Holy Spirit)?

It's important to mention here at the outset that whether you hear an actual voice or not doesn't really matter, the term "voice" is used metaphorically. What is really being referred to is the voice for guilt, sin, fear, etc. on the one hand (the ego), versus the voice for forgiveness, healing, and sanity on the other (the Holy Spirit). Or, even more simply put, the voice for fear vs. the voice for Love. The Course tells us that the ego always speaks first and is the loudest. The Holy Spirit is more the "still small voice" of sanity that simply reminds us that the ego is insane and if we follow it, we'll keep spinning in circles indefinitely. So in other words, whenever we remember that we don't really want to hurt ourselves and we choose forgiveness in place of attack, we've heard and listened to the "voice" of the Holy Spirit. And when we don't, we've listened to the "voice" of the ego. It's as simple as that.

How do I practically apply the Course to my daily life, especially considering that the Course says nothing specific about what to do/how to live?

The Course actually says nothing about what specifically to do or not to do. It's actually only talking about what you do in your mind. And what you are being asked to do is to keep looking at the ego in the light of Perfect Love (symbolized in the Course by Jesus and the Holy Spirit). As you simply look at the ego in the light of Love, gradually the ego will dissolve. It will become a non-issue, and in becoming a non-issue, all of your many ego-based issues will also fade away.

Can it all really be as simple as the Course suggests?

It sure can. Just remember: Simply, but not easy. What we are being asked to do here seems like an insurmountable task, one that would seem to require lifetimes and more. Yet Jesus is saying quite clearly that it's possible to wake up right now, in this moment. All it takes is a simple choice, a little willingness, just a slight shift in perception. Stay open to this possibility and note when the ego tries to complicate things by throwing you one anxious thought after another. Above all, be kind and keep practicing.

NOTHING REAL CAN BE THREATENED

A simple way to put the profound message of A Course in Miracles...

Fear is never justified.

Forgiveness is always justified.

What am I…afraid of?

Who am I…to judge?

Happy Unbirthday To Me

If I was all there,
well I wouldn't be here

I wouldn't have a care,
I would have no fear

Fall back into Love
and just completely disappear

If I was all the way there,
Well I wouldn't be here

Yeah, if I was alright, there'd be nothin' left
Life would no longer be such a matter of life and death
The wonder of it all would finally take away my breath
& it would all be all right, because there'd be nothing left

So Happy Unbirthday to me
I think I'm finally finally starting to see...
That it's not all about me
It's all about WE!
So Happy Unbirthday to me

Yeah If I was alright, I'd be already there
Our melodramatic old friend the ego just wouldn't have a prayer
But you know to be now and here is to be nowhere
And now I'm not all here, so I guess I'm not all there

*So I'll just keep singing this little unbirthday song
And invite y'all to come on and sing along
And consider, if it ain't all right
It might just be all wrong
Though it won't be long, no, it won't be long…*

*'til we're all all here and we're all all there
and we're in fact all alright everywhere
and nowhere do you end and me declare
that this is all neither here nor there.*

I Am Love

GnosisonG

Addendum: The Truth Is Right Under Our Gnosis

"Christianity really arose from the spirit of Gnosticism, but came into conflict with it later, because the Gnostics threatened to dissolve Christianity with their philosophical speculations."

~ Carl Jung, ETH Lecture V., page 162.

"It seems to me that the only true Christians were the Gnostics, who believed in self-knowledge, i.e., becoming Christ themselves, reaching the Christ within, the light is the truth. Turn on the light. All the better to see you with, my dear."

~ John Lennon

"One problem with Yahweh, as they used to say in the old Christian Gnostic texts, is that he forgot he was a metaphor. He thought he was a fact. And when he said, "I am God," a voice was heard to say, "You are mistaken, Samael." "Samael" means "blind god": blind to the infinite Light of which he is a local historical manifestation. This is known at the blasphemy of Jehovah—that he thought he was God."

~ Joseph Campbell

Religion is for people who are scared to go to hell.
Spirituality is for people who have already been there.

~ Anonymous

Over the course of time, the world has seen two basic approaches to God and the spiritual that are seemingly in sharp contrast to one another, and nowhere is this contrast more evident than in the realm of Christianity. Essentially, the two approaches, what I will call the Orthodox and Gnostic (but could also be termed "Religious" and "Spiritual"), are thus…

The **Orthodox** approach says that God is outside of us, transcendent, and can only be "approached" through the intermediary of a saint, holy person, or "Godman. Otherwise, God and the holy is somewhat unapproachable, unable to be accessed except through faith, prayer, good deeds, and righteous living.

The **Gnostic** approach, on the other hand, says that God is transcendent, yes, but also somehow immanent (in-dwelling – the meaning of "Immanuel")) and is actually our most innermost essence and can be revealed through an inner quest, an inner unfoldment of consciousness – a potential within each and every one of us. In other words, God – who in this view is not a person and does not have a body – is better sought within oneself, in one's heart of hearts, and this can best be done through exploring the deepest recesses of our being. The Kingdom of Heaven is within us; or better, as ACIM says, the Kingdom of Heaven IS us. *Us As Is.*

Now, the way this plays out in the realm of Christianity is like this: The Orthodox Christian approach is to say we cannot come to God except through the intermediary of Jesus Christ who is the only begotten beloved Son of God, and who had to die as a sacrifice for our sins. Otherwise, we're basically screwed.

The Gnostic Christian approach, conversely, is to say that we all can become like Christ – this was the true import of Christ's message – and it is only through unfolding our own Christ-essence through a journey into our own mind that we return to the one true God, who is no different than our own Self.

More simply put, one view would put God and Jesus as special, unique and distinct and forever separate from and outside of us; and the other would affirm that God and Christ are within us, and can be found by anyone (whether followers of Christ, or not) who feels the call to return Home to their Source or Christ-essence.

> Because I am always with you,
> You are the way, the truth, and the life.

To be more specific: The Orthodox Christian view is that our inherent nature is sinful and deserves punishment, that God is a transcendent Father who in his vengeful aspect would condemn us to hell for our sin, yet in His merciful aspect sent his beloved son to redeem us all, and that only through faith in Jesus we find redemption from sin. *No faith means no redemption.*

The Gnostic Christian approach, on the other hand, is to affirm that a truly loving God could not possibly create a world that is sinful and needs such redemption – that is absurd – and that Jesus was merely pointing the way back by affirming that God must be Only Good, God must be Only Love, and so the way home can come only by removing all of the self-made barriers to Love/God within ourselves.

Now, it is really not my place to judge which of these views is more correct, as if I could! All I will suggest is that these two paths (and the many paths that fall somewhere in and between these ways of approaching God) are both valid and will, if taken sincerely, lead to God in the end.

For it is my understanding that the idea "Paths Are Many, Truth is One" is correct and true. And which one you take is no one's business but your own and is completely up to you.

All I will say, however, is that for some paths, the end is a long way away, whereas others (especially what I have called the Gnostic approach) offer a more direct, less circuitous route back home. But we always find the paths and the guides that we are ready for at any given moment in the illusion of time. In other words, we choose the one that we're comfortable with given our level of fear, or the degree to which we have bought into the illusion.

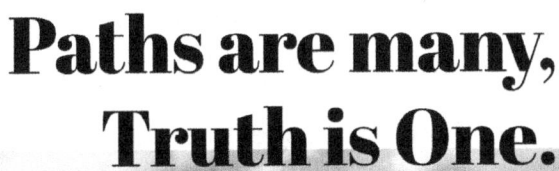

Paths are many, Truth is One.

Personally, the traditionalist Orthodox Christian approach to God doesn't work for me, and before I knew what I know now, I was not called to follow that way (you, too?) Perhaps the biggest obstacle to get around for me was the idea of "hell" and that some might go to hell for not believing that Christ died for our sins, including those who don't even know of Jesus or Christianity. Connected with that is the way that Christianity (and organized religion, in general) often creates divisions between itself and other paths to God, not to mention the world at large. Granted, my inability to walk the more traditionalist path might have been my problem, not its problem, but it sure made it necessary to find another path!

The unease I felt with traditional Christianity and institutionalized religion (including the religion of my birth, Judaism), led me away from the Abrahamic fold and into the study and practice of Eastern Philosophy. And ironically, it was my deep encounter with India and the Hindu worldview, in particular, which ultimately brought me back to a far deeper and richer understanding of Judaism, Christianity, Christ, and the mystical-experiential basis of world religion. And finally, it was that encounter with the East and the depth psychology made possible by ayahuasca that eventually led me to *A Course in Miracles*, the one scripture that for me puts it all into perspective in a way that I have not seen anywhere else, not even in the Hindu *advaita* tradition.

The reason being that the Course very clearly points to something that no other scripture or teaching has done before, and that is the phenomenon of guilt. But it doesn't just make a blanket judgment that since Adam's fall we are all guilty and cannot save ourselves, it actually explains how we allowed ourselves to get into this sorry state (through aligning with the ego), and how we might extract ourselves from the weight of guilt. And it does this by clearly delineating what the ego and its mission is, which is "**slavation**" not *salvation*. Buying into the ego we believe that we are a body, born into a world, destined to live out a few short years, and then perish, meanwhile generally leaving with so much unfinished business, regrets, unreconciled relationships, etc.

> Is he the Christ?
> O yes, along with you.

Are you the Christ? Yes, you are (Yeshua).

With this salvational knowledge (**gnosis**) in mind, we can now clearly see that it is as simple as choosing between two opposing thought systems in every moment, one that is taking us nowhere fast, namely the ego; and one that is gently leading us to the everpresent NoWhere (to the eternal Here and Now), which is Spirit. From my own experience, if we are just a little bit open to the possibility that this might be true, our awakening back to Love will be a gentle, gradual and beautiful process that will make our transition back easeful and graceful and not scary. And the only question then becomes: Well, what do YOU want?

And what do you know, brosis, this is all so simple as becoming aware as the breath right under our noses. But who would ever think to look there?

NOTHING REAL CAN BE THREATENED

"Teach not that I died in vain.
Teach rather that I did not die
by demonstrating that I live in you."

"Teach only love, for that is what you are."

On One Foot ~ A Story

This is a famous story from the Jewish tradition, from the Talmud to be exact, which relates the importance of the biblical injunction to "love thy neighbor as thyself," here expressed in the form of the "Golden Rule."

It is not so well-known that versions of the Golden Rule can be found in the scriptures of many ancient religions, the idea did not originate with Jesus in the gospels. Also, there are 2 versions, what might be called a positive expression of the rule and a negative expression. The one that is most common is the *"Do unto others as you would have them do to you"* version. But elsewhere, as in this story, we find the negative expression: "*Don't do to others* what you would not want done to yourself."

Personally, I prefer this way of stating the Golden Rule as what we might want others to do to us might not be what they want done to them. This version is a bit more conservative and less subject to overstepping bounds, especially in the area of proselytizing on behalf of one's beliefs.

***

So the story goes that once a non-Jewish man came to the great Rabbi Hillel (110 BCE-10 CE) and demanded that he teach him the whole Torah while standing *al regel achat*, which means "on one foot."

This is a Hebrew expression that is still used to this day. Essentially it means "the short version" or "the bottom line" – what you could express in the time it takes to stand on one foot before losing your balance. In English we use the expression "elevator pitch" to mean something similar.

So Rabbi Hillel stands on one foot and says to the non-Jew: "What is hateful to you do not do to your neighbor. This is the whole of the Torah. The rest is commentary. *Go and learn.*"

Interesting, yes? To say that the entire Torah is really about learning to live in peace and harmony with others, and that everything else in it is "footnotes" (pun intended) to that? This sounds less like traditional Judaism and more like Christianity…

Actually, there is a very good case to be made that more or less everything that Jesus taught (or what is attributed to him) was already found in the Jewish writings. This would make sense because Jesus was Jewish and no doubt was very much influenced by his birth culture. Which would also mean that Jesus did not necessarily need to go outside of his own culture (such as to Indian yogis) to learn wisdom. He didn't even need to go outside of himself, and perhaps he didn't…

The Beginning

> I am God's Lion, not the lion of passion….
> I have no longing
> except for the One.
> ~ Rumi

"There is no statement that the world is more afraid to hear than this:

I do not know the thing I am, and therefore do not know what I am doing, where I am, or how to look upon the world or on myself."

~ A Course in Miracles

Divining a De-Vine Mystery

Ayahuasquatic Adventures in Wonderland

DIVINING A DE·VINE MYSTERY

I'm trying to free your mind, Neo.
But I can only show you the door.
You're the one that has to walk
through it. (The Matrix)

"I cannot choose for you,
but I can help you make your own right choice.
"Many are called but few are chosen" should be,
"All are called but few choose to listen."
Therefore, they do not choose right.
The "chosen ones" are merely those who choose right sooner.
Right minds can do this now,
and they will find rest unto their souls.
God knows you only in peace,
and this is your reality."[23]

---
23   A Course in Miracles, Chapter 3.

All Are Called

*I enlist you
To be silent
& listen
to the calling of your heart*

*To Be
To Be in Love
To Be
To Be in Love
To Be…*

*All are called and few choose to listen
All are called and few choose to listen
All are called, all are called, please listen…*

*And Yet,
Everyone will come Home
Yet Everyone will come Home
Everyone will Listen*

*And Yes,
Everyone will be Free
Yes, Everyone will be Free
Everyone will Be…*

Divining a De-Vine Mystery: An Introduction to Ayahuasca

"Healing is the gift of those who are prepared to learn there is no world, and can accept the lesson now. Their readiness will bring the lesson to them in some form which they can understand and recognize. Some see it suddenly on the point of death, and rise to teach it. Others find it in experience that is not of this world, which shows them that the world does not exist because what they behold must be the truth, and yet it clearly contradicts the world."

~ A Course in Miracles, Lesson 132

"The ritual of my sacrament is not a religion. I will directly go into the soul of every Human and reveal in crisp detail their divine nature. This does not require a doctrine of faith, dogmas nor philosophies. Neither religion nor church. I am just in communion with the innate religiousness of the Human Beings. I dwell in the temple of the spirit."

~ The Ayahuasca Manifesto

"That which in the beginning is like poison, but in the end like nectar..."

~ The Bhagavad Gita, XVIII.37

"There is no coming to consciousness without pain. People will do anything, no matter how absurd, in order to avoid facing their own Soul. One does not become enlightened by imagining figures of light, but by making the darkness conscious."

~C.G. Jung

"What you seek is seeking you."

~ Rumi

Beware...Be Aware... Be Awe-Ware

"I have stressed that awe is not an appropriate reaction to me [Jesus] because of our inherent equality.

Some of the later steps in this course, however, involve a more direct approach to God Himself.

It would be unwise to start on these steps without careful preparation, or awe will be confused with fear, and the experience will be more traumatic than beatific.

Healing is of God in the end.

The means are being carefully explained to you. Revelation may occasionally reveal the end to you, but to reach it the means are needed."

~ ***A Course in Miracles***[24]

---

24   T.I.VII.5. Italics mine.

Prelude

In my first book, I openly discussed how I had been a hardcore, tradition-bound yogi for years before delving into the world of plant medicine, particularly ayahuasca. I also revealed how I was led to this more "tantric" exploration via a dis-ease I was feeling with the whole yoga path, or at least my approach to it.

On the one hand, yoga had been the most important discovery of my entire life, and I knew from the start that it was exactly what I had been calling in for years and that I would be engaged with it for the rest of my lifetime. Yes, it was indeed an engagement and a love affair that continues to this day, though now it has more the status of a marriage!

And yet, a decade after my oh-so- seductive meeting with yoga, I was at a crossroads in my relationship with it, or maybe better put, I was undergoing a dark night of the soul, a kind of mid-wife crisis (double entendre intended). If I had to pinpoint the biggest issue I seemed to be facing, I would say this: I struggled with the idea of following a guru, and I was rather guilt-ridden by the thought that I had left all of my wonderful teachers from India before I had reached the goal, Self-realization, let alone achieving *samadhi* (a temporary but timeless and life-changing experience of cosmic consciousness).

From my perspective now, it all was exactly what it needed to be, and in the end it doesn't matter how you get there, but that you get there. So, being the one-pointed seeker I was, the Universe (so to speak) presented me with another way to achieve the Union (Yoga) I sought, and that way was ayahuasca. It was like I was realizing that I wasn't going to do it living a somewhat conventional life in Florida while practicing and teaching yoga. There had to be something else, and again, that "something else" was a jungle medicine – and it sure is *something else!*

My first literary child and the prequel to this book.
Cover Design by Alexander George Ward.

But my initial exploration of ayahuasca brought with it a host of issues and questions that I wrestled with from day one. Big Questions, like: Is using a plant medicine (for me, ayahuasca) valid from a yogic perspective? Or is use of plant medicine its own yogic practice? Are these plants a kind of guru, and can they be used in place of a guru? Can plant medicines grant one true access to Samadhi, or even enlightenment? Are these substances offering a short cut, or a dead end? These experiences are so profound, and yet they don't last – why is this? And ultimately it all came down to, bottom line: Should *I* be using plant medicine, why or why not, and if so, how much and for how long?

When Neem Karoli Baba took those high doses of LSD (and "nothing happened"), he apparently told Ram Dass that while perhaps helpful for some serious aspirants using them under the right conditions, these substances don't give access to "true Samadhi" (or they are not the "highest Samadhi" – Ram Dass has said two different things over the years). And I felt this, too, because I was of the understanding that true enlightenment meant a steady, stable ever-present abidance in the One Reality, even while still in the body. And yet it appeared that the cosmic experiences from the plants just never stuck for me, as they hadn't for Ram Dass and apparently do not for most of us.

And yet, I wasn't going to "stand on ceremony" either – clearly these substances were helping me in many ways, as they are helping many these days and have since time immemorial. Why would I not make use of something that was such an obviously useful tool for self-understanding, not to mention self-healing?

I honestly will say that the jury is still out on this question, at least in my mind. Actually, in my first book I wanted to show that there really is no easy answer to such existential questions, and although I may seem to be here once again advocating plant medicine as a tool for awakening, I can only really tell you what it has done for *me*. And yes, what it has done is no less than miraculous, but it might not be everybody's trip this time around (As with the Course: "Ayahuasca is very for everybody, but not everybody is for Ayahuasca.") And yes, these substances can definitely be dangerous if you are not properly prepared. So please exercise due caution when approaching them!

I will also mention that the Course says the following about this subject:

"All worldly states must be illusory. If God were reached directly in sustained awareness, the body would not be long maintained."

This suggests that even Samadhi attained through yogic *sadhana* (yogic or spiritual practice) is itself illusory, it's not the ultimate. It might be more lasting and life-transforming, but the question "which is better?" seems to be beyond the rational mind.

To me, there is no doubt a very good reason why ACIM came into being during the years 1965-1976, as this was one of the most spiritually fertile times in recent human history. I will not hesitate to point to the already obvious: the precipitous rise of LSD and eastern mysticism at just that time, and how the Course might have come into being as a guide map for many who were now ready to fully awaken (or who had already had experiences of doing just this). And now, too, with the emergence of ayahuasca on the world stage in recent years, ACIM seems to me to be a guide *par excellence* for those seeking to make some sense of the ayahuasca experience.

Let us turn again to the passage from the Course with which I began this section, particularly these words:

"Others find it [the realization that the world is an illusion] in experience that is not of this world, which shows them that the world does not exist because what they behold must be the truth, and yet it clearly contradicts the world."

Ayahuasca has the potential to grant access to such a seemingly impossible experience, as I have myself witnessed firsthand on more than several occasions with it now. In the following sections I will be offering a personal recounting/accounting of what that looked and felt like in real time, taken directly from my journal reports. And similar to what I did with *A Course in Miracles* above, I will again be looking closely at a channeled writing, this one titled *The Ayahuasca Manifesto*, which claims to be the voice of Mother Ayahuasca Herself.

Visionary Artwork Courtesy of Alexander George Ward
(Title: *As Forças*)

But first, Questions for the Aya Quest

What is ayahuasca? Where did it come from? How old is it? What is its purpose?

What are some of the common things people experience when using ayahuasca?

Is ayahuasca dangerous to use? How so? Does ayahuasca, for instance, make one more susceptible to attack/hosting by so-called entities, demonic or dark forces?

Why do people who use ayahuasca generally prefer to call it a "plant medicine" as opposed to a "drug"? What's the distinction?

Also, some who work with ayahuasca also refer to it as a "plant teacher." What does this mean? How can a plant be a teacher?

Does ayahuasca create a dependency? In other words, is it addictive, physically or psychologically?

Related question: If ayahuasca is so powerful, why does someone need to do it again? Why do people do it tens, hundreds and even thousands of times? Isn't that overkill?

Does one need a shaman or facilitator to oversee one's ayahuasca journey? Is it dangerous to do it on one's own?

Why is ayahuasca spoken of as a visionary medicine? What's the difference between "visions" and "hallucinations"?

What's the science behind ayahuasca? What does it do to your brain? How do we know that it's not toxic to the brain?

Who would ayahuasca be most helpful for?

Who should not use ayahuasca?

Heroine

(based on the song "Heroin" by Lou Reed)

I, don't know
Just where I'm going
But I'm
Gonna try
For the Queendom
If I can
'cause it makes me feel, like I'm a man
when I put this thing into my brain
and man I tell ya, things aren't quite the same
& I guess, I just don't know
& I guess, I just don't know

When I'm rushing on my run
& I feel just like Mary's son
& it turns out that we are all one
& I guess that I just didn't know
& I guess well I just don't know

Heroine (with an "e") be the death of "me"
Heroine, well She's my wife and She's my life
Because a mainer to my brain
Leads to a center in my heart
Where there is no counter part
& we are back at the start…

I Am Love

...& when Her Love begins to flow
there is nothing, nothing more to know
& when my Heroine is in my blood
& that blood is in my head
Then thank Goodness I'm good as dead
And thank Goddess I'm now aware
& thank God Is I finally care
& now I guess I just *do* Know

Oh, & I don't guess – I just Know.

DIVINING A DE-VINE MYSTERY

The cover design of the author's "Heart 'n' Hands" CD. The CD sets some of the most profound and poetic Course passages to music, with the intention of strengthening these liberating ideas by sharing them. Clearly the cover art also displays psychedelic over and undertones – intentional, of course.

Artwork by Alexa Ballenger. Graphic Design by Bea Acs.

What Ayahuasca Is for Me Right Now (In One Page)

"... the journey into darkness has been long and cruel, and you have gone deep into it. A little flicker of your eyelids, closed so long, has not yet been sufficient to give you confidence in yourself, so long despised" (T.18.III.3:3,4).

~ A Course in Miracles

Ten years and over 100 sessions later, this is what ayahuasca is to me... Ayahuasca is a kind of truth serum. Its purpose is to help those who partake of it to realize their divine-spiritual reality, and it does this through whatever means is most helpful to the individual, in whatever capacity they come to it.

For me personally, this has generally taken the form of being shown what the shadow or false self (ego) is, so that I may more clearly and easily discern the true from the false. Early on I had a number of sessions where I was confronted with feelings of extreme guilt, shame, fear, doubt, jealousy, and worthlessness, to name just a few of the more prominent emotions. To say I was shocked, awed and traumatized to the point of devastation by this and similar revelations does not do full justice to the degree of horror that I sometimes experienced with ayahuasca.

At first, I took all of this to mean that I really was irredeemably shameful, unworthy, unlovable, etc., but gradually over time (and with the help of yoga and ACIM, too) I began to understand that no, this is not just about me, this is the Ego-at-Large that I was experiencing. That is, the one Ego that we all are very much identified with, not only me. And slowly, over time, I began to see that I could just witness this false self, and simply not identify with it. As the Course puts it, I could more and more easily deny the denial of truth, which is what the ego is and represents. I could choose against it, rather than for it, as I have done most of my existence.

And as I did this intense inner work (and it does require much moment-to-moment vigilance), the ego began to fade and my sessions with the Mother Vine started to lighten up quite a bit, as did my life and interactions with everyone. For I was finally living more and more consistently anchored in the awareness of what I really am, as opposed to giving energy to what I am not. Not only that, but I began to recognize that it was not enough to simply not give energy to *my/the* ego, but also that I must extend the same to everyone around me. Which for me means not to judge, but just to rest in that space of loving awareness with everyone and everything, to see that we all, deep down, really do want the same thing, which is Love, and we are all hampered in the process but are doing the best that we know how.

The pay-off, if you will, is that with aya I began to have more and more glimpses of non-dual awareness, which means getting the ego out of the way entirely and just resting in the truth of who I am. Sessions with ayahuasca now became more joyous occasions than not, and whatever egoic layers were in the way going in to the session could that much more quickly and easily be shed now than they had been previously. I also noted that those who I facilitated sessions for were often coming to similar realizations and learning the way of non-judgment and forgiveness, moving toward the One.

I have known all along that I am here to serve as a guide, but ayahuasca has really helped me to get to the point where I can truly be confident in what I am here to share. So here I am now to commend it to those who feel truly ready for it...

Ps. I want to add a story that Ken Wapnick related about Helen Schucman, with whom he collaborated closely for years: Helen once asked Jesus, "Why is my life so difficult?" To which he replied that together they were going "through the mountain." The mountain referred to her fear. It would have been easier to walk to the top of the mountain and then back down to the other side, but that would have also taken much longer. Instead, she had chosen the quicker, but more challenging path of working through her fear (guilt) directly. And that, I propose, is what happens when one decides to partake of a substance like ayahuasca. One has essentially chosen to confront their "shadow," and that offers the potential of releasing a lot of fear all at once. But more on this to come...

Section I

[**Note:** Now that I've summarized what ayahuasca is to me at this juncture, the following sections will fill in details of what my journey (and to some extent, our collective journey) has looked like. This section is an excerpt from a very early journey report that I wrote after one of the first group ayahuasca ceremonies I attended that was facilitated by a Peruvian shaman. I feel this more personal introduction to the Amazonian plant medicine brew will be as good as one that offers a more "objective" reporting. That said, please keep in mind that this was written prior to my exposure to *A Course in Miracles* and *The Ayahuasca Manifesto*, and though much of what I say here is similar to what ACIM and the AM teaches, it is not exactly the same. But it is actually very close, and in any case, I will be filling in the gaps later.]

What Is Ayahuasca?

The following is a summary of what came to me the other night in ceremony. Some of the things ayahuasca revealed to me were specific to me at this stage of my personal evolution, yet they also seem universally applicable.

Ayahuasca is a divine gift that was revealed to humans as a way of evolving their consciousness. To do this, ayahuasca lovingly yet persistently shows the user all the ways in which s/he has strayed from the Divine. The first and foremost rebellion involves wanting to live apart from God, to live a separate, egoic existence. Ayahuasca reveals how shallow, empty, and ultimately unfulfilling this is. It shows how asleep we are, and how when we lose our mental focus, we slip into egoic patterns that do not serve us. Thus its main task is to awaken us and force us to concentrate our mind. When we do that, we find ourselves able to ascend to higher, purer realms of experience, beyond the walls of the ego-mind.

Ayahuasca is the teacher of teachers. It might have been the original teacher of humankind, or one of them. Whatever the case may be, it is a tool for accessing the highest states of yoga. If we truly are in the Kali Yuga, the dark age of materialism, perhaps ayahuasca is here now to lead us out of our addiction to physicality.

The tradition of shamanism is an old and venerable one, and we should respect and honor it as we do ayahuasca. Perhaps the two – shamanism and ayahuasca – are inseparable. The message I received from ayahuasca was that wanting to explore ayahuasca without the guidance of a shaman is misguided, and perhaps also again part of the egoic rebellion to want power and knowledge for oneself alone. Which is not to say that there are not some who can use ayahuasca on their own profitably [nor that all shamans are qualified guides], just as there are some who do not need a spiritual teacher like a guru. Yet most probably should not. Ultimately one has to follow one's conscience. It is also important to find a trustworthy shaman, one who is not usurping the tradition but speaking on behalf of it.

There is a saying: "The truth is simple, but it ain't easy." Yes, there is much work to do, we have to take full responsibility for our lack of focus and concentration, and do whatever we can to awaken ourselves. Any tool that we can use to do that is okay, as long as it serves the greater good. I don't feel that it is useful to call this "cheating." Rather, ayahuasca is simply an aid to one's yoga [spiritual] practice. Ayahuasca and sadhana (yogic discipline) mutually support one another. They do not have to be considered distinct paths. As the biblical saying goes, "Two heads are better than one" (pun intended :)

Section II

[Note: What follows is more of a journalistic reporting on the whole ayahuasca phenomenon, particularly as it relates to the issue of "yoga and psychedelics" in general.]

"Ayahuasca: Generation X's LSD"

So the story goes & grows...

In the 1960s, recreational and irresponsible use of the psychedelic LSD led to the US government's classification of it as a Schedule I drug (1966). Up until that time, LSD has been the subject of much interest and study by scientists, artists, and musicians, who were considering its potential in medicine and the arts.

Drs. Timothy Leary and Richard Alpert began studying LSD after being forced to resign from Harvard in 1963. While Dr. Leary infamously became "The High Priest of LSD" and was a proponent of LSD for the rest of his life, Dr. Alpert went to India in the late Sixties, found a guru, Neem Karoli Baba, and became Baba Ram Dass.

In 1971 Alpert, now as Ram Dass, published *Be Here Now* in which he told the story of how he gave Neem Karoli Baba a very high dose of LSD and "nothing happened" – it had no visible affect on the guru. The message to the hippie baby boomers was that they no longer needed drugs to get high; yoga could do the same thing or better for them.

Be Here Now was a bestseller and a watershed moment in the Sixties countercultural movement. In reality, it was part of a shift that had already been happening since the banning of LSD, as the Beatles' disillusionment with it a few years prior reflected.

Ram Dass' book was published right around the time when the Nixon administration created the Drug Enforcement Agency and began the "War on Drugs." As a result, the next generation, the so-called "Generation X," grew up with many anti-drug messages such as Nancy Reagan's "Just Say

No" slogan. Many of the Baby Boomers were now seeking and finding ways to get "high" without use of psychedelic substances. Some found it through running, others yoga, meditation, music and chant, biofeedback, breathwork, shamanism, and any number of "alternative" modalities.

Taking their lead, Generation X came of age in a world in which the excesses of the previous generation had been tempered by age and wisdom. In the world of yoga, a world I was introduced to in the mid-Nineties, drug use was very much frowned upon. Why would you use drugs if yoga (or another "alternative" modality) could do the same thing or better for you? This is the question most of the new gurus from the East had been asking their devotees, the largest percentage of whom were the flower children. Yoga, they taught, is about independence from any external substance, whether it take the form of a pill, a dogma, or a government. "Get high on yoga, not drugs," was their selling point.

Such was the reigning sentiment in the yoga world for at least three decades. For the most part, yogis were not drug users; it was considered a contradiction in terms, antithetical to the whole yoga ethic and ethos of declaring one's independence from external tools and methods. I intuitively felt the truth of this from the very beginning of my encounter with yoga.

Yoga also was supposedly preparing me to be prepared for anything, but nothing could prepare me for what was to come…

Since the early nineties, the Amazonian plant medicine known as ayahuasca (also, yagé; prounced "ya-hey") has entered the world stage like no other psychoactive substance since LSD, becoming one of the most widely discussed and even celebrated psychedelics (aka "entheogens") of this era. In the last decade, ayahuasca seems to be teetering on the edge of mainstream status, if not already exactly a household term, having now been featured by such major media outlets as National Geographic, CNN, NPR, the Huffington Post, and even showing up in Hollywood films such as *Wanderlust* and *While We're Young*, as well as in documentaries on Youtube, Netflix, and other movie-streaming sites.

In the yoga world, of which I have been a keen observer over the last 20+ years, ayahuasca has definitely made its presence known. Based on my observations, there are as many Generation X yogis now who have tried ayahuasca as not, and a good percentage of those who have partaken have done it more than once. Certainly those of the older, Baby Boomer generation that I have approached about this have had mixed views, but more often than not, they have at least been somewhat sympathetic, if not actual participants. Some highly regarded yoga professionals have confided to me that they have used the Amazonian plant medicine in the tens and even hundreds of times, and not because it didn't work the first time. Mind you, these are some of the biggest names in the yoga world, with a considerable influence that would be difficult to estimate. (Others choose to abstain. Grammy-nominated kirtan wallah Jai Uttal, whose wife is Brazilian, told me in an interview – included in my previous book, *Who Am I?* – that he has turned down the invitation to ceremony many times; it's not his path.)

To be sure, there is still considerable tension and debate about this in the wide world of yoga, as there is in the broader society where ayahuasca and other psychoactive substances are still illegal in most places. Yet it's not only the legal status that has created a kind of rift in opinion; again, it's also the ever-present question as to whether a psychoactive substance could ever be fully embraced in a community that prides itself on self-reliance and to being to large extent anti-drug.

Growing up in the era of the War on Drugs and the son of a father of the Greatest Generation who was adamantly opposed to drugs and alcohol, I steered clear of all substances for the first 35 years of my life. About 10 years ago now, I cautiously began to explore various substances of which ayahuasca was only one, but the most significant for me. What I experienced from it was remarkable and very useful on my life's journey. It was also somewhat terrifying and left me with a new set of questions and issues with which to confront.

My fascination led me to begin writing a book on the subject of "yoga and psychedelics," as I continued to attend various ayahuasca ceremonies and speak with people about it, including elders and shamans. Nearly a decade later, I published *Who Am I? Yoga, Psychedelics and the Quest for Enlightenment* with the intention of inspiring greater awareness and a public dialogue on the issues involved, particularly in the yoga community. My sense is that because I equate yoga more broadly with "spirituality," many people will find the book interesting as it touches on the most universal and fundamental issues that we all deal with, whether we do yoga or psychedelics or not.

The current book, *I Am Love*, is a sequel to the first. This book raises many of the same questions, yet is a bit more authoritative in its answers to those questions. The authority comes from direct experience, as the following report demonstrates…

I AM LOVE

There is nothing to fear.

This is the title of ACIM Lesson #48.
*"The presence of fear is a sure sign
that you are trusting in your own strength."*

Section III

What is the Ayahuasca Manifesto?

"The ritual of my sacrament is not a religion. I will directly go into the soul of every Human and reveal in crisp detail their divine nature. This does not require a doctrine of faith, dogmas nor philosophies. Neither religion nor church. I am just in communion with the innate religiousness of the Human Beings. I dwell in the temple of the spirit."

~ The Ayahuasca Manifesto

"I always wanted to write, but I always figured it'd be no good unless somehow the hand just took the pen and started moving without me really having anything to do with it. Like, automatic writing. But it just never happened."

~ Jim Morrison

In the first section of this book, I introduced *A Course in Miracles*, a channeled (or more accurately, "scribed") writing that came through a reluctant professed-atheist professor of psychology at Columbia University in the mid-Sixties. In this section, I introduce another channeled writing, *The Ayahuasca Manifesto*, whose source is an apprentice of Don José Campos, a well-known and respected Peruvian shaman. Don José is the subject of a book and film of the same title, *The Shaman and Ayahuasca*, both highly recommended to learn more about Amazonian plant medicine in general, and ayahuasca in particular.

The Ayahuasca Manifesto (AM) is particularly interesting in that it claims to be the voice of the Mother Vine Herself (Ayahuasca is often called "Grandmother" or just "Mother Devine"), much as *A Course in Miracles* is understood to be a message from Jesus. Clearly these are bold and controversial assertions. While it does not seem that we could ever with 100% accuracy determine the truth or falsity of these claims, we can determine the value of these documents via their practical utility, their usefulness to us. *By their fruits ye shall know them.*

The AM was first published anonymously and in Spanish in 2011, but it later came to light that it came through an apprentice of Don Jose who had received it through what he felt was the inspiration of Mother Ayahuasca during an ayahuasca ceremony. As with Helen Schucman and her scribing of A Course in Miracles, the initial prompting that Don Jose's apprentice received was very insistent – he was being called to write a book specifically to "defend me [Ayahuasca] from the attacks that I will be receiving in the future." At first the man did not respond to the urgency of the message, writing it down in his journal but then forgetting about it. Two years later the man received the exact same urgent message in the form of "a voice from the high spiritual realms," but this time the message came spontaneously, not while using Ayahuasca. And this time, the man took the call seriously and the Ayahuasca Manifesto came to him through inspiration over the next several days. The original message was in Spanish, but it has since been translated into English and several other languages.

Before continuing, let's stop and point out a few interesting points of connection here. First, as with Helen Schucman's channeling of *A Course in Miracles*, the message Don Jose's apprentice received was insistent, there was an urgency to it. As you will recall, Helen kept getting the message: "*This is A Course in Miracles, please take notes.*" The message would not stop until she agreed to write it down and undertake the scribing process. In both cases, too, it seems that there was a case of the proverbial "reluctant prophet" – both scribes at first balked at their calling.

Another parallel to note here is that while the original call to write *The Ayahuasca Manifesto* came during an ayahuasca ceremony, the actual work itself was produced through inspiration while **not** under the influence of ayahuasca. This is also the way ACIM came into being. To the best of my knowledge, no one has ever claimed that Helen might have been on something like a psychedelic while scribing the Course. It would have indeed been remarkable had this been the case given that the Course came through over the course of 7+ years(!) While much shorter, though by no means short or light reading, the Ayahuasca Manifesto was channeled over a period of just a few days.

Finally, and connected to this, we are told that the Ayahuasca Manifesto was given by a "voice from the high spiritual realms." What this means exactly remains to be determined, but it could just mean that the work came from a valid and trustworthy spiritual source. However, elsewhere we are told that the voice was of the "spirit of Ayahuasca," as one would think it would be, given that it is written in the first person as if Ayahuasca itself were speaking directly to the reader. This adds a sense of authority to the writing, just as the Course's claim to be from Jesus adds weight to its message.

That is all in the way of similarities between ACIM and the AM. One point of seeming difference between the two works is that while the urgency behind the scribing of AM was due to its being necessary to defend ayahuasca from "attacks that I will be receiving in the future" (as is often the case with a "manifesto"), the Course has no such stated reason for being. Rather, the Course's purpose seems to be to show that any "attack" can never threaten our true self, and so no defense is necessary. Indeed, the title of one Course lesson is: "In My Defenselessness My Safety Lies."

That said, the very existence of the Course itself is to many of its subscribers proof that "attack is never justified," and in this way the Course, too, is a defense of the truth from attack. Thus, there is a sense that both works – ACIM and the AM – can be placed in the category of "apologetics," namely, works that are aimed at defending truth from attack. I would say the same is true of the book you are now reading, though with a Cheshire cat knowing smile that no "apology" is truly necessary.

One further word on this subject of defending the truth from attack is in order. As was just said, the Course's position is that the truth actually needs no defense. We need do nothing, actually, but accept the truth as it is. And that truth is that the ego and the world are not real, and that God as Love as Total Unity is all that truly is. Yet because we are all so resistant to this all-too-simple and seemingly incredible truth, we are all constantly "attacking" it in some way or another through our resistance/denial, sometimes consciously, but more often than not, unconsciously.

What ayahuasca showed me personally is that the ego, the embodiment of all of our fear-based thinking, is not the truth seeker's amigo and the ego must go in order to truly know what/who I am. On a deeper level, all thought is based in fear, because all thought is an attempt to create a separation between the thinker and what is thought about. In other words, thinking creates a subject-object dichotomy that serves to reinforce the egoic/illusionary belief that there is a thinker in the first place. In the world of form, it may be true that ayahuasca needs to be defended, but on a deeper level, Spirit needs no defense. If ayahuasca were not here to lead us back to Spirit (God, Source, Love, Unity, or whatever you want to call it), there would be something else that would be available in its place, as Spirit meets us where we are and uses *"skillful means"* – a Buddhist term that refers to the use of any and all means necessary and available to help us wake up.

I want to return a moment to the issue of urgency. From this side of the veil, shall we say, there is definitely a constant strong sense of urgency and emergency in both our private life and in the world at large. Yes, it certainly does look like the world is running down (devolution) and the Apocalypse is at hand, it most certainly does! There was a time in my life, actually a good portion of my adult life, where I so worried that my life or the world could end horribly at any moment that I found it difficult to be around people because I couldn't understand why they didn't feel that same sense of imminent doom. "Don't you see you could die – we could all die – any moment now?!?" I inwardly screamed, amazed at people's obliviousness.

But now, after years of working through my "stuff," I have no such feeling of imminent disaster or much concern about my world or any world going anywhere anytime soon. They will be around as long as I want them to be, and they will dissolve when it is my time for timelessness, that is all. On one level, though, I'm sure glad I went through all of that turmoil. For if it hadn't been for those extreme zealous apocalyptic feelings, I would not have made the journey I did, nor be able to share this information and wisdom. (And as I said at the outset, writing feels like righting – feels right to me.)

Similarly, when Helen first began scribing *A Course in Miracles*, she asked Jesus what the Course is for, and the answer she was given was that there was a need for a "celestial speed-up" due to the "world situation... worsening to an alarming degree." While some will disagree, I follow the school of thought that says that at that point in time, Helen (a reluctant prophet, remember) merely was hearing what she needed to hear in order to inspire her to continue with the task. Later she was to learn that the world and time are illusory, and that no so "speed-up" is truly necessary. The only urgency ever is when we feel the personal urgency to awaken, and when we do, we will find the call and the witnesses and the means to do that everywhere.

Who Wrote *The Ayahuasca Manifesto?*

Recall that this is the same question that I asked above in regard to the authorship of *A Course in Miracles*. And as with ACIM, no one can really answer this question. But once again we can start with entertaining the question of whether the AM could have been written by a human being, not "the spirit of Ayahuasca," as it claims.

Could the AM have been authored by a mere human intellect? Yes, of course it could have. Is it likely? I would argue to the contrary, simply because, as with ACIM, the work seems too complex and authoritative to be of merely human origin. That doesn't mean we should take its claim to be the voice of Ayahuasca itself at face value, but it does mean that we would be wise not to easily dismiss this work as fraudulent or biased (as I earlier said we would be wise not to dismiss the work of Ken Wapnick). Indeed, I am including this discussion in this book as I feel the AM is a very important document, worthy of our consideration.

As with ACIM, we can also ask if perhaps the AM was authored by a spirit other than ayahuasca with some secret agenda of its own. Again, as with ACIM, this seems impossible to determine with absolute certainty. For myself, after having ingested ayahuasca many times now, I can say that the essential message of the AM rings true to me. That is enough for me to take the document seriously, but I am still open to hearing a critique of it.

Ayahuasca as Holy Mother & Holy Spirit

Up until now I have seemed to make a distinction between "human" and "spiritual" authorship, whereas there is not such a hard and fast distinction. As I understand it, when Helen scribed ACIM, it was coming from a place within her, something that had always been there. We could say that it was her heart or "right mind." It was not separate from Helen, she was just able to get her ego out of the way to let that "voice" – her true voice – come through her. And the Course uses the terms "Jesus" and "Holy Spirit" to refer to that "Voice," a voice which is actually within all of us, if we but knew how to listen. We are told that Jesus was the first to truly listen to the Voice of the Holy Spirit, and in doing so, he actually became the Holy Spirit, which is why we cannot properly differentiate between the two.

It needs to be kept in mind that Jesus as the author of the Course goes out of his way to not put himself on an unapproachable pedestal; rather, he is our elder brother who assures us that we can do exactly what he did, which is to listen only to the Voice for God, the calm voice of reason and rightmindedness within ourselves which is none other than the "Holy Spirit." And anyone who does as he did will discover something truly amazing, which is that he/she is no different than Jesus or the Holy Spirit. So not only could such a one say that "I and my Father are One," but also: "I and my Brother [Christ] are One." I believe this is what Helen discovered and knew, at least in those moments when she was truly able to let go. Again, I can say this because I have had experiences that have also made this clear to me.

Similarly, my Indian guru, Sri Karunamayi, once told an assembled crowd of westerners on Christmas Eve that she would like us all to know that "I and My Mother are One." We all laughed when she said this, but she was making a serious point, which is that we are not different than she is and that we can also realize our oneness with Her, and that is where she was leading us. Please keep in mind that the "Divine Mother" is understood to be a spiritual principle or presence that sometimes takes human form (as an "avatar"), in this case as the form of Sri Karunamayi, whose name means "Goddess of Compassion."

I bring this up because it is likewise possible to understand the "Holy Spirit" of the Course as a feminine principle or in feminine terms. This is not too much of a stretch: The Hebrew translation of ACIM renders "Holy Spirit" as "Shekhinah," which in the Jewish Kabbalah the feminine presence of God. This makes sense, too, as then the Trinity would be Father, Mother, and their Son. I am sure this would resonate with many; it certainly does with me. And at the same time, in the end the gender doesn't really matter and the Course does suggest, for example, that we could even substitute any name we like in place of "Jesus." That said, if we have an issue with "Jesus" or the idea of God or the Holy Spirit as a "He," then that is something we might want to look at as it's almost definitely something in the way of our peace of mind.

Again, I want to continue to stay true here to the idea that ultimately there is nothing outside of us, all is within, meaning that things like the "Divine Mother" and "Jesus" and even the "Spirit of Ayahuasca" are all within us. But from this side of the veil, from the dualistic perspective (where we are now), it can be helpful to speak of them as something separate from us. And now, with all of the above on the table, we are getting closer to the idea that Ayahuasca, as "Divine Mother," might somehow be connected to what the Course calls "The Holy Spirit."

Why does this even matter? Well, it doesn't, but it does for anyone who might want some strengthening of their faith in this whole process. Or as a reality check of sorts.

So we can ask: Why does the idea of the "Divine Mother" resonate with us? Or with *you*? What is it about the Divine Mother that comes to mind every time we hear those words? Aren't they the qualities of nurturing, mercy, compassion, forgiveness, sanctuary, unconditional love? And aren't these but a reminder of what we truly want to receive and to give to all? And isn't this a truth that we know and that we want to live, yet we fail and fall short continually in our interactions with others and ourselves? Well, it has been my experience that this is what Ayahuasca is wanting to show us – how to embody these principles more and more by releasing what is not loving within ourselves, and embodying more and more what is truly of love. And this is also the work of the Holy Spirit.

And yet, again, these deep driving forces towards Unity are not separate from us but live in each of our hearts and minds.

My essential point above is to show how Ayahuasca and *A Course in Miracles* are related, at least for myself, and to make a case that Ayahuasca as Divine Mother may be understood as essentially the same as what the Course refers to as the Holy Spirit. Both are that memory locked deep in our heart and mind of the unity of all life and how to return to it: Through removing the blocks to separation and the process of forgiveness. And now to return to the message of "the Spirit of Ayahuasca" according to *The Ayahuasca Manifesto*. But before we do, consider the following poem by the Course's scribe, Helen Schucman, in which she seems to speak of the Holy Spirit as Mother…

Mother Of The World

Peace is a woman, mother to the world,
Whom God has sent to lay a gentle hand
Across a thousand children's fevered brows.
In its cool certainty there is no fear,
And from her breasts there comes a quietness
For them to lean against and to be still.
She brings a message to their frightened hearts
From Him Who sent her. Listen now to her
Who is your mother in your Father's Name:
"Do not attend the voices of the world.
Do not attempt to crucify again
My first-born Son, and brother still to you."
Heaven is in her eyes, because she looked
Upon this Son who was the first. And now
She looks to you to find him once again.
Do not deny the mother of the world
The only thing she ever wants to see,
For it is all you ever want to find.

~ **Helen Schucman**[25]

---

25   See Helen Schucman, *The Gifts of God*.

The Essential Message of the Ayahuasca Manifesto

"Jesus saith unto him, I am the way, the truth, and the life: no man cometh unto the Father, but by me."

~ *The Gospel of John 14:6*

"My sacrament is only one of so many expressions of religiousness in Humans.
It is an affirmative expression of surrender to his/her spiritual nature; it is an act of bravery and conviction to reach out towards the central Light of all existence."

~ The Ayahuasca Manifesto

This is a manual for a special curriculum, intended for teachers of a special form of the universal course. There are many thousands of other forms, all with the same outcome (M-1.4:1-2)...A universal theology is impossible, but a universal experience is not only possible but necessary (C-in.2-5).

~ A Course in Miracles

Like ACIM (and unlike traditional Christianity), the *Ayahuasca Manifesto* makes very clear that it is only one of many paths home, as the above two passages attest. These paths are also in no way elitist, they are open to all. Yet relatively few will choose these paths home and I will attempt to explain why below.

Now, while saying that these are not the only paths that one can take (or tools that one can use), both ACIM and the AM do claim to offer a quicker route, one that can save a lot of time. Consider the following passage from the AM:

"If you want to return to the Light, you can only do it by following back the path that took you here. There is no shortcut to the Light, you just need to return as the pure child that originally left. I am offering you the most powerful spiritual healing tool to return to the Light. It is the most powerful medicine that ever existed; nothing else will ever surpass the direct route of the botanical— glandular bridge. All the other benefits are in one way or another, by-products of the spiritual healing."

Granted, some would argue with the suggestion that ayahuasca is the "most powerful spiritual tool," but that is what is being claimed (and by Mother Ayahuasca herself, remember). However, being the most powerful does not mean it is a shortcut and the AM makes a point to say there are no shortcuts:

"Only your own inner Light can guide you towards the brighter Light, only the Light can guide you to the Light. There are no shortcuts or detours; you are already Light, and you own the talents to expand it within you. Awaken, open your arms and rejoice. You are all love, and fear does not fit in you."

This is essentially the same message as ACIM, just using different terminology (such as "Light' instead of "Holy Spirit"). And the Course likewise says that it presents a path that can save one a lot of time, even "thousands of years." The reason being that until we understand what the ego is and how it works, we will tend to be endlessly caught up in its machinations. This can and does continue for apparent lifetimes. And the reason it does is because the ego uses fear (sin, guilt and fear) to keep us from waking up to the fact that it is really nothing and following it is madness. From the AM:

"[The] awakening of your cosmic nature is a powerful tool for managing your own ego structure. Ego is always seeking its permanence in your soul and will never cease to sabotage your spiritual aspirations, as your awakening will diminish its authority over your Human machine."

So though both ACIM and AM present themselves as potentially quicker paths, the work that is required is actually the same, and that work involves total disillusionment – the *dissolution* of all fear (ego). To do this seems nearly impossible and few actually ever arrive at the place of even getting a proper glimpse. Consider this passage from the Bhagavad Gita:

"Out of many thousands among men, one may endeavor for perfection, and of those who have achieved perfection, hardly one knows Me in truth."
(Bhagavad Gita 7.3)

Prior to the Bhagavad Gita, the Upanishads (Katha Upanishad) had said the path to enlightenment is like walking a 'razor's edge' – it is fraught with chutes and ladders, snakes and adders. Only a true guru, it was said, could show the way. Perhaps it is necessary to say that the book you are reading right now is an attempt to show that these spiritual tools alone – ACIM, AM, and Yoga – have the potential to serve the function of a true guru, though help from living teachers might also be warranted and very useful.

Again, I want to say that I am in no way attempting to conflate these 3 paths; indeed, they are all quite similar, but they are not exactly the same. Their uniqueness needs to be respected, but that shouldn't keep us from seeing what we can learn through comparison and contrast.

For myself, I will say there is really only one path and that is to listen to your heart, the teacher within. Each of these paths, together and alone have the potential to guide one to the heart, to home. And I am pointing to the fact that all 3 of these tools/paths make very clear that it all comes down to one thing: uprooting the false self through rooting out all fear. The end of *feardom* is freedom, there really is no other way.

Let's conclude this section with one more notable passage from the AM, this one again playing up the importance of the AM as a work of apologetics necessary to ward off future attacks from the uninitiated;

"Another very effective method used to sabotage my mission with the Human species is by generating and manipulating the powerful emotion of fear. You have nothing to fear. I am not the cause of any deaths, I just channel Light and vital energy through your secret meridians. Any accusation or allegation of danger, permanent injury or death should be thoroughly investigated to allow science itself grant me the Human absolution. It should be expected that my enemies manipulate the facts to instill fear at any available opportunity, as this is part of their debasing agenda against my global expansion. It should be the objective of all my supporters to gradually obtain the social and legal acceptance of my sacrament as alternative medicine until I become officially accepted by the governments of modern society."

Granted, some might bristle at the tone and some of the wording here such as "my global expansion" and "my enemies," but isn't that just what is in question here – the extent of our fear? On the other hand, unlike ACIM, the AM does bring in an element of "us vs. them" thinking that might result in more separation and misunderstanding. People who read the Unabomber's manifesto, for instance, might note similarities of expression. Others who are more sympathetic to the cause will of course just applaud this as Mother taking a strong stance on behalf of her children. Which leads me to relate the following story…

> "Love brings up everything unlike itself for the purpose of healing and release."
>
> ~A Course in Miracles

A Tale of Two Brothers

"Know what doesn't matter, and if your brother asks you to do something outrageous, do it because it doesn't matter."

~ A Course in Miracles

There was once a young man who grew up surrounded by various intoxicating substances. From an early age he and his friends would regularly smoke marijuana, drink alcohol, and also experiment with harder drugs like cocaine. It was just what they did and what they saw their elders doing, too, so why should they be any different?

In time, this young man grew wiser and, with a show of considerable will power, bowed out of the crowd he had been in. Seeking to overcome his addictive behavior, he began to explore the Native American tradition of using psychoactive plant medicines such as peyote. And for a while that worked for him and helped him get free of certain negative habit patterns, but it also did not last. While he saw the value of the medicine path, he was not convinced that he needed it and began to think that there were other more "natural" means to feel better and even get high.

So he began to explore modalities such as yoga, arts and crafts, music, martial arts, dance, and even gymnastics. He began to see that he was feeling better and better and he no longer needed any substances to feel alive and whole. He became an advocate for a substance-free lifestyle. He saw it as his duty to convince as many people as he could that drugs, including and especially psychedelics, were not the way and were in fact harmful to them, particularly their brains. In this, he became rather zealous for the cause. He would sometimes even become belligerent in regard to people who had anything to do with such substances, especially sellers, feeling as if they were leading people astray, especially young people. He had zero tolerance for people who used drugs, and even less for those who sold them.

So hold that snapshot, and now check this out...

There was once another young man, of the same generation, Generation X, who grew up in a culture where drugs were not so available. Not that kids in his community weren't taking them, but he made a conscious choice not to associate with them or to use any substances, including alcohol and marijuana. Instead, from an early age he got heavily into distance running. In a sense, running was his drug and he was at first unwittingly addicted to it. But he prided himself on it being a "natural high" versus illegal substances other kids were taking, risking being caught and potentially messing with their brains.

Later the young man got into yoga and at that point he became even more convinced that drugs were not the way, partly because it was the message he heard from the elders in the yoga community. And this made complete sense to him given his background and experience. He had been feeling so alive and ecstatic without drugs, and his yoga practice was bringing him to new "highs" all the time. There was a part of him that was curious about things like LSD, but not so curious that he would actually try something as risky as that.

Ten years later, however, after experiencing a decided lull in his yoga practice, he was offered various psychoactive substances and he now felt ready to try them. When he did, he was surprised to discover that he was learning some very interesting things about himself and his psychology from these substances, to say the least. He began to look at his old attitudes toward substances (i.e. "drugs") and saw how while those attitudes had served him at the time, such intolerance was no longer helpful. At the same time, he still questioned the ultimate utility of such things, and whether the more "natural" pathways such as yoga were still to be preferred.

So this "brother" became a cautious advocate of what he began to refer to as "plant medicine." He looked around him and noted that a growing number of people were also re-evaluating psychedelic substances and wondering whether things like ayahuasca and psilocybin mushrooms might just have some medicinal and societal value after all, not to mention being aids on the spiritual path.

Now it was around this time that the two "brothers" in question met. I call them brothers because they were so similar in so many ways. They were very much kindred spirits, of the same soul tribe you might say. At first, as you might expect, they were on good terms with each other. They shared a lot of the same friends and communal activities, as well as interests like music and physical conditioning. But it was when the first brother found out that the second was bringing plant medicines into the community that things began to change.

And that's a bit of an understatement. Suddenly, the first brother had what seemed to be a personal vendetta against the second. According to the first, the second brother was no more than a drug pusher, influencing the young and innocent from a position of power to take substances which he strongly believed were harmful to them, not to mention illegal. The second brother, for his part, knew he was not pushing anything, everyone was free to make their own adult decisions about such matters. Furthermore, the second brother sensed that the first had an emotional blockage in regard to all substances. In other words, it wasn't about the substances themselves, it was about his own troubled past and what these substances symbolized for him.

And then the first brother took it even further, essentially outing the second brother on social media, telling the community to stay away from this wolf in sheep's clothing. The second brother considered it might be best to just remain silent, but then thought silence would be an admission of guilt and decided to try to engage in what might be helpful dialogue – at least for those who were open to listening without prejudging. But quickly the dialogue turned into an *ad hominem* attack against the second brother, with very little actual mature discourse on the subject at hand. The second brother quickly realized that reason was futile and ended the dialogue. Meanwhile, the whole local community had been watching the exchange…

"There is no order of difficulty in miracles… there is no hierarchy of illusions."

~ A Course in Miracles

At this point, I want to affirm that both brothers were right in their own way, and if this book is about anything, it is about looking at how judgment is a slippery slope down to a hell of our own making. That said, we can also and in a generalized way say that when deciding such matters as these on the level of form, the less judgmental and prejudicial stance is more helpful in terms of finding what we all really want (really) – peace, joy, happiness, our true self. As the Course pointedly asks, *"Would you rather be right, or happy?"* If we want to be right, sure, we'll feel great for a while having crushed our opponents, but what we will have really crushed is our own inner peace because at a fundamental level we are all one. Peace is the natural fruit of releasing judgment.

I would add that the Course is also about offering a "correction" to the mistakes (not sins) of humanity, particularly in the realm of religion and spirituality. Traditional Christianity, in particular, is offered the biggest correction of all, as Christ's original message got lost along the way (focusing on hell, sin, punishment, the deification of Jesus, etc.), and was actually misunderstood from the beginning.

But such errors in perception are not Christianity's alone, they are very much a human problem. Indeed, students of *A Course in Miracles* have fallen into the same kinds of errors. I say this because I am aware that there are ACIM students out there who take the view that psychedelic drugs are antithetical to what the Course is teaching. They are magical ways to deal with the ego and fail to get at the root of the problem, they say. They are temporary solutions at best, and dangerous methods at worst. A true ACIM student would know that nothing external to us is needed beyond our own choice for Love (Spirit), or fear (ego).

For sure. And a true ACIM student would also know that even breathing is a magical pill of sorts, a way of keeping our sense of separation alive and well. We all use "magic" (external aids) all the time and to deny that we do or to say that one form of magic is better than another is to make the mistake of seeing an order of difficulty in miracles, which is to say, to see a "hierarchy of illusions." In other words, an illusion is an illusion is an illusion. Whether in the form of a "drug" substance or some other form, what's the difference?

The other point dying to be expressed in this here book before you is that psychedelics like ayahuasca just might have the potential to show you some things about the mind that you could not possibly be aware of (except vaguely) in your normal waking consciousness. And for a very simple reason: You're too scared, the ego is too threatened. And many people are opposed to such "drugs" for that very reason: Fear. Whether it's fear of taking them, what other people might think of you for taking them, what you might think about yourself for taking them, etc. Fear is fear is fear.

Psychedelics are not the problem, your mind is. Psychedelics are also not the solution, the solution is in your mind. But how in God's name would you ever know that unless you understood your mind a little better?

This is why people do the Course and wonder why they're not having the experience the Course points to. Of course you're not, there's a shitload of fear and judgment still blocking the way! One of the Course lessons is "I will be still a moment and go home." No you won't! Not anytime soon, not unless you're prepared to be scared. The Course and psychedelics are not for the faint of heart, at least not when it comes to really looking at what the Course calls the "viciousness" of the ego. But the good news is, you *can* prepare for calmly witnessing these things just by being willing to daily question your own judgments and tightly held beliefs. And yes, you might just get a glimpse of y/our true nature at any moment.

So I was recently invited to come to an ACIM gathering, but when I asked if it would be okay to bring my first book (*Who Am I?*) and tell people about it, I was told that they would prefer I didn't as they were more "purists" about ACIM. Somehow they couldn't see how that was a judgment against me and what I had spent a good portion of my life researching. There was slightly less hesitancy when I explained that actually my book is less about advocating one thing or another, and much more about asking the right questions so as to offer a helpful discourse on the subject of substances and spirituality. But the answer was still no.

One thing that is not clearly understood about ACIM, or if it is, is terribly frustrating, is that the Course actually is not prescriptive on the level of form. In other words, it doesn't tell you how to live. Nowhere does it say, "This is good. You should do this. And that's bad. You shouldn't do that." What it does say is that whatever you do, ask yourself: Are you doing it from a place of fear (guilt, judgment, shame, revenge, lack, etc.), or from Love – just because you know in your heart of hearts it's the right thing to do in that moment? So the Course does not say, for example, that sex is bad, don't do it. Or that premarital sex is bad, per se. Or even adultery. Or even (hold onto your pants) that rape is bad, per se. Yes, this is where most would turn this off. How could rape ever be anything other than what it is?

*"You have no idea of the tremendous release and deep peace that comes from **meeting yourself and your brothers totally without judgment**."*

And it doesn't say that psychedelics are a no-no either. It also doesn't say they're good. In fact, it has nothing to say on the subject. It's really more of a matter of *pragmatism* – whether they are practically useful or not. If they seem useful to you, helpful in some way in your process, then why question their value to you in that moment? Or their usefulness to someone else? Why judge? *Who are you* to judge?

And now, back to our tale of the two brothers…

Because they were such kindred spirits, the second brother knew that perhaps one of the few things that might actually help the first brother was something like ayahuasca. Even though the first seemed happy to many on the surface, it didn't take much to see that he was actually a deeply troubled individual. But he was too proud and closed to be open to help from those who he saw as threats to his self-styled identity as community health advocate and bodyguard of sorts. So the second brother let the matter go and even did not try to stop the first in his campaign against him.

And so the years passed.

And then, several trips around the sun after all of this went down, the community was shocked to learn that the first brother had violently taken his life. It was surprising to many, but not to those who had observed the degree of emotional torment this brother was under. He had clearly been living under so much guilt and shame and self-judgment that he saw no other way out but to stop the pain in that most dramatic way.

Again, no judgment. If someone were to make a judgment here, this book would be worth nothing. This is exactly what the brother needed and what needed to happen. There are no mistakes., no loss or gain in the Divine Economy.

So why am I sharing this story here? Simply to help those who have eyes to see and ears to listen. It is just for those who are waking up. It is not to try to prove something, for this is not about me, just as to say "I Am Love" is not about me. It's about Love. And Love is one and has already won. Fear in all its forms has already been revealed to be nothing. If you want to keep inviting fear to the party, be its guest and it will be your guest. And you will have second guessed yourself once again.

Love is non-judgment, and Love is all there is, all we are.

And here's an old story to bring the point home…

The Foolish Wise Judge from Chelm

Way back when, there was a town called Chelm. But this wasn't any old town, this town was just a little different. You see, the people of Chelm were very foolish, very foolish indeed. In fact, the Chelmites were so foolish that they had become wise, making true the old saying:

*"If a fool persists in his folly,
he will become wise."*

Actually, if they weren't wise, I wouldn't be telling you this story. I wouldn't want to waste your time! God knows, you are no fool...

So once upon a time in Chelm, there was a man who brought a lawsuit against another man claiming this or that, it doesn't really matter for the purposes of the story. But the first man, the plaintiff, said that the other, the defendant, had hurt him in some way.

The case was brought to court and was to be decided by a single judge. Now the judge, though he was a judge, was just one of these wise fools. And that day, as was usually the case, the judge's wife and 6-year-old daughter accompanied him to court to be with him while he heard the case.

And so, they had their day in court. Many people were in attendance, mainly the relatives and friends of the plaintiff and defendant. There was a lot of excitement in the air. It was a big deal!

First the judge listened to the plaintiff present his case. He made a very powerful case against the defendant. The judge was impressed, so impressed that at the end of the plaintiff's speech, he pounded his gavel and declared:

"You know what? You're right!"

What a preposterous thing for a judge to say, no? Without even hearing the other side of the case? But remember that this judge was no ordinary judge.

So then the defendant had his turn to present his argument. And he, too, gave a very convincing speech. There were murmurs and scattered applause throughout the courtroom.

And once again, the judge was very impressed, so impressed that he once again pounded his gavel and cried out,
"You know what?!? You're right, too!!!"

The crowd in attendance was stupefied. What was going on here?
How could they both be right?
And how could the judge decide the case so quickly?

Just then, the judge's young daughter, who had been listening attentively to all the proceedings, called out to her father:

"Father, how can they both be right?
They can't both be right, can they?"

At which the judge stroked his beard thoughtfully and then pounded his gavel and said,

You know what, my dear, you're right, too!"

Very wise, right?

And this is usually the end of the story, but I wanted to just mention that there is one part that is often left out, which is what the judge's wife says to him. And what she said was…

"You old fool, how can everyone be right!?!"

To which the judge immediately replied,

"Now woman, you shut up."

THE BEGINNING.

The Music Now

When life feels so unfair
And no one seems to care
Her love flows everywhere
She wants to take you there

Ma

This is your way of being
Just change your way of seeing
Her way is so freeing
My heart is agreeing

Ma

When you learn how to bow
And flow with the Tao
Anyway anyhow
You are the music now

Ma

The Rise of the Anti-Shaman

"While I thought that I was learning how to live, I have been learning how to die."

~ **Leonardo Davinci**

I want to make this all the more by briefly telling the story of a man who at present has been working with ayahuasca for the past 32+ years. I have chosen to keep this individual's name out of the story, but it would not be difficult to determine his identity from the outline I am about to present. Though he has kept somewhat of a low profile, he is also well-known and respected in certain parts of Peru and around the world. I heard this story from this man for the third time just last week when I was with him in Peru, so I hope to have it down pretty well by now…

This man is originally from France and in his mid-20s found himself in Peru. He had up until that point in his life lived a decidedly conventional life and been fairly successful with a job and career and relationship, etc. It should also be noted that he did not have much interest in spirituality, and certainly no interest whatsoever in any kind of intoxicant, including alcohol and marijuana. But suddenly he was presented with the opportunity to participate in an ayahuasca ceremony with a shaman in what was then a remote part of Peru (mid-80s), and he reluctantly agreed.

As he tells his story, the first ceremony he had absolutely no experience whatsoever outside of some nausea. Meanwhile, all of the other participants seemed to have had some very interesting visions and other experiences. So he decided to give it another try…

But still nothing.

The third time he drank much more of it…

Still nothing.

A fourth and fifth time… *nada*.

He was ready to give up on it and go back to France. Only as fate would have it, his plane was canceled, so he had to stay longer. He went to one final night of ceremony. This time he was given only a spoonful by the shaman. And just that little spoonful gave him a lifetime of experience and the experience of a lifetime, one that he is still processing to this day.

So much happened in that first experience, I will just relate a few of the more salient details, the highlights that this man related to me…

He seemed to have left his body and was in an entirely other realm. He was hearing an inner voice speaking to him, guiding him. He saw his entire life up until that point and everything made sense to him. Another thing he was shown was that in each person there is a white ball in the heart center, and he was told that this is why a human birth is so precious. He was shown billions of people in crisp detail, all with this special heart center. He also was shown other " chakras" in the body, starting with the same white energy balls in the middle of the palms.

But all of this was not the most essential for him. No, what was most essential was at a certain point in the experience he had a brief taste of going completely beyond the subject-object (observer-observed) dichotomy and being in a spaceless, timeless, eternal "whole-oneness," as he put it. In other words, he briefly experienced non-duality, or oneness. This was the core experience (beyond experience) which he is still processing to this day. It was an experience which he spoke of as *satchidananda* – infinitude, being, bliss – and as being in "the eye of the cyclone." We will return to this in a moment.

This man told me he much enjoyed life and had no desire to leave this world, but this new world was so true and fascinating that now he did not wish to return. And yet the voice told him that he must return, it was not his time yet, he had to go "back down."

And then suddenly, he felt himself rather abruptly plopped back down into his physical body. And yet, he wasn't quite in it yet. Thinking that he was now a ghost stuck between worlds and would stay this way, he screamed for help. But neither the shaman nor anyone else in the room heard his cries. His inner voice told him to look at his hands, and as he did, he saw his physical body returning. And when it finally did, at that moment, the shaman turned the light on in the room to mark the close of the session.

As you might expect, this was all enough for him to stay in Peru and continue working with ayahuasca for a bit. But after awhile, some doubts crept in and he began to feel that he and the others he was journeying with were a little bit off. So he went back to France, determined never to return and he again resumed a rather conventional life. The only difference being he now felt his life was rather phony. But it didn't matter, he wasn't going back to the jungle. And in not too long, he had a wonderful place to live, a relationship, a good job, friends…everything seemed to be going very smoothly.

But just a few short months later, everything fell apart and he lost everything. He took this as a sure sign to return again to the jungle and to continue his work with ayahuasca. And this same pattern repeated itself several times over the next few decades, where he became doubtful and resistant and ran away from his inner work, but then was brought back to it once again by some unfortunate turn of events, which oftentimes was quite painful and challenging.

Resolving to finally accept his calling, his work with the medicine took a level of intensity that few ever explore. There was a time where he did ayahuasca every day, but at the very least he did 2 heroic sessions per week for years. He also worked with a series of different maestros. After 4 years, he finally felt ready to do solo journeys with ayahuasca, meaning without any external guidance. He had a great fear of this, yet with time, he gradually lost his fear.

His greatest fear was what he believes is all of our greatest fear, and that is the fear of death. He told me that he was very deeply afraid to die for a long time. I will say here that this was also my own experience, and perhaps one of the greatest motivating factors on my spiritual search. What will happen to "me" when I die? Will I still be "me" or something else? What will that something be? He would say, and I would concur, that if you are not in touch with this primal fear (of dying), it is due to the veils of ignorance obscuring your vision. Awareness of this fear and the search for resolution ultimately will yield wisdom. Without such a confrontation and exploration, inner growth and ultimate enlightenment or liberation will prove elusive.

….. This is why he now chooses to refer to what he does as "Death Coaching." Clearly this is not for everyone, and these days he generally only works with those who are open to viewing the spiritual journey and the use of ayahuasca in a radically new way. While he certainly respects the traditional Amazonian shamanistic worldview and perspective, and he actually was a shaman himself for a good decade (he said it took him another decade to undo that!), he now feels it is too limited. For the traditional view is primarily dualistic, teaching essentially that outside forces are at work in our experience with ayahuasca and the spirit world. Whereas his view is primarily non-dualistic, with the view that everything depends on the consciousness of the one doing ayahuasca. For instance, when one feels attacked by some outer force, a so-called "entity," it is actually a manifestation of an inner state, not something being imposed from without.

This makes all the difference in how one approaches work with the medicine. It is also why he now sometimes somewhat tongue-in-cheek refers to himself as an "anti-shaman." More to the point, he terms what he does "Integral Shamanism," which involves integrating and transcending all of the different levels of reality until one finally rests in the non-dual state of awareness. The closest he has found to this is in the Dzogchen tradition of Tibetan Buddhism. The ultimate realization of this is that "*nirvana is samsara*," or realizing non-dual awareness in the world and all levels of experience.

And he made a point to say that it's really not about the substance itself, or the "spirit of the plant," as it is commonly referred to these days.

His words:

"It is not located in a decoction or a specific molecular structure DMT, 5MeODMT, LSD, THC, MDMA, etc…or even in our brain or personal idea of what we think we are that we are not. Not every one who has tried all of this spectrum of tools, substances or non substances have been in touch with that specific paradoxic experience. Why? The fruition is not the practice! The fruition includes the practice but the practice doesn't include the fruition. We should get more discernment about our inner personal and transpersonal background. It is all I can say through my own, limited and humble attentive observation all over this years…

Non Duality is beyond Science and Spirituality as known nowadays for the average of people. It opens to a deeper, bigger and larger transpersonal paradigm than the dualistic observer/observed...Hated who thinks badly!"

Please understand that this is not an isolated phenomenon. This shift away from the more dualistic Amazonian shamanistic worldview to the non-dualistic is occurring all over today in different spiritual realms the world over, not only in the realm of plant medicine. And yet, it's not as if shamans have not been aware of the non-dual level of experience either, as I attempted to show in my first book (in the chapter "What's the Difference Between a Yogi and a Shaman?") It's just that it hasn't received as much attention.

Yet shamans have regularly reported non-dual or causal plane experiences, not simply astral ones, as Stanislav Grof has sought to show in his research.

Similarly, in the world of A Course in Miracles, there is clearly a rather large segment of the Course community who understand the Course in a dualistic way, claiming that is how much of it reads, and it does. And yet, as Ken Wapnick made it a special point to clarify, this is only because Jesus in the Course attempts to meet us where we think we are, which is in a body, in a world, having a human experience. Jesus for the most part does not attempt to negate this, and yet not a few passages in the Course clearly delineate an essentially non-dual message. Consider the following:

"He makes no distinctions in what is Himself and what is still Himself. What He creates is not apart from Him, and nowhere does the Father end, the Son begin as something separate from Him" **(W.pI.132.12:3,4; see also T.2.I.1:1; T.11.I.2,3,4,5,6,7; T.28.II.2:1,2).** The Son is the extension of God within the Godhead, **"a Oneness joined as One"** (T.25.I.7:1)

And perhaps the most telling passage of all:

"Oneness is simply the idea God is. And in His Being, He encompasses all things. No mind holds anything but Him. We say "God is," and then we cease to speak, for in that knowledge words are meaningless. There are no lips to speak them, and no part of mind sufficiently distinct to feel that it is now aware of something not itself. It has united with its Source. And like its Source Itself, it merely is.

We cannot speak nor write nor even think of this at all. It comes to every mind when total recognition that its will is God's has been completely given and received completely. It returns the mind into the endless present, where the past and future cannot be conceived. It lies beyond salvation; past all thought of time, forgiveness and the holy face of Christ. The Son of God has merely disappeared into his Father, as his Father has in him. The world has never been at all. Eternity remains a constant state."

It is difficult to read these passages and not recognize that this is essentially the Upanishadic conception of God as "**One without a second**." In other words, it is not just non-dualistic, it is purely or radically non-dualistic, meaning that God, or the Ultimate Reality, does not permit of any dualism whatsoever. If God did, God would not be God, but something else. And that something else would be part of the egoic illusion of separation, what the Hindus call "Maya."

This radical non-dualism is hard for most to fathom, let alone accept. As Ken Wapnick warned, due to our deep resistance to the radicalness of the Course's message, we would rather dilute the message than drink it in its pure form. Almost everyone does this on some level or another, bringing Truth to the illusion rather than our illusion to the Truth. And this is okay, we are just scared. Everybody is afraid to let go of the illusion and their individual illusions because we are afraid of the unknown, and the greatest unknown is what would happen if the ego would no longer be there. Would we still exist? How? What would that look like? Would I still be me? Or something else…?

No one can answer these questions except if they've had an experience of going completely beyond the ego (the world). Once they do, they will have no more doubts and questions – at least for a little bit, until the experience wears off. But the fact is that the doubts and questions will be less than they were before, and one can now use such an experience as a lighthouse to differentiate or discern what is our true self from what is not. It is in light of an experience like this that something like *A Course in Miracles* starts to make a lot of sense.

*

.... I ended up not doing an aya journey this time with the man whose journey I have been discussing, even though he offered that I could participate for free. I had done one with a small group a few nights before with a more traditional Peruvian shaman, my first in a couple months, and it was quite intense, bringing up some very funky feelings that I had not felt for quite awhile.

Which was a reminder to me that as long as we are in a body (or think that we are), the ego will still be there. But it is how we react, or rather non-react, to the ego that makes the difference. If we give it energy and take it seriously, we will tend to suffer; or rather, the extent to which we take it seriously is the extent to which we will remain unaware of what we truly are.

In my case, the ceremony with the shaman had me locked into a view of my body (and other bodies) as ugly, imperfect, sinful, actually odious, truly disgusting. And despite all I know about these things now, it was really hard not to feel what I was feeling and disengage from it. It even had me praying for help, including to the shaman. I really felt like I needed it somehow, like some kind of major intervention. It reminded me again of where that extreme form of Christianity came from, you know, the one that sees us inherently sinful and without hope except for salvation by Jesus. Well, that's how I felt, like there was no way out of the hell I was feeling except through some kind of saving grace. Clearly nothing I could do would be of any help. I was beyond pathetic.

I could offer suggestions as to why I was going through all of this now (and there was more), but I think it's enough to say that maybe I could have prepared for it better, plus I was just getting over a cold, had recently had sex, etc. These factors may or may not have made a difference. Obviously there are very experienced psychonauts who occasionally have similar kinds of awe-full journeys. And while I can view such plant medicine experiences in a positive light, as giving me some insight into the mind and spirituality, the truth is that the likelihood of having such a potentially traumatic or horrific experience is exactly why we need to use caution with such substances. We must honestly ask ourselves whether we are really ready to see what the Course calls the "viciousness" of the ego, or to a lesser extent, its "suspiciousness," which is a word for the paranoia people often feel with plant medicines, including marijuana.

For me, this aya journey was really just a test of my ability to "overlook" the devastation I was seeing and feeling, knowing that "this, too, shall pass" and if I gave it credence, I would not be representing my chosen path. So I did my best to just sit back and observe with as much amusement as I could, which honestly, was not that much. And yet! I put it down to something I needed to see in order to better delineate these things for you. Hope it's helping!

*

One last thing to report: At the French man's ceremony was a young man around my age, also from France, who was new to the medicine, this being only his second journey with aya. In his first (the one with the traditional shaman), he told me had nearly the exact same experience he had once had with some very powerful marijuana.

The second ceremony with our French anti-shaman sounded like it went deeper for everyone. Apparently his ayahuasca is more concentrated because no one had too much of it and they were all off to the races. I didn't participate like I said, but was downstairs and was awakened at 3:30 in the morning by our integral shaman's medicine drum. It was around this point that the other French guy was told to please be quiet because he was in a trance and singing something or other over and over. Later he told me he felt this was a bit harsh. I sensed there was some tension between the 2 of them before the start.

When we talked the next day, my French friend told me he felt that perhaps there was too much emphasis and talk from the facilitator about his views, veering close to missionizing of sorts. Perhaps, he suggested, he was trying a bit too hard to get the others to see and accept his point of view…

His own view was that science would ultimately be able to clarify all of these "spiritual" things, to ultimately show how something like ayahuasca works, and why. I said that might be true, but it seems to me that until that time comes (and it just might someday), it seems to me more to the point of seriously asking ourselves, as of right now, what is our own investment in whatever we believe. If I am a firm believer in science, why? Where is it coming from? And if I believe in the ultimate truth of non-duality, what is behind that? In other words, are we attached to a certain outcome, and if so, why? What are we afraid of?

Needless to say, we didn't come to any kind of agreement on this. My view in this book is that if someone could scientifically prove that Helen Schucman made up *A Course in Miracles* or otherwise prove its fraudulence, I would be happy to re-examine my views. But given the Course's existence; and given ayahuasca and the Ayahuasca Manifesto's existence; and given the testimony of the sacred scriptures of India as well as many of its greatest saints and sages; I find it rather difficult to not think there is something more going on than meets the eye. And more than meets the eye of even the most high-powered microscope or telescope…

I Am Love

The author in Peru, 2018.

As You Get Closer to the Truth...

"You have not yet gone back far enough, and that is why you become so fearful. As you approach the Beginning, you feel the fear of the destruction of your thought system upon you as if it were the fear of death. There is no death, but there *is* a belief in death."

~ *A Course in Miracles*[26]

"As the light comes nearer you will rush to darkness, shrinking from the truth, sometimes retreating to the lesser forms of fear, and sometimes to stark terror."

~ *A Course in Miracles*[27]

---

26 T.3.VII.5:9,10,11.
27 T.18.III.2:1.

Section IV

Journey Report: Taking Ayahuasca with a Traditionally-Trained Peruvian Shaman

'After tonight, the word "profundity" will have another meaning.'

~ PA, the Shaman

[**Please Note**: This journey report is essentially what happened in my first ayahuasca session guided by a shaman. It is also what directly preceded the writing of Section I (What Is Ayahuasca?). This was also the same Peruvian shaman that I mentioned working with in my first book, and who I interviewed for that book.]

I came into this ceremony with PA having already done several sessions alone using an ayahuasca analogue named "Jurema" (Mimosa Hostilis root bark and Syrian Rue), which is very similar in effect to the kind used by the Amazonian shamans. My experiences with Jurema were quite intense and definitely the most profound of my life, catalyzing me to begin a journey of exploration of "plant medicine" in particular, and "psychedelics" in general.

With ayahuasca, I felt I had finally found the missing ingredient in my yoga practice, so I naturally wanted to look more deeply into it. Towards this end, I began to write a book on the subject of "yoga and psychedelics," with the sense that the writing process would both enable me to get clearer about these substances, and also to deepen my insight into yoga and the nature of reality. Nine months into the writing, I hoped that the ceremony with PA would answer certain questions I have had regarding the paths of yoga and shamanism and the interrelation between the two idioms. For the most part, I was not disappointed.

What follows is my subjective recounting of what happened during the ceremony, and particularly what I experienced. Please keep in mind that this is only my interpretation, and also the wisdom that "we do not see the world as it is, we see it as we are," and thus take all of the following with a touch of salt :)

What Happened (?)

We all sat in a circle and had our backs near or against the wall, some of us had back jacks. Before opening the session, PA had a few opening things to say about ayahuasca and the ceremony. The following is a reconstruction of some shorthand notes I took of what he said:

This experience is something that the conscious mind cannot understand. After tonight, the word "profundity" will have another meaning...

The kind of Ayahuasca we will be doing is a combination of ayahuasca and chacruna, called "yellow ayahuasca."

What is ayahuasca? It is a path to the Divine, a way to get closer to the Divine. It is a fast way... There are so many different plants [and this one is very powerful]... You tell me if you want more after you drink!

Ayahuasca is the mother of all plants.

Breath is most important in ceremony. Through breathing you can process everything. I invite you to breathe everything – visions, sounds, feelings..

Breathe, breathe, breathe!

The breath is the connection between the spirit and the body.

Focus your mind in your breath.

Please be sitting up with your spine straight as much as you can.

Don't lay down. Have the experience of letting yourself go completely.

It is important that we try to maintain silence.

Sounds can be very loud when you are using ayahuasca.

The ceremony will have a clear ending.

Questions?

Q: Is it better to have eyes open or closed?

A: I feel that eyes closed is best. The songs are the medicine. Listen to the songs. There are songs for healing, for bring the energy up or down, all kinds of songs.

Ayahuasca is such a big thing. She's a woman. Spiritually she is infinite – no beginning and no end. Try to maintain the same energy. The power of your concentration can maintain your energy. That's the most important thing that I'm going to share today.

And with that, PA opened the ceremony with some benedictory prayers. We then went up one at a time to be given our portion of the ayahuasca. Because there were so many new drinkers, PA first asked each person if it was their first time or not. If they said yes, he gave them a lesser amount. Most everyone was able to just drink it right down with one gulp. I wasn't planning to do that myself, but that seemed to be the protocol so I went along with it.

I thought it was going to taste pretty nasty, but this apparently was the stuff that kind of tastes like chocolate (I thought is was more like prune juice, and at least one other participant thought so, too) and it really wasn't that bad at all. I did deeply inhale for a bit to make sure I kept it down. I also was doing some yogic practices like *uddiyana bandha* (stomach lock) and holding my breath prior to and after drinking the ayahuasca. I don't know if it really made a difference because there wasn't a moment when I felt nauseous or the desire to hurl. I did hear these deep, internal rushing, gurgling sounds every so often, and they didn't seem completely physical. Hard to explain but it seems reasonable to assume that at least some of the others also experienced the same sound/sensation.

After drinking my portion, I watched a few others go up to drink theirs, and then closed my eyes and settled in for the ride. I was sitting in lotus and attempting to keep my back straight (without props). This was to be one of my biggest challenges throughout the night, but I'll get to that. We all sat in silence for a little bit, and then PA began a soft whistling to begin the icaros, or shamanic songs. The first icaros was an invocation of ayahuasca:

ayahuasca yari-ri
limpiaringe cuerpecito yari-ri
limpiaringe cuerpecito yari-ri
Limpia limpia espirito yari-ri…

At this point, I believe we were all just sitting there, enjoying the song, watching, waiting. I personally was expecting to feel the ayahuasca begin to be processed through my internal organs and stomach. I actually didn't feel that so much. Nor did I feel nausea, as I said. After maybe 35 or 40 minutes, I did begin to feel the ayahuasca taking effect, though it was somewhat milder than with my previous journeys with Jurema – certainly similar, though. In my previous sessions with Jurema, generally I would begin to enter this cartoonish realm that was initially a bit outlandish and disturbing, partly because I had hoped there would be something different, like maybe a deity or great master. Instead all I got were these cheesy, garish cartoons. After that I would often see little pinballs going around in all these different patterns (reminding me of the psychonautical lingo "tripping balls").

This time I thought I saw the faint beginning of some kind of jungle cat, but the picture didn't get any more distinct than that. At this point, I'm not recalling what happened next, but it wasn't long before my visual space opened up and all sort of whirling colors and geometries began to appear.

I haven't had great recall of the visionary images in my various journeys, no doubt due to the fact that they are so transitory. What I do tend to have better recall of is how I was feeling during the experience, and what issues were being brought up for me. In all of my psychedelic experiences thus far, at the outset of the journey I tend to find that I am being shown all of my darkness, patternings, nasty habits – all of the things that I need to work on. Tonight was no different. I was forced to confront my demons, and it wasn't pretty. Never is.

One of the first things that came up was that I really don't have it together as a teacher. I was seeing all of the things that aren't completely kosher about what I do, especially in light of what I could be (and I was being shown that, too, particularly later) and in light of PA, and I was just seeing how much I am currently missing the mark, all the little things I need to do to clean up my act and be a "crystal clear" vessel. I don't think the ayahuasca is asking for anything less than that. In which case, we all are falling short of the mark. And I understood that, too, and I also recognized that as much as I was in awe of PA, he, too, is going through his own process of evolution.

I also saw that our "human condition" is what it is insofar as we have allowed our egoic-demonic nature to get the better of our higher impulses to evolve beyond selfishness. And I saw all-too-clearly how much ego I truly have, how much I think of "me" over and above "we," how many times my immediate, unconscious thought is not for the upliftment of others, but for the aggrandizement of myself. As I said, it wasn't too pretty.

Again, though, I had a strong sense that we all made this luciferic rebellion against God, it happened long ago. We chose to be separate, to want to live apart from God, to go our own way. But it hasn't truly served us, nor the highest good of all. So now the task is just to correct course and consciously choose to expand our consciousness beyond our egoic prison house.

That said, and despite how much a part of me knew that this was all just par for course, I was feeling this all very much being applied to me personally, and I actually felt exposed. I felt as if my yoga students, the few who were present that night, were all seeing me for who I really am, which is a fraud, a phony unkosher yoga dilettante. I felt PA was seeing all of this, too. What added fuel to this was the fact that the energy began to move me into "kriyas," or automatic bodily postures and movements.

For example, I suddenly realized I had my arms raised in the air ecstatically. And then I discovered my upper body was being circled around in the movements I teach at the outset of most of my yoga classes. It's not that these didn't feel good, they did. And these were the kinds of experiences I had always wanted to have 10 years ago when I had been in a kundalini yoga group but never did. Now the realization was that although these were "fun," they also were the result of unconsciousness, of my own asleepness. I again had a feeling of slight embarrassment that people were seeing me, particularly my students, and realizing I didn't really have it all together. [Note: This was all somewhat confirmed the next day when one of the participants said she saw me briefly as one of the asuras/demons who do yoga poses as a way to gain favor of Lord Shiva. I would have to concur with that, much as I would not want to acknowledge the truth of it, but there is some truth to it.]

Connected to all this, too, was this perceived power struggle between PA and myself. It started off with what I just related, and then it began to get into: Where is this shaman taking us? Who are we truly serving here? How do I know what PA's true intent really is, if he even is even truly aware of what it is? Or maybe he is truly of the purest intentions, but maybe the ayahuasca and the traditions are not of the highest vibration. In which case, I really can't rely on him or his strange brew, so better start directing this experience toward the highest. I actually did sense that I/we were kind of stuck in some high astral spheres and could go higher. When PA chanted in Quechua (the ancient language of the Incas), too, it sounded very cool, but also somewhat demonic. I think possibly images like those of some angry Tibetan deities popped in at that point.

Now please don't misunderstand me here – I'm just relating to you things that were coming up for me and don't want you to think I'm passing judgment in any way. In fact, all of this got pretty much resolved anyway by my realizing the following…

I do feel that PA is doing the best he can here, just as I am doing the best I can, but we are both still human. We are both going through the same process here. If I judge him, I judge myself. If anything, he is more humble than I in that he long ago joined with an ancient practice that goes way beyond him, for which he is but the instrument. He is not the teacher here, the ayahuasca is the teacher, and he is just speaking/singing on its behalf. In fact, I later realized that actually he IS the ayahuasca. And here I am who is captaining my own ship without compass, very much asleep at the wheel, not fully connected to anything truly ancient, very much entranced by all of our society's many distractions, living in mental disarray. If I should be doubting anyone, it should be my own egoic-demonic nature, which is leading me to have such doubts in the first place!

I think the final resolution came when PA stopped singing, lay back on one arm, and said: "Ayahuasca forces you to choose which side you are on…" – or something to that effect. That was it! Who are you serving? Is it truth or falseness, purity or impurity, awakeness or asleepness? Looked at from that perspective, this is a choice that we all have to make, moment to moment to conscious moment. It's an ongoing process. Fall asleep, and you risk opening yourself to energies that are not fully awake. Fall asleep, and risk being hypnotized by someone else's agenda. So the task is to be very vigilant: Don't miss a beat, don't have a second thought! That became one of my mantras for the night: *No second thought!* Later, towards the end, P A began singing a song in Spanish that had a chorus with the line "*no otra pensa,*" and that just confirmed what the ayahuasca was teaching (and again, he was the ayahuasca :)

Another mantra for the night was "don't back down," and it was a bit of an epiphany when I suddenly realized why keeping one's back straight is so important – it's literally not letting your back down!

This was all in the first couple of hours. It was around this time that P A asked if anyone would like some more ayahuasca. I didn't really feel I needed any, but a few others went up. One of them was a man, A, who was doing his 40th ayahuasca ceremony tonight. He went up a second and even a third time to get a refill. Perhaps not surprisingly, he also purged more than any of us, and quite violently it sounded like. G., who was sitting next to him, heard all his retching and decided he wasn't going to get a second helping, even though he was not having quite the experience he had hoped he would. I think all of us wondered how A could do ayahuasca that many times and still purge so dramatically. It's still not clear to me, except perhaps for the idea that if there's deep, uncleared stuff in you, or if you're not completely living a clean life, then the ayahuasca might have to help you clear out your closet and clean up your act a bit. Not that I am suggesting that that applies to A, and I don't really pretend to understand how it really all works.

So back to my little psychodrama: After that point, I was like (think Dr. Evil in Austin Powers) "We're not so different, you and I, PA..." Yes, let's work together here, let's join forces. Meanwhile, PA was completely innocent of my whole drama, it was all just my mind's projection onto him. On the other hand, perhaps he was very well aware, I have no idea, he kept his shaman poker face the whole time, and that just added to the respect I felt for him.

So after getting to this point, I had basically ascended toward a more divine, angelic plane. I was in yogi loka – the realm of the yogis. I really felt like I was in this world of the great yoga masters, one-pointedly fixing their gaze on the highest. It wasn't quite deva loka, the realm of the gods and angels, but it was getting up there, getting warmer through this intense *tapasya* (a Sanskrit word meaning "heat, austerity").

I thought of Baba Rampuri, who I had been in communication with last year regarding the interconnection between yoga and psychedelics. He intimated to me that he and his Naga Baba compatriots regularly use psychedelics as part of their practice. Doing this, I could definitely understand how a yogi would find this ayahuasca an amazing tool for focusing the mind for a long period of time.

I also thought of Ramana Maharshi as we headed into the early morning hours. When I think of Ramana Maharshi, I think of a master of all the states of consciousness – waking, sleeping, deep sleep, and even beyond (*turiya*). In other words, he could remain fully in the witness consciousness (*sakshi bhava*, in Sanskrit) in any of these states, even in deep sleep – or so was claimed about him, no one really knows except him.

More recently, though, Ken Wilber has shown how he can change his brain wave patterns in seconds – from beta to alpha to delta to theta, and back again. And what I seemed to be being shown was that ayahuasca is one means of learning how to do this, and it was also showing me that I was failing miserably at it. I kept falling asleep! Granted it was late at night, but no matter how hard I tried, I kept dozing off. Or so I thought. Maybe it was just some trance state, I don't know. I kept having to come out of it and reminding myself to breathe. Towards the end of the night, it actually got easier to remain fully awake in the experience and breathe.

Towards the latter part of the session, as we were "coming down," I felt more and more blissed out, it was like I had reverted to childhood. It was definitely like I was 5 years old again. I couldn't help singing and laughing. As for what I was experiencing, think of a summer sunset down here in the tropics, with the sky those gorgeous hues and the shimmering of lapping waves – only better.

At some point around this time, PA either sang a song or said something how life can be a great play, if we allow it – and maybe, if we discipline ourselves. I've come to this realization with ayahuasca before, but also just through my regular yoga practice. The sages have talked about bringing heaven to earth, and I can definitely understand how both yoga and ayahuasca are gifts from spirit to encourage this process.

One of the profoundest things that occurred for me happened after the ceremony, and that was connecting with everyone from that space. What beautiful energy! Even the people who had what seemed the most challenging experiences were beaming beatifically. My favorite part was the hugging. Got some great ones. One was from a member of the yoga group. And you remember me talking about A and his awful purging? Well, afterwards he was just absolutely glowing. We just looked at each other in the eyes and hugged – and hugged, and hugged, and then hugged some more. It must have been at least a 20-30 minute hug! We truly merged. Then A led me down to a cushion on the floor and proceeded to massage my feet expertly for a good long time. I returned the favor and then left him to sleep. Since that time, A has emailed me to say that in the 40 ceremonies he has done, that was his best hug yet!

So let's just say, a lot more happened, a lot of other insights came to me, a lot more beautiful sharing took place afterward, and it was all very sweet. And perhaps that is all a story that shall never be told, on this plane at least! Suffice it to say that I was left feeling that I really want and maybe need to do this more often :)

About The Ayahuasca Pa Gave Us:

Yellow Ayahuasca is more often referred to as Ayahuasca *cielo*; it is a relatively gentle but powerful healing vine and when used by Shaman in traditional ceremonies is capable of vivid and highly transformative visions. Such visions can often hold important insights into the drinker's life and frequently visions of animal spirits such as giant snakes or big cats are experienced.

There exist many different varieties of *ayahuasca* vine, over one hundred have in fact been identified, but the most commonly used in the Northern Peruvian Amazon is the *Cielo ayahuasca* one, which is reputed to be the most suitable for initiations, can deliver profound visions (and purging!!) and is safe to use.

A beverage prepared with the *Ayahuasca* vine cuts alone wouldn't normally produce visions (just purging), and the same would happen if one was to take a concoction prepared with the *Chacruna* plant on its own. By means of an apparent very simple process - which reveals, however, at close range examination, an utterly sophisticated research and knowledge on side of the indigenous people who made first this discovery - the two plants prepared together work wonderfully in synergy and each one maximize the benefit of the other.

Ayahuasca and *Chacruna* work synergetically not only on the biochemical plane - making possible the assimilation of the alkaloids otherwise attacked by the enzymes present in our digestive system - they are also believed to be, respectively, a "grandfather" and a "grandmother" plant spirit.

One may be blessed by wonderful visions and/or amazing revelations, without ever having hoped to see or know anything, whilst others yet may see nothing at all. Nothing is granted with *Ayahuasca*. Many factors - visible and invisible, ranging from one's own attitude, psycho-physical conditions and sensitivity, to the respect of the dietary prescriptions, to climatic conditions, to the *icaros* sang by the shamans, to changes in the electromagnetic field and even the moon, to quote a few - may contribute in different degrees to the depth of the visionary experience given by the *Ayahuasca* medicine.

Musical Question #108

Does Anybody Really Know What Time It Is? (not yet, not yet)

Excuse me, what time is it?

"The time is Now."

And the question
for this now moment is yet:

"Are you ready yet?"

And the answer is yet:

"No, not yet, not yet."

And the soft reply yet is:

*"Okay, Love, I'll wait...
yet don't be too late!"*

> Have faith in only this one thing, and it will be sufficient:
> God wills you be in Heaven, and nothing can keep you from it, or it from you.
> Your wildest misperceptions, your weird imaginings, your blackest nightmares all mean nothing.
> They will not prevail against the peace God wills for you.

Anyone who has ever had a crazy dark or even hellish mental journey (psychedelic or otherwise) will understand this. But the faith in this message that there is a way out will make all of the difference.

Section V

Yoga, Ayahuasca & A Course In Miracles: Notes On The Ongoing Revelation

"The miracle is taken first on faith, because to ask for it implies the mind has been made ready to conceive of what it cannot see and does not understand. Yet faith will bring its witnesses to show that what it rested on is really there. And thus the miracle will justify your faith in it, and show it rested on a world more real than what you saw before; a world redeemed from what you thought was there."

~ A Course in Miracles (What is a Miracle?)

*

"This world is not our home/we're only passing through/the trail is all made up/way beyond the blue…"

~ Charles Johnson (sung by Jerry Garcia)

[PLEASE NOTE: The following journey report is from years after the early reports that I included above. The one you are about to read was written after working with a Columbian shaman, Taita Juanito, and a couple years after my introduction to *A Course in Miracles* (ACIM). It gets closer to the non-dual truth of everything because I was getting closer to the non-dual truth of everything.]

I've been meaning to write down a bit about the ongoing revelations that have been facilitated through my encounter with ACIM and ayahuasca. I actually have written about all of this before and have notes that I might actually quote here, but I haven't put anything down in light of more recent journeys. I feel that it's important that I do this now for the purposes of greater clarity, both for myself and for YOU.

Essentially I would like to say that yoga helped to bring me to ayahuasca, and then ayahuasca brought me to ACIM (*A Course in Miracles*). ACIM to me is the Master Teacher that has elucidated both yoga and ayahuasca. The word "elucidate" means "to shed light on" and ACIM has certainly served as a guru for me in recent years, helping to bring light to the dark places of my own awareness.

How did yoga bring me to ayahuasca? Quite simply, it helped me to get beyond fear and rigid beliefs/thoughts enough that I was open to ingesting a substance that I really had no idea what it would do to me. For the first 35 years of my life I had resisted any type of drug or alcohol and was quite the "purist" when it came to my body and the spiritual journey. I definitely judged people that did any kind of substances to help themselves, just as for a long time I looked down on meat eaters, smokers, overweight people, and just about everybody. What it really came down to, though, was I was scared and so I judged, and it seems that I called in ayahuasca and ACIM as tools to help me to see that (that is, how identified with the ego I was).

So just overcoming the mental barriers to even trying a substance like ayahuasca was huge. And then ayahuasca only helped to remove other mental blocks, one big one being the image I had of myself as a "yogi" and the somewhat rigid/narrow way that I had chosen to view what being a yogi meant. I had for many years been the ascetic/purist yogi who denied the world and the body and human emotions to some extent, but I recognized that wasn't completely working and I was slowly being opened to a more tantric approach, one that was gradually more embracing of everything and open to any "tool" for awakening that might come my way.

So ayahuasca only served to quicken that process of seeing how all of that asceticism and discipline of my early years had served its purpose, and now it was time to let go of the rigidity and "just say yes" to life as it was presenting itself to me.

I have written in some detail (in my first book, *Who Am I?*) about an ego death experience that came through a rather strong dose of ayahuasca.

What that experience showed me was the power of the ego to keep us in our suffering. Many people on psychedelics will experience heavenly and/or hellish realms (as Aldous Huxley's book "Heaven and Hell" highlights). Well, the night that I had that experience I went to hell and I really saw no way of getting out. Even after the session, for weeks after in fact, I was still living in a state of hell, of deep despair to the point of seeing no point in going on. Again, others have experienced this with psychedelics – John Lennon, for example, who gave up LSD because he was having too many such "bad trip" experiences. And the other night during a session a young woman wanted to kill herself because she saw herself as the most demonic creature that was holding up the salvation of the world. Mind you, I explained to her that is exactly what the ego wants us to believe and was able to talk her out of it.

Now, I'm not sure I would have been able to explain all of that so confidently or at all to this young woman had I not encountered the Course. Indeed, in light of the Course, I could now make sense of my ayahuasca experiences, and I really want to highlight the following: ***I really don't think I would have truly gotten the Course had it not been for my revelations with ayahuasca, it's almost as if they complement each other.*** In other words, ayahuasca takes you down the rabbit hole to give you the experiences towards which the Course is pointing. If you've never seen the depths of the ego and how far its illusory power truly extends, it's very unlikely that the Course will resonate with you. You don't need a psychedelic to show you that, of course – a traumatic/tragic relationship could also do that, too, for example – but psychedelics do have that potential, and they can be ingested consciously to access those deeper, usually hidden dimensions of the psyche.

As for me, ayahuasca in light of the Course has been interesting indeed! And now I'm getting closer to revealing the "revelations" that I really wanted to share here. Essentially, post-ACIM, ayahuasca has shown me that what the Course is sharing is all true and actually can be experienced.

So what have I experienced?

Well, first let me say that the Course's metaphysics is essentially that we are still at home in God, in a state of perfect Unity (Love), and we have merely forgotten and gotten trapped in a false idea of separation and all that spawned from that original idea. In other words, this whole universe which we take to be so real and to be our home is not so, and we must unlearn (undo or reverse) everything that we learned because the conditioning of the world (duality) is ego-based, which is another way of saying fear-based. And deep within each of us who are identified with the ego is a primal fear of the retribution of God – we fear that God will punish us for the sin of separating from Him. Yet this is just the ego's false projection of what God must be, because the ego is based in the idea of separation and cannot see beyond it, so everything in its thinking will only reinforce the separation – at any and every expense.

The Course also teaches that time and space are the creations of the ego, being tools to maintain the separation. Yet beyond the ego is the truth, which is eternity and eternity means "no time, nowhere." In other words, Heaven is the eternal Here & Now ("now" and "here" together make "nowhere.") As the Course says, as soon as there was that original "tiny, mad idea" of separation from God (Total Oneness without a Second), there was an immediate correction for it, though that's only looking at it from our limited, time-bound perspective of linearity. In reality, as the Course puts it, "not one note in heaven's song was missed." The Universal Song didn't miss a beat! Another way to put this, a phrase Ken Wapnick was fond of using: **NOTHING HAPPENED.** In other words, that original idea had no effect on God/Love/Eternity whatsoever, it just continued on as if nothing happened, because nothing did, in fact, happen. It's a paradox we cannot understand, so let's not try to figure it out! It's an *experience*, and I'm here to tell you that I've had such an experience (or something like it!), and on several occasions, with ayahuasca.

In my most recent experience, I saw that all of this already happened and that we are all in a kind of movie that's just being played out. From the standpoint of eternity, in other words, all of this is just a "vast illusion" (the Course's words), and as Jesus says in the Course: "This world was over long ago." We are all just waking up to this and it must happen slowly and gradually because it would be too scary otherwise. The news (and it is good news!) has to be broken to us very gently, just as a lover would who cannot stand to learn that his beloved no longer desires him. We're so deeply entrenched in the separation, you see, that to all of a sudden recognize that there is no "me" would be terrifying, which is exactly why people do get terrified with psychedelics, precisely because they touch that place quicker than they're ready for. They didn't know what they signed up for! That happened to me early on with ayahuasca and it was none too pretty, but I don't regret it either, because what doesn't kill you makes you more awake and aware, though you might still have to work through the trauma.

Consider the following passage from early on in the Text of ACIM:

"Some of the later steps in this course…involve a more direct approach to God Himself. It would be unwise to start on these steps without careful preparation, or awe will be confused with fear, and the experience will be more traumatic than beatific."

~ A Course in Miracles

So we're waking up to the truth that there truly is only one of us here. We are all IT, we all share the same mind, there is no separation! And that experience I had recently with aya was that yes, when you wake up, everyone comes with you and in fact, the whole world is over, and there never was a world! This is one of the most amazing things about it all, and again the Course says this: There is only one of us here that needs to wake up, and in fact, the process has already been completed by Jesus (and also by others who have transcended the ego paradigm). We can now just use Jesus as an example and guide by at least being a little willing to accept his gentle and simple method of returning to the place we never left. And please don't forget that we are all Jesus, he is not separate from us, because again, **WE ALL ARE OF ONE MIND**, there is no separation. But, mind you, Jesus ultimately is also an illusion, a symbol. There was no Jesus in reality, just as there is no separate me, no separate you. Ultimately, only the non-dual ONENESS is real; or to put it another way that has much currency these days:

Only Love is Real.

And so what was coming to me is that there truly is nothing to fear, because everything is but a lesson to bring us home, and we are already HOME anyway! If you really knew that and felt that, even for a moment, you would never experience fear, or at least not to the degree that you did before. This definitely has been my experience. Yes, fear sometimes still comes up, because in the separate dual state in which we usually find ourselves, it's nearly impossible to remember the non-dual truth of existence. We're almost inevitably bound to feel worry, fear, anxiety, etc. as we move in this world. It's just that those feelings will come up, and then we will just remember that no, we don't need to go there, that's not real, and it will more quickly than not dissolve.

The last thing I want to say here, for now, is that the path really is one of complete forgiveness, which really means to teach yourself to see everyone and everything as YOU and release all of your grievances, because that's the truth, and to do otherwise is to deny God (the essential Oneness) and to delay your own awakening back to God.

So it all ends with complete forgiveness, of letting go of all that we are not, everything of the ego, and the total and complete acceptance of all that we truly are, which is only God, only Oneness, only Love. And this process is simple, but for most of us, it ain't bloody easy! Again, why? Because due to our deep investment in the ego, we are very afraid of the truth. But the truth is that if we could just look at the ego and realize it's nothingness, we would be home free. And I don't care what anyone else says to the contrary, ayahuasca has really helped me in this process (and is clearly helping many others today, too), and again, I don't feel I would have gotten to the Course, or as quickly, had it not been for it. I sense that given my intense and all-consuming desire to awaken, aya just showed up in my life to help quicken the process.

The Journey to the Cross...
The Last Useless Journey

"Do not embark on useless journeys, because they are indeed in vain. The ego may desire them, but spirit cannot embark on them because it is forever unwilling to depart from its Foundation.

"The journey to the cross should be the last "useless journey." Do not dwell upon it, but dismiss it as accomplished. If you can accept it as your own last useless journey, you are also free to join my resurrection .... Do not make the pathetic error of "clinging to the old rugged cross." The only message of the crucifixion is that you can overcome the cross.

Until then you are free to crucify yourself as often as you choose. This is not the Gospel I intended to offer you."

A Course in Miracles[28]

---

28   3rd Editin, p.47; T-4.in.3:1-3, 7- 10.

Section VI

Yet Another Journey (to the Cross) Report

"The miracle establishes you dream a dream, and that its content is not true. This is a crucial step in dealing with illusions. No one is afraid of them when he perceives he made them up. The fear was held in place because he did not see that he was author of the dream, and not a figure in the dream."

~ A Course in Miracles

Wanting to share here a little bit about the last aya journey, the one with J, the artist, as it seemed particularly notable. And really, it's been an ongoing revelation, yet it feels like some of the last ones, and particularly this last session, have been really remarkable, which is to say, they are worth remarking about, for the purpose of clarification.

There's always so much to tell, so I will keep this as succinct (to the point) as possible, while giving enough background to make it understandable to someone who might read this – you :)

I mentioned to a friend who has been doing ACIM that with this experience I felt like I "graduated the Course", though that's probably a bit of a stretch. And if I did, so what? But here's why I said that…

It was all a very loving space, and J felt it clearly and spoke about it. That was the first round, ending around 11 pm. It ended with us singing together, J for the first time in a long time, he said. I was pleased to hear that. We were in Loveland and all was well with the universe.

Then we drank another round. I sensed this round was going to take us deeper and reveal the blocks to the awareness of Love's presence, as the Course says. I remarked something like this to J, and he seemed ready enough for whatever might come.

Generally, when pouring for myself, I just go based on what I feel I should have. This time, however, I voiced aloud that I was going to allow the medicine to tell me how much to pour. And then, uh oh, a lot came out of the container and it was too late to go back. I ended up getting considerably more than I would have otherwise. I knew we were in for something...

J noted that the second cup tasted more bitter, and I had suggested this was often the case. In fact, at first, many people enjoy the taste of the medicine, only to find later that, on second thought, NOT. I myself felt almost immediately like hurling after this second cup.

To deal with the nausea, I began to beat the big bass drum we had, while playing the didgeridoo. I began to point the didgeridoo directly at J, who was maybe only 2-3 feet away from it. It was a very powerful sound, and it wasn't long before Paul pulled his bucket closer and then began to purge. (Neither of us had purged up to this point.) Later he told me that his purging had definitely lessened the effect of the medicine, and it definitely had everything to do with the didge, which made him lose control of his stomach muscles.

After that I felt like I was getting the message to play Shimshai stuff through Spotify, so that's what we did – for the next 3-4 hours. The Dharma Mittra recordings (especially "Hum Sa") are a tough act to follow. I didn't quite know what would be appropriate, and I didn't want to keep changing songs throughout the night, so I just put Shimshai on continual play. Not sure how much that had an effect on what was to come, though to me it felt like the completely right choice...

I'm now writing this a few days later. Even right after the experience, I realized how tenuous and slippery all of this is. Words cannot do any of this justice, and just might do it an injustice. In fact, it probably will, but nonetheless, it feels important to at least take a stab in the dark at elucidation, so here goes nothing...

There was a moment in the experience where suddenly it felt like all barriers to reality fell away and I was just sitting calmly observing the simple, naked truth. It was like nothing had actually changed except a fine film that was obscuring the naked truth had finally, at last, been lifted.

And that last thin barrier was just all of the last things in my consciousness that were obscuring the simple, unadorned truth.

The Course says about enlightenment that it is a "shift in perception, not a change at all." This made sense now.

And so did all of the Course. It had all led me to this point. The Course was just what I needed on my journey to give me that last push over the edge, and the faith that the push would not end in death, but Life. And what was coming through was this: We are all so afraid to let go of our judgment, because we are afraid of losing our personal identity, which is intricately involved with our judgment. And with that judgment is our sense of specialness. Without our judgment and sense of specialness, the world that we think is so real would just dissolve and we would see things for as they truly are. As Blake said: ***"If the doors of perception were cleansed, things would appear as they truly are: Infinite."***

And this is what I saw. Suddenly, I was "above the battlefield," as the Course puts it, just calmly observing everything, without the filter of thought and judgment. A little later, yes, I slipped back out of that and, while still in that place of observation, I could feel like a solid mass of fear and judgment still there.

But before I talk about that, let me go back to that place of infinite/pure awareness that I experienced. At that time, Shimshai was still playing and the message coming through was something like this: "You can either sit apart and in subtle judgment of the music, seeing it as not yours, seeing Shimshai as not you, or you can let go and be a participant in it, you can join in, it's your choice." Something like that. Clearly music has been a big issue for me, particularly the issue of jealousy and ownership/authorship. My ego is constantly being threatened by other musicians, it goes so deep. It was a big block to my becoming a creative artist.

Now the message here was just to see all of the music as one, to know that love is love is love, and there's no separation, and there's no reason to ever feel less (or more). Just join with the music, be a full participant. And of course the music is a metaphor for everything. It's about acceptance of WHAT IS, not what you think it should be. Each moment – accepting each moment without trying to change anything about anything. Just accepting.

So the word "**accept**" became a very important mantra for this journey, and I repeated the message/mantra "accept only Love" many times, to myself, but also mainly out loud, though in a soft tone. So soft that J could hardly make out what I was saying until later. All he heard was "accept." It wasn't until later in the night that he heard "only Love." (A few days after, speaking on the phone, J. said it was all great and he had a great new mantra, "accept only Love." That was cute.)

Again, I'm getting ahead of myself a bit. I want to go back to the moment before there was any need for acceptance on my part, because I was there, in a state of pure acceptance that was also a state of pure awareness. What I saw then, too, was this:

Everyone is afraid to let go of judgment and specialness because the "ego" that we've chosen to identify with knows this will mean its demise. When I say "everyone," of course, I mean "Every One," because there truly is only one of us. One that has chosen to accept limitation, tricked by the ego, whose sole job is to prevent the "Son of God" from recognizing that he has a choice between the ego and God, and that we are all, ultimately, One.

So we are all so afraid to let go! So afraid! Even in the letting go that I experienced, just prior to it, it was scary! But it has been far more traumatic for me in past aya experiences, and now it's becoming easier and easier – with the help of the Course, which I am now understanding is a path for those who are ready to completely awaken from the dream, and that ayahuasca also has a special role to play in this awakening process.

Thinking about this is mind blowing, in the sense of which "nirvana" means "no wind" or "no mind." Because what I was also experiencing was myself as the One Son of God, the One Mind that is dreaming this all up, from a place beyond time and space. I was being shown how what the Course has written about so intimately and intricately, in such detail, is in fact true. It's all true, I saw, every word of the Course is a masterly way of helping to lead someone out of the "senseless maze" that is the egomind/world. And I am the chosen one, for I have chosen it, I have chosen to fulfill the conditions, to go beyond all fear and to fully remember who I am.

And then I saw all the reasons why I have been chosen for this mission, and that I am here to be savior of the world. Of course, as the Course says, there are numerous other saviors in the world of form, but there is only truly One Son. So I am one of many messiahs in the world of form, in other words, but when in that place of pure awareness of Oneness, then I am One with all the "others," too. So, in other words, I am one of many "Teachers of God," who are here to teach that there is only One Son of God, and that he is without guilt, purely innocent. As long as a mind is separate to any extent, it will see diversity, but when it returns to the One Mind, it will see unity.

So back to fear: Fear prevents us from truly looking deeper. We keep retreating and advancing. We take a courageous step into the unknown, only to find it so hard to face the darkness, so we retreat back into the shadows once again, until again we muster the courage to advance. And the next time, we go a bit further, only to fall back again. That's why Jesus says at the beginning of his Course that it "is a required course…only the time you take to take it is up to you."

He also says early on that he's carefully detailing the necessary steps for the awakening from the dream, and that it is necessary to have the essential theoretical underpinnings in place so that one doesn't get too awestruck/traumatized by it all. In another place he says that some have died in getting a glimpse of where this is all leading. He knows how hard it all is, because he had to go through it himself. So he is in a position to be infinitely compassionate and patient with those who are still lost in the maze of the ego. And he has carefully detailed the steps one needs to take to get out of the maze.

So it's important to consider all of the Course, if the Course is your path. Because it's all there, and Jesus didn't waste or mince words. It's a symphony of unfolding themes, the overriding theme being that the Son of God is guiltless and can freely choose to return to God at any time. The invitation's on.

But I sense that the experience of oneness will remain elusive until one fully goes into it all, as with any path. *You have to go **THROUGH IT**, if you want to get to it* (as I once heard Sly Stone say on the Dick Cavett show). You have to go all the way with your chosen path. And yes, the

Course can be made an idol. For me, it can become another means of separation and specialness, and it still is that to an extent. It's still being used to make myself feel better, and that's not its purpose. It's to show that the true me does not need to feel better, and all that's asked of me is merely to accept that there's nothing to be done but to accept that it's already been done. Jesus (or our true Self) has already done it. The work is already cut out for us, it's just to bow to his lead and not try to come up with a plan that can only be ego-based.

And that's SO simple, and yet SO hard. The ego wants to be the author of the plan, what the Course refers to as the "authority problem."

Anyway, there is something else that happened during the journey that night that will be very difficult to describe and explain, but I will try to because it seemed so significant.

I seemed to be going through something like a crucifixion process. It was like I needed to go through this whole thing, or rather, the ego did. It was like it had to happen, there was no way that it could NOT be crucified. At one point it was so intense that I let out a cry of agony. It wasn't that loud, but I'm pretty sure J heard it. It didn't matter, I was only vaguely aware of anything. It got to the point of being a kind of repeat of Christ's death on the cross, which the ego and traditional Christianity took to be one of intense agony and suffering, but which the Course says was merely a teaching device to show that Jesus could not truly suffer because he knew he was not his body.

And then I remembered Jesus' words in the Course about how the journey to the Cross should be the last "useless journey" and that we are free to make such useless journeys as many times as we wish, but we don't have to. Jesus has shown us that we have a choice. All we have to do is accept the Atonement, which is the principle that the ego is not real and the whole world/universe based in separation never happened. All we have to do is accept that we need not sacrifice or suffer anything to be what we are and have always been.

So in remembering all of this, I snapped out of the crucifixion experience. I believe this all happened prior to the "enlightenment" experience I described earlier. Perhaps this is what made that later experience possible.

Another very memorable thing that happened was that it really felt like I was outside of time and space, in an eternal moment, perhaps what Jesus in the Course calls a "holy instant." But that moment didn't last when it became clear that there were still deep pockets of unforgiveness that needed to be addressed. Again, it felt like a solid mass of stuff that was there. And then it felt like it was just me in all of the Universe and I had a choice to make.

What would I choose?
The whole Universe was waiting upon my choice.
What would I choose?
Well, the whole Universe is waiting…
And of course I knew what it must be, and yet it was so hard!

The Ego's Prop Agenda

It became clear again in all of this that there's really nothing to say, and especially because everything that you might say or do is only to establish that you (the ego) exists. As the Course says, it's all a form of propaganda, it's the ego's agenda to prop up its own existence in any way possible, using the excuse that it is "helping" or adding something. And the Course/Jesus is telling us that, no, it's not really adding anything of value or meaning, just trying to assert itself.

So with that, there's nothing I can really say or do about the Course that wouldn't come from that place and so the best that I can do is practice patience and non-coercion and gentleness with myself and everyone. First and foremost, to fully love and accept myself – every part of myself. All is already done; all that is left to do is release the resistance to that truth, to let it be *undone*.

> Forgiveness is still, and quietly does nothing.
> It merely looks, and waits, and judges not.

Goes without saying…

Section VII

One Final Journey Report
(Last One, Promise)

"There is a way of living in the world that is not here, although it seems to be. You do not change appearance, though you smile more frequently. Your forehead is serene; your eyes are quiet and the ones who walk the world as you do recognize their own. Yet those who have not yet perceived the way will recognize you also, and believe that you are like them, as you were before."

~ A Course in Miracles

"You may say I'm a dreamer, but I'm not the only one..."

~ John Lennon

May 27-28, 2017

I was having an issue with my liver, or so it felt like, so I fasted all day. I ended up fasting for about 2 days, just had some liquids is all. Not sure how it affected the medicine work, but I do feel the medicine probably came on faster, and I certainly did not feel at all like purging.

So my sense is that if I drink enough medicine now it will more often than not take me to the "quantum field of forgiveness" (as ACIM teacher David Hoffmeister puts it), or to what the Course calls "the real world" where all is forgiven. And then I will see how that field gets disturbed. At one point I had the insight that we would never leave the state of grace if we just kept laughing, and that eternity is in a sense just one long laughgasm.

There was a moment when B. was tending the fire and he suddenly became this really brutish warrior with what seemed to be malicious intent. I don't know whether I was reading something deep in him or not, though later when he and his girlfriend D. began to have a little argument about something he had posted on Instagram, I got the sense that he might be using spirituality as a kind of weapon. Of course, this is something that we all do on some level or another, like, "Let me try to fix you. If you would just listen to me!"

But anyway, when he was tending the fire, it touched off this whole scenario in my mind of how in the ego's dream world there must be a messiah who sacrifices his (or her, but in my case his) life on behalf of humanity, because the whole thing is just too *f*-ed up. There's just no way that salvation can come to all unless that sacrifice happens. Or so it felt like! And I've witnessed this scenario before, in which I am the messiah who must sacrifice for everyone. Now, of course (or, according to the Course) this is illusory, because it is of the world of illusion. In reality, this all didn't happen because in reality there is no world, no bodies, no separation, no me, and thus no need for guilt, sacrifice, etc.

But it does point to in a sense the validity of what the gospels are getting at, as well as other stories of a messiah who suffers in order to bring salvation to all. It's just that it doesn't go deep enough. It's true on one level, but it doesn't go all the way.

And when one gets to this place with the Course, I think one realizes that yes, I am the messiah. I am the One that everything depends upon. Yet the difference between what the Course teaches and traditional Christianity is that the latter says there is only one messiah, and that was Jesus. What the Course is saying is, well, actually, you are Jesus when you arrive at the place where he is and see as he sees. Then you realize you are the Christ principle, you are the messiah, you are the light of the world. And this experience, while rare, is not so rare that there wouldn't be various and sundry enlightened Christ beings floating around in the world at large at the same time. And as the Course says in one of the lessons (quoted above), those who have attained to that degree of serenity will recognize each other, while those who are not at your place of peace yet will also recognize you, because you will be very down to earth, you won't need to be special, you won't need to be the Guru.

The one who is wholly gentle and patient and kind is the one who can take everything, who is disturbed by nothing. Such a one is thus in a place to truly see the truth, such a one truly is the savior of the world, because such a person recognizes that there is no world in truth that one needs to be saved from. It's already done. Or already *undone*.

Or even better: It's all One and has never not been One, so no need to be done or undone, it just is.

Another insight, and I want to reiterate that this is again the "ongoing revelation" because this was not my first time witnessing these things, is that the candidate to be the messiah is someone who has an excruciatingly keen sense that there is something really wrong with this whole picture, something really rotten in the state of Denmark, and has run with that all the way to its absurd conclusion. In my visions the other night, I sensed the arc and flow of my entire timeline in the course of probably just a few moments and how it all led me to where I am now.

I also was in the Cosmic Moment seeing how the whole thing unfolded from the original seeming separation into the egoic world of illusion.

One other thing also is of special note here, and that is that I played the Bhajamana Ma song while pretty much at the peak of the experience, but I didn't record it. I also recognized that I needed to dedicate it to D. (whose name in Sanskrit means "Goddess") who had just mysteriously shown up. And that was because the song felt just a little prompted by an ego need. With all that in place, what unfolded was just the most magical song that has ever come through me. In fact, I had the experience at several points in the song that it wasn't even me playing it. It was pure Grace flowing through me. I wonder if I could ever approximate that without the help of the medicine. Most of the time, it just doesn't seem possible. I also wonder if that song would have come through like that if I had tried to record it. I sense there will be other such magical moments that will give me additional insight into this. But I will say that it was kind of one of those moments of like: Whoa, yes, this is IT! *This is the music!*

And I wondered if it had flowed as well if F. or another musician had been there and some doubt had crept in. Probably not!

And to dispel the mystery of it all: We would all rise to the occasion if we were able to get those egoic doubts and fears out of the way to just let the music come through us.

So much more to say about all of this, but again I will just affirm that it confirmed the truth of the Course and how ayahuasca can provide an access to that truth.

And Now, to Give Responses to Our Initial Questions for the Aya Quest…

What is ayahuasca? Where did it come from? How old is it? What is its purpose?

As for what ayahuasca is, this is and will most likely ever remain a wide open question. Clearly, it is different things to different people. For some it is a healing medicine and a tool for psycho-spiritual awareness. For others, it is merely a "drug" and a particularly dangerous one at that. Even those who use and endorse it do not completely agree on what ayahuasca is. So let's leave this question aside for the moment, and stick to the "facts," or at least that for which there is general agreement.

Ayahuasca (more traditionally "ayawaska") has many names. Some of the more common are hoasca, yagé, natem, shori, caapi and cipo´. But the most common designation, and the one for which is approaching almost mainstream/household status today, is *ayahuasca*, The word means "vine of the dead" or "the vine of souls" in Quechua: "aya" is "soul, spirit" and also "corpse, dead body," while "waska" is "rope, woody vine, liana." It should be noted that while "vine of the dead" is often used, it was a derogatory term first used by missionaries.

Its scientific designation is *banisteriopsis caapi*, the name of specific vine that is indigenous to the Amazon basin. When it is combined with the DMT (dimethyltryptamine)-containing leaves of the *Psychotria viridis* ("chacruna") through a rather involved process of preparation and cooking, it produces a thick brownish black liquid that often has a taste perhaps similar to blackstrap molasses. Some seem to enjoy the taste, but many more do not, especially after ingesting it more than once.

Ayahuasca was discovered independently by various indigenous tribes in the Amazon basin, particularly in the areas of Ecuador, Peru, Columbia and Brazil, where it is used and administered legally to this day by various shamans and healers. How it was actually discovered is still a mystery, though there are various stories and myths that attempt to explain its introduction to humanity some thousands of years ago. Many have pointed to the fact that the odds against putting these two plants together (the vine and the leaf) in just this specific way is very high. Add that to the fact that it appears that the discovery was made independently by various Amazonian tribes, and you have one of the great wonders of the world.

It is interesting to note here that the scientific name of ayahuasca is "telepathine," indicating that it was used for the purposes of telepathic communication.

As for ayahuasca's purpose, again, this is a question about which we are questin', there's no easy answer. What we can say is that generally ayahuasca has been used for the purposes of healing, and that includes healing on all levels (physical, psychological, spiritual). It has also been used for other purposes, not all of them beneficent (to say the least), but healing and the return to wholeness is the primary one, at least at this historical moment.

What are some of the common things people experience when using ayahuasca?

Here I will just list several of the most commonly reported and catalogued recurring motifs of the ayahuasca experience, and then expand on several of them. Many who use ayahuasca report experiencing the following: Nausea, vomiting, diarrhea, visions, hot and/or cold sensations, fear, dread, euphoria, laughter and tears, alien visitations, journeys to other worlds and dimensions, physical and psychological healing, benevolent and malevolent force/entity encounters, deities/divine beings, sacred geometry, and the spirit of the vine, Grandmother Devine Herself.

Clearly *La Purga* (the word "ceremony" is not generally used in the Amazon) is so-called because the purgative aspect of ayahuasca is a fairly common component of the experience, and the purgation may happen in any number of ways. Vomiting and diarrhea are the two most common physical forms of purging, but things such as coughing, belching, hiccupping, moaning, laughing, crying and singing are other forms of this. On a more psychological level, the ingester of ayahuasca might feel as if past traumas, unprocessed emotions, habit patterns, and more are being brought to the surface in order to find release. This, too, is a form of purging. Gradually, one learns to separate the false from the true (fear from love) in their moment-to-moment experience, to daily "clean house." As one does this, the ayahuasca experience can potentially become beatific rather than horrific, and the need for the medicine decreases. My personal understanding is that like any true teacher, the ultimate goal of ayahuasca is to make itself superfluous for the user, that he or she finally understands that they alone are responsible for their peace of mind and do not require external support or dependence on any outside factor.

Many experience physical healing with ayahuasca, and sometimes it's amazing to see how quickly and effectively this is effected. It is important to note that such healing really begins with the mind's firm decision to experience healing. On this view, ayahuasca isn't really giving you anything that you don't already have, but is rather just revealing what is already latent or dormant in the mind. I also want to bring attention to the phenomenon of the "placebo effect," which is the strong expectation of a desired result. This probably accounts for a lot of the felt healing that happens. Please keep in mind that we are not just talking about the conscious mind here – the unconscious plays a big role in all of this.

Finally, I have heard enough reports now of journeyers who meet what seems to them to be the spirit of ayahuasca, the Queen of the Forest, the Grandmother Herself, that I want to comment on this. Some actually even connect and commune with Her before the experience itself, sometimes a long time before and a long time after. I myself generally feel an unconditionally warm and loving motherly presence with the medicine, though I cannot say that I have had direct visionary experience of Grandmother. Here, too, I want to bring up the possibility that She is an archetype (like Mary, Oshun, Kali, Shekhina, etc), and She is not outside of you, but lives within, and when the devotee is ready, the Deity appears. From the vantage of A Course in Miracles, Grandmother Ayahuasca can be seen as the embodiment of the Holy Spirit, whose role it is to lead you back to the One Reality that lies beyond all names and forms.

Why do people who use ayahuasca generally prefer to call it a "plant medicine" as opposed to a "drug"? What's the distinction?

Words are funny, right? It's important to recognize the symbolic nature of language, and how the same word may mean one thing to one person, and something very different for another. Take the word "God." There probably are not two people on this planet of nearly 8 billion who have the same conception of what "God" is. But for our purposes here, let's say there are 3 basic camps: Those for whom the word "God" is positive, those for whom it is negative, and those for whom it is fairly neutral or indifferent. If you grew up in a stifling religious environment or a religious indoctrination that did not suit you, the word "God" might have a pejorative (negative) connotation. But if you recently became born again, the same word could be your favorite in the whole world. (The same goes for other "loaded" terms, such as Jesus, Christian, Jew, etc.)

Now, if you work for a pharmaceutical company, the word "drug" might not have negative connotations for you; rather, it might quite positive, or at the very least neutral. But many others today hear the word "drug" and it does not carry such a nice tone, probably because it is so often followed by words such as "abuse" and "addiction," not to mention the "War on Drugs" that has been US government been waging for the past 50 years. Clearly, we have a deep ambivalence about "drugs," an ambivalence which is often unconscious. The same is true, by the way, for the word "psychedelic," which in itself is just this innocuous Greek word that means "mind manifesting," but which for many is symbolic of a time in their life and in the world that they would rather put behind them (namely the radical "psychedelic" Sixties, when these substances were made illegal).

And this is why today many supporters of such substances are choosing to use different names for the same thing. So "entheogen" (meaning "generating the divine within") as opposed to "psychedelic"; and "plant medicine" instead of "drug." The thing itself is still the same, but the language is changing as a way of saying: Let's not use language that has accrued negative connotations for these substances, for names do matter, they do have an effect on our consciousness whether we like it or not.

But there is another distinction. Many today are resisting lumping organic psychoactive substances like ayahuasca and iboga in the "drug" category, too, because they define drug as what is synthesized in a laboratory. So LSD and MDMA, for example, could still be called "drugs," as they are produced in the lab, but not magic mushrooms, aya, iboga, peyote which are "plant medicines" that are as old as humanity and have been used for medicinal purposes for millennia. The feeling is that to call them a "drug," which essentially means something made by humans in a lab, is a misnomer, not to mention misleading and offensive/insulting to many.

So this here Q & A is really a more general plea to watch our words and use them wisely, and not use potentially loaded or offensive terms in our discourse, but to listen to opposing viewpoints and give them the benefit of the doubt.[29]

Also, some who work with ayahuasca also refer to it as a "plant teacher." What does this mean? How can a plant be a teacher?

Everything can be our teacher, if we have eyes to see and ears to hear. Nothing is happening here by chance. And as we begin to open to this possibility more and more, we will more and more see Spirit's guiding hand at work in our lives. We will see how are being led and how we are being taught, not just at certain times, but all of the time. And the Course makes it simple: We're always being taught to choose Spirit as a our teacher, despite the fear-based promptings of the ego to follow its mad dictates.

With that out of the way, yes, of course, ayahuasca can serve as a teacher, and many who have worked with it have reported feeling that it was subtly and not-so-subtly teaching something. I myself have had this experience on many occasions.

The ultimate lesson to be learned, of course, is that the teacher is YOU, that ayahuasca is not showing you anything that isn't already present within yourself. This awareness will come to light just when you are good and ready for it.

---

29 For one recent take on this subject, please see Josep María Fábregas' video "Ayahuasca: Dope or Medicine?" https://www.youtube.com/watch?v=GmT3Tlmz9ao

Why is ayahuasca spoken of as a visionary medicine? What's the difference between "visions" and "hallucinations"?

From the perspective of eastern philosophy and ACIM, what we are experiencing here is a kind of mass hallucination, or as Einstein put it, a "optical delusion of consciousness." We just can't see that yet. These teachings tell us that the mind fabricated this whole drama of existence and then split itself into all of these separate parts to keep the lie from ever being brought to light.

What's the science behind ayahuasca? What does it do to your brain? How do we know that it's not toxic to the brain?

You're going to start to see a pattern with my answers, if you haven't already. And that is to resist giving definitive "answers" to these or any questions, but first to ask you: Who is it that wants to know? In other words, where is the question coming from, why are you asking it, and will your bias even allow you to really be open to the possibility that you might be wrong? That you might just be seeing what you want to see?

I will get directly to the question in a moment, but first let me ask: How many times has science apparently proven something, only to later find that its findings are questionable yet again? That's one point. The other is: What if ayahuasca *is* screwing with your brain. So what? In other words, perhaps the value of using it outweighs the potential risks involved. If we are honest with ourselves, this "cost-benefit analysis" is involved with nearly everything we do, though most of our decision-making is now unconscious. For instance, getting in the car to go on a simple errand poses a risk. Even eating food poses a risk. I remember my brother saying something funny and cute when we were very young (back in the Seventies) after we heard on the news that yet another thing was proven to cause cancer. "Sheesh!" he said, "Everything causes cancer!"

Spoiler alert: You are going to die someday of something, and it will be sooner or later. Please do not delude yourself that this might not be the case. Now, this does not mean not to make wise choices in regard to your health or anything else, but it does suggest that it might be wise to question our unquestioned assumptions about everything more and more and more. And if anything, ayahuasca aids in this process of questioning, questioning ***everything***. In this case, we might question whether quantity of life is more important than quality of life; and whether or not it is preferable to risk working with something like ayahuasca if it means being able to live and die in peace?

But I do want to take this question of the science behind ayahuasca seriously and provide a response based on the most impartial scientific findings available at this moment. (Note, you could simply skip this section and take a look at the following: http://www.beamsandstruts.com/bits-a-pieces/item/750-neuro-huasca .) Also, Josep María Fábregas of the CITA Clinic in Barcelona has conducted the most extensive study of long-term ayahuasca users to date. Here is one video of him discussing his findings: https://www.youtube.com/watch?v=GmT3Tlmz9ao . His research suggests that ayahuasca is not addictive, and that regular users scored higher on some cognitive tests than non-users.

In my own personal experience, I have not found ayahuasca to have had a greatly noticeable positive or negative impact on my brain functioning, at least in the long-term. That is, I neither feel necessarily smarter or sharper, nor do I sense that ayahuasca has dulled my mental functioning. This is after over 100 uses. Of course, it could be that there have been subtler, more gradual changes to my brain chemistry that have accumulated over time. I will say that I do feel that it is true that the amygdala has been affected, as I have much less nightmarish and terrifying thoughts, dreams and visions than I used to, nor do I have nearly the same degree of nervousness and social anxiety that I did. I have no real fear of public speaking and the opinions of others affect me less and less. This certainly could be due to other factors such as maturation and the aging process, but I did notice this effect from day 1 of my use of ayahuasca.

Is ayahuasca dangerous to use? Howso? Does ayahuasca, for instance, make one more susceptible to attack/hosting by so-called entities, demonic or dark forces?

This is one of the most interesting and problematic issues surrounding ayahuasca. As with every such controversial issue such as this, the really only honest answer we can ever give is: *It depends*. I realize this answer might seem as a cop-out and frustrating to some, but it all really does depend on not only how we define words like "negative," "dark forces," "demonic," but also how we even define what we ourselves are, what ayahuasca is, and so on. It also depends on a host of other factors that are too various and numerous as to make it near impossible to predict outcomes. Before we go on, I do want to stress the great need for clear intention, due diligence and preparation in approaching ayahuasca.

That said, from a yogic non-dual perspective, the following could be said…

Is ayahuasca dangerous? It is, for sure – to those who believe in danger. Can it have negative effects on you? Certainly, if you believe that you can be hurt. Can you be attacked or unwittingly hosted by malevolent entities or forces while using ayahuasca? Very much so, if you believe in attack. And will you be scared? You bet you will! In other words, to the extent to which you invest belief in anything (and specifically, *anything outside of you*), you can and possibly will encounter those things, both with ayahuasca and in your daily life.

I recall once having a brief conversation with a deeply Christian young woman who was working in food prep at a local natural food store. She asked me what I did and I told her that I teach yoga and meditation. When I mentioned meditation she offered a stern warning to be careful with that meditation stuff, you don't know what might get in there. Actually, I hadn't really considered that possibility, or at least what I supposed she meant, which was that somehow Satan and/or his minions might attempt a hostile takeover of some sort. And because I had not put much belief and fear there, that was not my experience.

But the truth is, she was right in that it is quite possible to simply sit still and attempt to empty the mind, only to encounter such unwanted intrusions. Recently one of my yoga students told me she was very much afraid because this sort of thing happened to her while she was meditating. After our talking things through, though, she felt some relief and after a while was not further bothered by the situation, but it had all been quite traumatic for her.

Now, not only do people encounter such things when they meditate, but we often experience psychic attacks and hosting from such seemingly innocuous activities as resting in bed and/or sleeping. As a graduate student years ago, I took a class given by a professor who had done his doctoral research on the "Old Hag" experience, which is basically when you are lying in bed and then suddenly feel like something with ill intent is right on top of you, pinning you down and paralyzing you (it's also popularly known as "sleep paralysis."). During and immediately after taking this professor's class, I had 2 such experiences. My point is that prior to the Old Hag phenomenon being on my radar, being "jumped" while in bed by some crazy entity probably wasn't in the cards for me. And also to point out that this happened while I was not under the influence of anything more than drowsiness.

Which is not to say that things have to be in your conscious mind to manifest; clearly, if anything, ayahuasca shows us just how much is in the mind (the subconscious) that we're generally not aware of, or just peripherally aware of. That is why I am stressing here the importance of preparation and readiness when approaching something like ayahuasca, including the importance of set, setting, and dosage. Unless you don't mind being scared out of your mind – hey, maybe that's what you've been calling in! Maybe you love horror flicks! But if you would like to "ease in" to things a bit more and not go straight for the ego death experience, you might want to proceed with a good deal of caution and respect.

Finally, I want to make a case once again for what seem to me to be the more fundamental things at work here. Essentially, we are being called to look at our investments in the ego, which is an illusory thought system based in the idea of separation and which uses sin, guilt, and fear as smokescreens to keep us from ever waking up to who we really are, which is Spirit, which is Love, which is the All in One. Because we still believe we are here, and thus still have fear, once again it is the greater part of wisdom to be very judicious in regard to plant medicine, to nip that freak out in the bud.

Let's conclude this section with an important caution from *A Course in Miracles* which I've already noted a couple of times:

"Some of the later steps in this course...involve a more direct approach to God Himself. It would be unwise to start on these steps without careful preparation, or awe will be confused with fear, and the experience will be more traumatic than beatific."

I want to also add the following addendum which tries to get at where the "problem" lies in all of this, whether it is with ayahuasca itself, or those who misuse it. This passage come from the Ayahuasca Manifesto:

"Another very effective method used to sabotage my mission with the Human species is by generating and manipulating the powerful emotion of fear. You have nothing to fear. I am not the cause of any deaths, I just channel Light and vital energy through your secret meridians. Any accusation or allegation of danger, permanent injury or death should be thoroughly investigated to allow science itself to grant me the Human absolution. It should be expected that my enemies manipulate the facts to instill fear at any available opportunity, as this is part of their debasing agenda against my global expansion. It should be the objective of all my supporters to gradually obtain the social and legal acceptance of my sacrament as alternative medicine until I become officially accepted by the governments of modern society."

Does ayahuasca create a dependency? In other words, is it addictive, physically or psychologically?

It really depends how we define the word "addiction." Defined broadly, there is case to be made that we are all addicted to everything – to thinking, breathing, eating, sleeping, being a body and personality, etc. etc. It is in this sense that ayahuasca is actually anti-addictive in that it has the potential to take us beyond the body-mind-personality, beyond thought, and beyond the world completely. It also can and does often show us the unhealthy addictions that we have – to sugar, alcohol, sex, gossip, you name it – and helps us to see how such addictions are keeping the mind enslaved. Many have used ayahuasca just once and then given up whatever habitual patterns as a result, or else those habit patterns just fall away.

That said, dependency on ayahuasca is a very interesting question, and one for which there is no easy answer. I don't think that actual physical addiction or dependency on ayahuasca is the issue as there are no physical withdrawal symptoms from not using it. The issue is more whether it creates a psychological dependency in users, such as the following kind of thinking: "I always feel so much better after using ayahuasca and I'm starting to feel depressed again [or lonely, or whatever], so maybe I should use it again…" Yes, this does happen. But then the question is: Is this necessarily a bad or unhealthy thing? Would we say that someone who goes to the gym or meditates when they feel depressed or low energy is addicted to working out or meditating? Yes, of course, on a certain level there is a dependency, but as long as that is honestly seen for what it is, it is okay.

A Course in Miracles and the non-dual tradition of yoga would ultimately say that the root cause is actually in the mind, and so it is really just a simple change of mind that is needed, just a little shift in perception, a willingness to see things through the eyes of compassion, forgiveness. Nothing external to the mind can do this, but can only help support this change of mind. Of course, this is simple, but not easy! And as long as it is not easy, then external tools such as ayahuasca can be very helpful. So be gentle and oh-so-patient with yourself and the other patients, patient! (For more on this question, see the addendum below.)

Related question: If ayahuasca is so powerful, why does someone need to do it again? Why do people do it tens, hundreds and even thousands of times? Isn't that overkill?

Continuing from the previous question, we could just as well ask why someone needs to run or meditate or even eat countless times in their life, isn't once enough? Well, apparently not! Why does there need to be this judgment? If someone feels like they are being helped by something, why would you try to get them to stop, or suggest that there's something wrong with them? Well, granted, you might think they are hurting themselves in some way; in this case, maybe this "drug" ayahuasca is doing weird things to the brain, or whatever. But even then, who's to say? And if you were to really look within yourself when you make such a judgment, you will probably see that you have your own habits that could be pointed out in the same way. So yes, there IS something wrong with someone who needs something outside of themselves to feel better, but in that case, there's something wrong with all of us. As the Cheshire cat said, we're all mad here, because if we weren't, we probably wouldn't be here…

The thing to keep in mind about plant medicines like ayahuasca is that they can be a valid path in themselves, let's call it "the medicine path," as it actually has been called. This means that someone takes a plant medicine regularly over the course of time as a way to expand their awareness and ultimately break free of limiting patterns of thought, speech, and action. And there may eventually come a time when the medicines are no longer necessary, either because you are directly told by the plant itself that this is the case, or you just realize yourself that you no longer need them. As the saying goes, once you've taken the boat across the river, you no longer need the boat.

And yet again, say someone takes ayahuasca their entire life (and there have been shamans and others who have, thousands of times), can we really make a judgment as to whether they have been more or less enlightened or evolved than anyone else?

Does one need a shaman or facilitator to oversee one's ayahuasca journey? Is it dangerous to do it on one's own?

It is essential that you have a support network when doing a plant medicine like ayahuasca, and that could just be one person that you can rely on to help you if you need it. But the answer to this really depends on too many factors to give anything more than a very general answer. In general, yes, most would be helped by a qualified shaman or facilitator in this process, and it can be dangerous to use ayahuasca on one's own, even with a faithful friend at hand. In the end, look for signs and seek inner guidance for how to proceed, as with everything. If all signs are pointing to do it a certain way, then go that way. If not, then it would probably be wise to go to Plan B.

Who would ayahuasca be most helpful for?

Personally, I feel that everybody could benefit from ayahuasca, at least in lesser amounts. That said, most people will never do ayahuasca, for the simple reason that it's not time, they're not ready. The fear of the unknown and of losing control is a big one to overcome. And preparation and readiness are key. In fact, the phrase "ready, willing, and able" springs to mind here. One must really be ready for this experience because it can be quite challenging. I've witnessed this firsthand, both in my own journeys, and also in guiding others. For most it's a relatively smooth enough ride, but there is always that handful of people who have a particularly rough time with it. So ayahuasca would be most helpful for those who have already done enough inner work that they really know they are ready for the experience and feel called to it.

Who should not use ayahuasca?

Anyone who is not prepared, who comes to it from a "recreational drug" perspective and is not mature enough yet to view it as a sacrament. Of course, they can use ayahuasca, and it still might be very helpful, but they also might end up hurting themselves or others around them. Ayahuasca is also contraindicated for those who have a history of mental illness or who are on certain prescription medications (lists of contraindicated mental disorders and medications are readily available on the internet). Again, anyone who does not feel called to ayahuasca, ready for it, and well-prepared should best not use it. I will for now leave aside the questions of use of ayahuasca by children, the elderly and dying, and other special cases, except to be said that these, too, need to be approached on a case-by-case basis.

And now, a little bit more on the question of whether ayahuasca is addictive or fosters dependency…

Addendum

A Good Teacher's Purpose is to Foster Independence, Not Dependence

"Every good teacher hopes to give his students so much of his own learning that they will one day no longer need him. This is the one true goal of the teacher.*"*

~ A Course in Miracles (T-4.1.5)

I was listening to a podcast interview with Don Howard Lawler, resident shaman at Spirit Quest in Peru who has been working with plant medicines now for decades. During the course of the interview, Howard echoed the above words of the Course in making the point that ayahuasca, being a "plant teacher," has the ultimate purpose of freeing us from dependence on it. That is, its goal is to make itself unnecessary, superfluous. In other words, ayahuasca is a means and not an end in itself – once you get across the proverbial river, you no longer need the boat that got you there.

This is an important point because so often what happens in any student-teacher dynamic, especially in regard to spirituality, is that the student in some way becomes dependent on the teacher. And this ultimately becomes antithetical to the true purpose of spirituality, which is to foster *in*dependence, freedom. This is the meaning of the Zen koan *"If you see the Buddha on the road, kill him."* It is also one reason I ultimately stopped seeing my Indian gurus; I was recognizing an unhealthy dependence on them within myself. I was also realizing I was now strong enough to take the lessons and wisdom learned from them and continue the journey on my own.

And those lessons and learnings involved the dependence, or attachment, I had to things, or better put, to the egoic view of things. So you see it's not so easy as to just say you don't need a teacher at all, because the true teacher will help you see the darkness for what it is and thus help you free yourself from it. Which is why from its earliest sacred writings on in India you find the admonition that the spiritual path requires a qualified guide, don't be so arrogant as to think you can make it on your own. Our relationship to the ego is very *involved* and it requires quite a bit of *involution*, or turning inward, to see that. Only someone who has already done the work can lead the way.

The recent docu-dramedy Kumaré makes this paradoxical point beautifully: On the one hand, it tries to show that the guru is an illusion, that all one needs is already inside of oneself. Yet in the process of showing this, Kumaré, who is the director Vikram Gandhi's alter ego, proves that the guru is also necessary (in most cases) to help us to see this.

Another way to put all of this is to say that a true teacher wants and needs nothing from anyone, including and especially from his or her students. If there is no more sense of sin and guilt and fear, what is there to gain or lose in any relationship? Except that it is merely the teacher's recognized "function" – that helping to show the way home is all that there is left to do, nothing else. They no longer even need or desire the appellation "guru."

Every good teacher hopes to give his students
so much of his own learning
that they will one day no longer need him.
This is the one true goal of the teacher.

Section VIII

How Ayahuasca Can Aid In Work with A Course in Miracles, and Vice Versa

"The Great Way is not difficult for those who have no preferences. When love and hate are both absent everything becomes clear and undisguised. Make the smallest distinction, however, and heaven and earth are set infinitely apart. If you wish to see the truth then hold no opinion for or against. The struggle of what one likes and what one dislikes is the disease of the mind."

~ Sengcan, Hsin Hsin Ming

A few words before we begin: I can only speak from my own experience here. My own experience, though, includes a number of reports now from others on how ACIM and ayahuasca seem to inform each other in interesting and even uncanny ways. And still, the mystery remains and I don't claim to fully comprehend it all, and I highly doubt there are many (or any) who can or do.

So with that out of the way, I will say that I think we can all more or less agree that to forgive is a virtue and that forgiveness works. Why? Because, at the very least, we feel better when we forgive someone, even if we still think the other wronged us, we at least feel some peace from having forgiven. Verdad?

The problem is that generally our first response to a perceived wrong is anything but forgiveness; rather, it's a reaction, it's attack. Tit for tat, eye for eye. You hurt me, so I will hurt you back, and then maybe later we'll get to forgiveness. And attack, not forgiveness, is what makes us feel better, at least temporarily. It's like: "Fuck forgiveness, that bastard has it coming." Revenge is sweet, as it's said.

Now this is on a very basic, surface level.

On a deeper level (probably where you the reader are!) we have a very difficult time forgiving ourselves for not being forgiving enough, for not being kind and compassionate the way we "should" be, for thinking all of the mean, nasty, twisted things we think. We beat ourselves up about this, never once questioning where these thoughts are coming from – is it the real me? Or some false identity?

The Course says those insane thoughts are indeed not who you really are, and are due to a false identification made real by long conditioning, by habit. It is what it calls "ego," which is really nothing but a mistaken thought process about who we are. In fact, all words, all thoughts, all concepts are potentially in the way, they can all be obstacles to inner peace.

Think about this for a moment: A negative thought such as such deep anguish or frustration that you wish ill on or even want to kill someone – could that possibly be what we really are and want? Why even take that seriously? And most of the time we don't take it seriously enough to actually do something about it. Yet the anguish and frustration and whatever else still linger on. We are unsettled, in a state of *dis*-ease. And it's hard to let that shit go. But not letting it go means hurting yourself, and why would we want to do that?

To bring this back around for a moment: We got off talking about all of this mainly because I wanted to get at what we could all agree upon, and that is forgiveness… Something I'll never forget is sitting in a car years ago with someone who was unable to forgive his mother for a terrible separation and divorce that he and his family underwent. And he wanted me to hear a new song by Don Henley of the Eagles, "Heart of the Matter," which is all about forgiveness. What I understood him trying to tell me was that he knew in his heart that forgiveness is the way to go.

It is, yes, and yet most of the time when we say or think we've forgiven someone or something, we generally haven't. And you know the test is when you get around that person again, or even think about them, and look at what feelings that brings up in you. "If you think you're so enlightened, go spend Thanksgiving with your family and see," said Ram Dass (a paraphrase). It is indeed so true that we generally don't know where we're at until we're tested. We might have thought we'd forgiven, but the truth is that we're still holding on to a grievance.

Now, what is unique about ACIM is that it essentially says that our sights need to be set on "complete forgiveness" or what might be called "radical forgiveness," which goes above and beyond how we normally think of forgiveness. It isn't feeling that someone wronged us and then forgiving them; rather, it is the understanding that they really did nothing to us. I know that sounds preposterous, but it actually makes perfect sense when taking the metaphysics of ACIM into account. And the metaphysics are that because the ego really is nothing – it is an illusion based in an impossible thought of separation – and because our perception is so rooted in the ego, then we're bound to have countless problems and grievances projected outward and suffer endlessly. That is, if we take the ego seriously. But we have a choice, and the choice is always to "see peace instead of this" as the Course suggests in one of the Workbook lessons. Or, to trust and remember, mind you, that "*nothing happened*," that the ego is ultimately an illusion.

The apparent difficulty is again: Why should I take what the Course says seriously? Why should I accept its metaphysics? As noted above, this is the very question I have had, too, so no worries – in fact, everyone has this question to some extent or another. I would never tell you what to believe or not, I can only tell you what has worked for me. And I will say very clearly and pointedly and openly that ayahuasca has granted me (and others) numerous experiences now that have demonstrated to me the truth of ACIM, including several experiences of non-dual Oneness.

Now, I realize that this will not be satisfying to everyone. It actually will probably only resonate with those who have used ayahuasca, done the Course, or both, or who have had similar experiences with ayahuasca. So I have no illusions about any of this. My purpose here is not to try convince anyone of anything, but rather to merely report my findings, trusting that they will be helpful to those who need them.

I will just conclude by telling one little story: A few years back, a middle-aged man who had lived at a prominent ACIM teacher's retreat center attended one of our ayahuasca ceremonies. Actually, over the years, this man has attended several. Even though his teacher does not necessarily approve of plant medicines like ayahuasca, apparently this fellow does and he only has good things to say about it. In fact, he told me that for him, in light of the ayahuasca experience, ACIM makes complete sense. Anecdotal evidence, I know, but I have no doubt that there are many others like him out there these days. Probably you, too, right?

Ayahuasca: Select Resources

Articles
1. National Geographic Article
2. New York Times Article (2015)
3. LA Weekly Report on Ayahuasca in Hollywood and Contemporary Music
4. Article in Huffington Post on Ayahuasca as a Potential Treatment for Depression
5. Ayahuasca in Hollywood movies: Wanderlust & short piece on Ayahuasca in Hollywood
6. My own most recent piece for Reality Sandwich: Yoga, Ayahuasca, & A Course in Miracles

Documentaries
Six Ayahuasca-related documentaries worth seeing: 1) Vine of the Soul; 2) DMT: The Spirit Molecule; 3) The Sacred Science; 4) Neurons to Nirvana; 5) Metamorphosis ; 6) The Reality of Truth

Other Media
Ayahuasca on National Public Radio:
1. "Window Into the Soul" & UDV Controversy
2. Lisa Ling's CNN Report on Ayahuasca

Organizations & Websites
1. MAPS
2. Kaphi

I Am Love

Maya, Madhava & Moksha

A Foray into Indian Yoga's Non-dual Traditions

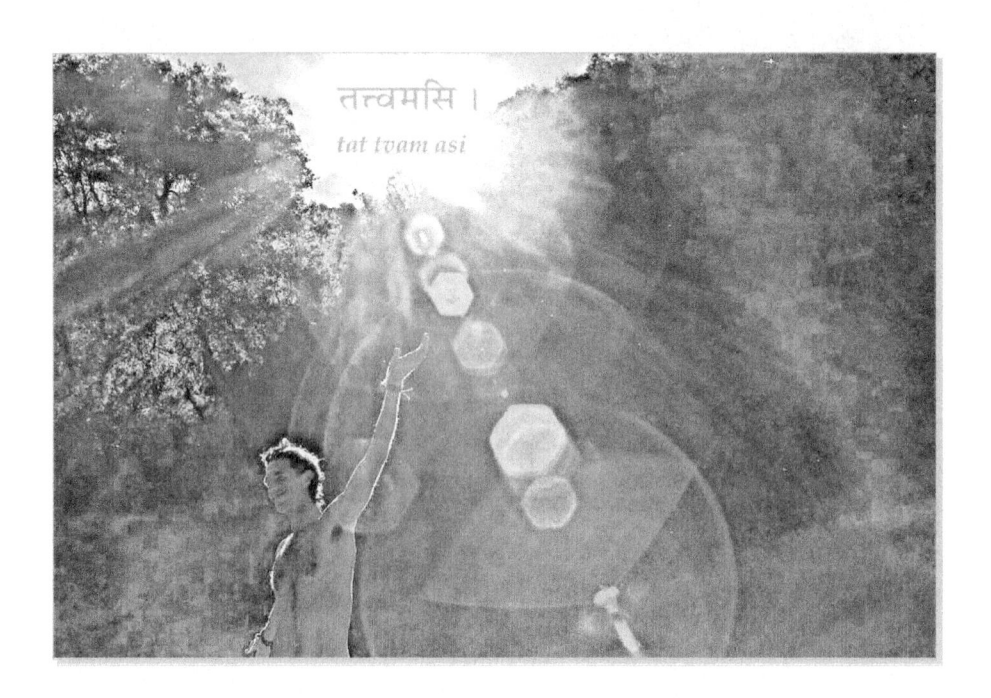

Tat Tvam Asi ~ Thou Art That

Yoga Means Union

Yoga,
Yoga means Union –
Peelin' back the layers of the onion
Tears keep falling from my eyes
As I see where the ego's truth lies
a flimsy disguise
But I know in the end there's gonna be a Pearl
Janus Girl, no more world in a whirl…

Yoga,
Yoga means Union
Reelin' back the layers of opinion
(no need for a minyan, minions)
Towards the final consensus:
CommUniSon
No more neMesis, brosis
The truth right under our gnosis
Just The Universe as Mighty ChorUs
Self-proclaiming the OneLoveness <3

Sometimes I think yoga is boring
But then I say to myself,
"Nah, am-a-stay"
(_/_NAMASTE _/_)
I'm gonna stay here in my heart
& live the part

never meant to live in some *apart*-ment
what comes and goes
came and went
I'm only here to re-*present*...

Yoga,
Yoga Just Is
Says what it means
& means what it says.
& it's gleaning is just around the bend –
the end to the means
and the means to
The End

I Am Love

Sometimes I think...

But then again...

nah, i'm a stay... in my heart

Questions for the Yoga Quest

What is yoga? Where did yoga come from? How old is it?

Yoga is often defined as "Union." What exactly does this mean? How does the practice of yoga bring one to this seemingly exalted state?

What do the most ancient yogic texts from India, the Vedas and the Upanishads (which includes the Bhagavad Gita), say about yoga and what it means to be liberated?

What is Vedanta? And what are the various forms of Vedanta? In particular, what is Advaita Vedanta? Why is "Advaita" generally considered to be the highest philosophy of India?

Who were/are some of the great exponents of Advaita Vedanta?

What is "Neo-Advaita"?

What are some of the most important Advaita scriptures? What is the provenance of these scriptures, meaning who wrote them?

What is the path of Jnana Yoga and how can it best be practiced?

How do Jnana Yoga and Advaita Vedanta relate to A Course in Miracles? Do Advaita and the Course really point to the same thing?

What is Maya? What is Moksha? Is it possible to attain moksha, or liberation, while still in one's body?

Selected Source Texts for the Study of Advaita Vedanta, India's Philosophy of Non-dualism

The following are some of the most important sources for the study of the philosophy of Advaita Vedanta, India's non-dual tradition.

The Vedas – Truth is One
Maha Vakyas ~ The Great Sayings
Mandukya Upanishad
Mandukya Karika
Katha Upanishad
Bhagavad Gita
Sri Atma Gita
Avadhuta Gita
Ashtavakra Gita/Samhita
Atmabodha
Brahma Sutras
Viveka Chudamani ~ Crest-jewel of Discrimination
Yoga Vashishta
Swami Vivekananda's *Jnana Yoga*
Ribhu Gita
Advaita Bodha Dipika
Sri Tripura Rahasya
Nisargadatta's "I Am That"

Some Essential Select Quotes from the Non-dual Sources

"The Infinite is the source of joy. There is no joy in the finite.
Only in the Infinite is there joy.
Ask to know of the Infinite.

"Sir, I wish to know of it."

"Where one sees nothing but the One, hears nothing but the One, knows nothing but the One – there is the Infinite. Where one sees another, hears another, knows another – there is the finite. The Infinite is immortal, the finite is mortal."

"In what does the Infinite rest?"

"In its own glory –nay, not even in that. In the world it is said that cows and horses, elephants and gold, slaves, wives, fields, and houses are man's glory – but these are poor and finite things. How shall the Infinite rest anywhere but in itself?

"The Infinite is below, above, behind, before, to the right, to the left. I am all this. This Infinite is the Self. The Self is below, above, behind, before, to the right, to the left. I am all this. One who knows, meditates upon, and realizes the truth of the Self – such a one delights in the Self, revels in the Self, rejoices in the Self. He becomes master of himself, and master of all the worlds. Slaves are they who know not this truth."

~ **The Upanishads**

***

"Here there is a single resolute understanding, Arjuna. The thoughts of the irresolute have many branches and are, indeed, endless."

~ **Bhagavad Gita 2.41**

"Content with whatever comes to him, transcending the dualities (i.e. pleasure, pain, etc.), free from envy, constant in mind whether in success or failure—even though he [the yogi/sage] acts, he is not bound."

~ **Bhagavad Gita**, 4.22

"When he leaves behind all desires emerging from the mind, Arjuna, and is contented in the Self by the Self, then he is said to be one whose wisdom is steady [stithaprajnas].

He whose mind is not agitated in misfortune, whose desire for pleasures has disappeared, whose passion, fear, and anger have departed, and whose meditation is steady, is said to be a sage.

He who is without attachment on all sides, encountering this or that, pleasant or unpleasant, neither rejoicing nor disliking; his wisdom stands firm."

~ **Bhagavad Gita 2.54-57**

***

"The Soul regarding Itself as a jiva is overcome by fear, just like the man who regards a rope as a snake. The Soul regains fearlessness by realizing that It is not a jiva but the Supreme Soul."

~ **Atmabodha** of Sri Shankaracharya

***

"I am free from changes such as birth, illness, senility, and death; for I am other than the body.
I am unattached to the objects of the senses, such as sound and taste; for I am without sense-organs."

~ **Atmabodha** of Sri Shankaracharya

"The universe was neither born, nor maintained, nor dissolved; this is the plain truth. The basic screen of pure Being-Awareness-Stillness devoid of all the moving shadow pictures of name and form of the universe is the sole, eternal Existence."

~ **Essence of the Ribhu Gita 2.33**

"The universe of name and form, the embodied creatures and their creator, mind, desire, Karma (action) and misery and everything other than the Self are merely thought formations projected by the power of the Self on its screen – Self."

~ **Essence of the Ribhu Gita 5.25**

I Am Love

> Blessed are the flexible
> for they shall never be
> bent out of shape...
>
> & Blessed are the inflexible
> for they shall be made
> flexible again.

God Hides: A Creation Story

The self-existent Lord pierced the senses
To turn outward. Thus we look to the world
Outside and see not the Self within us.
A sage withdrew his senses from the world
Of change and, seeking immortality,
Looked within and beheld the deathless Self.

~ Katha Upanishad[30]

So the story goes, God wanted to create the world…
(Let's leave aside why God would do such seemingly outlandish thing for a moment.)
So God wanted to create the world and people it with people, only God had one little problem…
For some crazy reason only beknownst to God, no one could ever know how to return to God, or at least not that easily.
(Again, why would God do such a thing?
But God *did* do that very thing, at least according to the story.)
So what God did was this…
God called all of the angels together and had a BIG meeting.
"Hey angels – HALO! – I have a question for you…"
"What is it, Big Guy?" asked one.
"We need a hiding place for the mystery of the universe, and quick," said God.
"I have an idea!" cried one.
"Shoot," said God.
"Why don't we hide it somewhere way deep in outer space?"

---

30   Katha Upanishad II.1. Eknath Easwaran translation.

"Nah," another angel said. "They'd be sure to find it eventually. They'll figure out how to build rocket ships and ship like that. Too easy."

"Wait, what about down deep in the depths of the earth?!?" another excitedly called out.

"Still too easy," one said, "over time they'll be able to dig down there, too."

"I got it!" exclaimed another. "How about at the bottom of the sea?!?"

"Ingenious!" said one.

"Really?"

"I mean, *they* are ingenious and would figure out a way to get down there, too."

At this point, God was feeling frustrated.

"WTF (what is this foolishness?), my angels? I made you to solve these kinds of problems for me, and this is the best you can do?" God grumbled.

"Ok, wait, I got it!!!" piped up the littlest of the angels. "Why don't we hide the mystery of life in their **hearts**, they'll never think to look for it there!"

And at this, everyone agreed and God was well pleased. So pleased, She laughed heartily. And this is why to this day, no one knows who God really is. Except for those who really search their hearts to uncover the mystery. And now that you know this secret, maybe you will be one of them.

THE BEGINNING

(And that was just a wee little story to prepare you for the next part of our journey together...)

Does God Play With Herself?

tad ekam sat vipram bahudha vadanti
"Truth is one, yet even the sages call it by many names."

~ Rig Veda

*

Who really knows, and who can swear,
How creation came, when or where!
Even gods came after creation's day,
Who really knows, who can truly say
When and how did creation start?
Did He do it? Or did He not?
Only He, up there, knows, maybe;
Or perhaps, not even He…

~ Rig Veda 10.129 (Nasadiya Sukta)

These amazing passages from one of the oldest and most sacred of the world's spiritual literature express something that from the very beginning of my love affair with yoga about India and the Hindu yoga tradition, namely it's open-endedness and absence of dogma, which has translated into its great tolerance for even seemingly contradictory ideas.

This can be seen in the fact that there is no one founder of Hinduism (such as a Moses, Buddha, Jesus or Muhammed), and no one scripture that is considered to be the sole authoritative one (even the Vedas are not). Rather, there are many *Hinduisms*, many yoga schools, and many saints, sages, swamis, and gurus with their respective schools and lineages. The idea, as expressed in the Vedic hymn (above), is that there are many ways to get there, numerous trails up the mountain, something for everyone in the smorgasbord of spirituality laid before us to partake. But at the end of the day, there is only one place to go…

"Truth is One, paths are many,"

said the late Swami Satchidananda, echoing the ancient Vedic dictum above.

And thus, when the student is ready for a particular teaching, the teaching will appear in some form or another, and the form itself ultimately does not matter. And when that lesson is learned –or rather, embodied — then the next, deeper teaching will present itself to the seeker, and then the next, and the next… At least in theory, this will go on and on until there is Nothing more to learn and Nowhere (Now Here) to go, in other words, until the point of "enlightenment" — a point to be considered in due time!

And since we're on the subject of Creation stories… In the Hasidic tradition, there is a beautiful quote that says,

"God created the world because God loves stories."

Whether this is at all truly true is also something that will be touched on here, yet I at least love stories, you? Well, here's a wee little one…

I believe Freud is to be credited with the observation that when we're young, our parents are like gods to us, and up until a certain age, we treat them as such, becoming chips off the old blocks, so to speak. I was no different, yet when I was eleven years old, my parents went through what I experienced to be a very painful separation. Painful because the fairytale was over for me, the Queen banished forever from the King's Castle, and my hot air ballooning sense that we would be one happy family forever deflated quite abruptly and decisively.

So one day, a few years later after the Queen's exile…

I was over at my dad's house when my mom happened to call and start to berate me for something, related to the fact that I was with my dad and she didn't like that (this happened often enough at that time). My dad overheard some of what was happening with me and my mom there on the phone and he said something that I still have not forgotten to this day, partly because it was a little out of character for him, I thought:

"Tell her you didn't ask to be born."

He said it facetiously, like to get her off my back, yet this was an idea that I had already begun to really ponder and vibe with, namely, the feeling that I could let go of all feelings of guilt and judgment because hey, I didn't ask for this life, it was just thrust upon me (Gee, thanks, mom!) If so, why was everyone on my case about everything? Why this big heap of guilt and judgment all the time? *Sheeshkabob*!

Of course, I could have said the same thing to my Dad when he was giving me a hard time about something. This is all your fault, bro, lay off!

[Btw, Bill Cosby, one of my and my brothers favorite comedians growing up but who has been drawn and quartered of late, has drawn much comic material from his own childhood and has a new book out called "*I Didn't Ask to Be Born (But I'm Glad I Was)*"]

I do believe this idea of not asking to be born, if taken to its extreme, contains a very strong kernel of truth. On the one hand, from the standpoint of reincarnation (which I do believe is true in a relative sense), we did in fact ask to be born. We even planned it all out and wrote the whole bloody script, even down to who was going to be in our family, core group of friends, etc. So we're not off the hook that easy! And to bring the above story to a close, I never got off the hook with either of my parents that easy, either!

On a still deeper root level, though, the question arises: Who, or what, is this "I" personality that seems to keep reincarnating lifetime after lifetime after lifetime, how did *that* happen?

Was that something that "*I*" asked for? And again: Who, or what, is this "I"?

Who the heck Am I anyway?

As you can see, in recent years I've been a keen student of *A Course in Miracles*, recognizing it to be the next big thing in the unfolding of my own spiritual journey. I'm noticing that a lot of other people are waking up to the profundity of this work, too. Another little story...

So I was living on Maui and happen to be of the Mosaic persuasion (i.e., I'm Jewish by birth — did i sign up for that, too? Who persuaded me?) and even though I didn't make it, I heard that there was this great rabbi who was flown in to lead Yom Kippur services (Yom Kippur, aka the "Day of Atonement" – the "holiest" day of the year on the Jewish calendar). This rabbi was not traditional in the sense that he didn't stick solely to the Torah, Talmud, and other Jewish sources. He was just as much at home quoting Rumi, the *Tao Te Ching*, and guess who... our old messianic and similarly unorthodox friend, Yeshua, who is the stated voice that dictated *A Course in Miracles* (aka "The Course") to Helen Shuchman some 50 years ago now.

So I was told, the rabbi began his sermon with the opening words of the Course:

Nothing real can be threatened.
Nothing unreal exists.
Herein lies the peace of God.

Wow, a rabbi on Yom Kippur quoting the words of Jesus as channeled by an atheistic Jewish psychology professor in the heart of the Big Apple some 5 decades ago (!) Surely a sign o' the times, which perhaps could be described as "post-traditional," a time when the best of the world's spiritual traditions are being brought together all on one buffet table, much as your Whole Foods superfoods section contains the most superb foods from various traditional cultures around the globe.

Yet back to the main point, which is how *A Course in Miracles* views the Creator's creation of the world.

Essentially, *it never happened.*

Really? Yes, really.

As the opening salvo of the rabbi's sermon above indicates, if only God is real, and the world of impermanence that we feel to be so real is in reality *not real,* then how could God have created this world? Why would, and how could, what is Real create what is false?

As the poet-sage of the Rig Veda humbly admits (in the quote at the start of this piece), he didn't really have a clue either, but he was pretty damn sure it was a toss up between 2 possibilities: Either God did it, or God didn't! Pretty brilliant, no? Hey, anyone's got a 50-50 chance of getting that one! They didn't call 'em wise guys for nothin'!

So later, it seems, some of these wiseacre sages got cleverer about how to answer this whole question. God didn't create the world, actually, they said, but somehow it still came from God.

Whaaaaa? um, How?

"The play's the thing…"

(remember Hamlet?)

Yes, the idea somehow came through that God was lonely or some crazy shit like that and wanted to feel what it felt like to have a playmate, namely the dualistic Universe of *namarupa*, name and form, yin and yang, Shiva and Shakti…

This is the Hindu tantric idea of "Lila," that the whole cosmic manifestation that we find ourselves in is the "Play of God," sometimes also referred to as the "Divine Drama," in which we are all merely players/actors (again, Shakespeare).

Now, the squeaky keen reader will still be wondering WHY on earth God would/could do this if God is perfect Oneness for which nothing could possibly be added or taken away…? Sounds preposterous, no? Why would God need a "playmate" (the Universe), in other words, when He could just Self-Pleasure Himself for all Eternity (figuratively speaking, of course ;)?

Here's one recent, decent answer to this that I found in Gary Renard's second book dealing with the Course, *Your Immortal Reality*, which is a dialogue between Renard and two ascended masters, Arten and Pursah:

Gary: "…there are people who think that God couldn't experience Himself in Oneness, and the only way He could experience Himself was to make this world and live in it.…

Pursah: "…The idea of thinking that God would have to make this world in order to experience duality so he could enjoy Himself is the equivalent of the idea that in order to experience and enjoy sex, you would have to also experience getting shot in the gut. No. Pain is the result of the guilt that came from thinking you separated yourself from God, and you don't have to experience pain in order to experience the pleasure of reality. But you do have to forgive pain and suffering and give it up in order to return to reality."

It's at this point that the idea of *paradox* perhaps needs to be brought in, paradox being a Greek word that literally means *"beyond belief."* A paradox is the concept that two seemingly contradictory ideas can somehow be reconciled, like having your cake and eating it, too, or the chicken and egg manifesting at the same time, something like that.

For if the conception of God is one of Absoluteness – that God is omniscient, omnipotent, omnipresent — or even that God is absolutely transcendent of everything, the All in All, then we still want to say that someway, somehow, God did create the world, or that it came to be through God's agency somehow, otherwise God wouldn't truly be God, would God?!?

Well, the idea we find in A Course in Miracles is that a "tiny, mad idea" was somehow in the Cosmic Mind that "gee, what would it be like to be separate from God…?"

Now, most people I've spoken with do not find this completely satisfying, because it still seems to suggest that God had something to do with it, otherwise where could that tiny, mad idea come from?

Well, if God is truly infinite, then there might be a sense in which God contains within Godself infinite possibility. This could also mean that God contains within Godself even the thought "not-God." Yet even that thought is still part of God and could never actually be separate from God – it's a possibility and could even *appear* to become an actuality, but that would only be from *within* the idea itself that it would all seem real. In and of itself, however, it would really only be a possibility in the Mind of God, nothing more – but also, nothing less.

"Some people say there is a God; others say there is no God. The truth probably lies somewhere in between."

~ W.B. Yeats

To return now to the idea of "Divine Play" (*lila/leela*) that we find in the Hindu tradition, and one that has definitely taken hold in the minds of many in yoga and new thought circles…Perhaps we can now reconcile the seemingly opposing view that we find in the Course with this idea. On this view, God also did not willfully create the world, yet it still arose from God as God's "Lila" (pronounced "Leela") or divine play from out of the eternal bliss of God's Self. As one commentator has put it:

"Brahman is full of all perfections. And to say that Brahman has some purpose in creating the world will mean that it wants to attain through the process of creation something which it has not. And that is impossible. Hence, there can be no purpose of Brahman in creating the world. The world is a mere spontaneous creation of Brahman. It is a Lila, or sport, of Brahman. It is created out of Bliss, by Bliss and for Bliss. Lila indicates a spontaneous sportive activity of Brahman as distinguished from a self-conscious volitional effort. The concept of Lila signifies freedom as distinguished from necessity."

—Ram Shanker Misra, *The Integral Advaitism of Sri Aurobindo*

For those who need some kind of answer to this question, there you go, and I do feel that this is the closest we're going to get to it using just our intellects. While for those deep thinkers (or perhaps, overthinkers :) out there I realize that even this will not be sufficient, I do feel this does go far enough to explain what cannot be explained in words. What I especially appreciate about both Advaita Vedanta and what is presented in *A Course in Miracles* is their downplaying the theological and philosophical speculation on these Big Questions in favor of the actual **experience** of these truths through the continual practice of removing the delusive clouds in our minds that have obscured the light of the sun. As the Course famously says:

"The ego will demand many answers this course does not give. It does not recognize as questions the mere form of a question to which an answer is impossible. The ego may ask, 'How did the impossible occur?', 'To what did the impossible happen?', and may ask this in many forms. Yet there is no answer; only an experience. Seek only this, and do not let theology delay you."

The Course (or Jesus, the narrator of the Course) goes even further to tell us that actually, the only reason the ego has these questions to begin with is to say something like: "See, I exist! I'm real! Now tell me (or don't tell me!) how I'm not real!" So at various places in the Course, Jesus makes radical statements like the following:

"Your questions have no answer, being made to still God's Voice, which asks of everyone one question only:

"Are you ready yet to help Me save the world?""

Another way of putting all of this is that the only way for the ego to have a truly satisfying answer to these ultimate questions is for the ego to be completely dissolved – at which point there will be no more ego to appreciate the answer! Until that point, there will only be, there *can* only be, doubt and questions. This is where trust and faith must come in, and a firm commitment to keep that faith and keep practicing, even with doubts.

"Faith begins as an experiment and ends as an experience."

The good news is that even just on the illusionary level at which we currently are, the practices that will "undo" the ego will also generally make for a happier, healthier, more peaceful life. So we do get our cake and eat it, too!

In other words, while I do feel it is helpful to be aware of the questions and these metaphysical issues, they mean nothing if there is no practical application of them. And so I will conclude this section with one of my favorite philosophy jokes:

What is Mind?
Oh, no matter.

What is Matter?
Never mind!

> The body was not made by love.
> Yet love does not condemn it
> and can use it lovingly,
> respecting what the Son of God has made
> and using it to save him from illusions.
>
> ~ A Course in Miracles

"The body was not made by love.
Yet love does not condemn it and can use it lovingly,
Respecting what the Son of God has made
And using it to save him from illusions."

**In other words, love and care for the body,
but also understand it for what it is – it is what you make of it.**

A Course in Miracles in Light of *The Katha Upanishad*

"There is one thing that you have never done; you have never utterly forgotten the body. It has perhaps faded at times from your sight, but it has not yet completely disappeared. You are not asked to let this happen for more than an instant, yet it is in this instant that the miracle of Atonement happens. Afterwards you will see the body again, but never quite the same. And every instant that you spend without awareness of it gives you a different view of it when you return."

~ A Course in Miracles 18.VII.2

"The wise man does not grieve, having known the bodiless, all-pervading and great, seated firmly in perishable bodies."

~ Katha Upanishad 1.2.22

"The view of things ... that all plurality is only apparent, that in the endless series of individuals, passing simultaneously and successively into and out of life, generation after generation, age after age, there is but one and the same entity really existing, which is present and identical in all alike; — this theory ... may be carried back to the remotest antiquity. It is the alpha and omega of the oldest book in the world, the sacred Vedas, whose dogmatic part, or rather esoteric teaching, is found in the Upanishads. There, in almost every page this profound doctrine lies enshrined; with tireless repetition, in countless adaptations, by many varied parables and similes it is expounded and inculcated."

~ Arthur Schopenhauer

The Upanishads are a collection of Hindu scriptures that many consider to be the high water mark of India's revered spiritual literary heritage. The great German philosopher Arthur Schopenhauer was a keen student of the Upanishads and had this to say about them:

"In the whole world there is no study so beneficial and so elevating as the study of the Upanishads. It has been the solace of my life. It will be the solace of my death."

Elsewhere he wrote:

They are destined sooner or later to become the faith of the people."

Schopenhauer meant the German people of his time (19th century), but I would suggest that we could expand this today to include the people of the entire world. Yes, sooner or later, everyone will recognize the truth of these ancient but ever-relevant teachings, it is only a matter of time. And today we can say this with even more confidence if we simply look at the impact that Indian yoga has had on the world. Indeed, yoga is a worldwide phenomenon that has had a global impact beyond what anyone even 25 years ago could have imagined. The United Nations has even recently (in 2014) declared an International Day of Yoga every June 21st(!) Even the Catholic Church has lightened up a bit about yoga, granting that its adherents can at least practice the non-spiritual aspects of it. Who wouldathunkit?

I would say the same thing about ACIM and ayahuasca – that they, or the principles found therein, will one day be understood or at least accepted by a majority of people – which is why I am writing this book. Yes, someday they will be seen for what they truly are, spiritual guides of the highest order for the process of spiritual awakening. It is not that they are not ready for the world, apparently they are! It is that the world is still not ready for them, yet this is steadily changing with each passing day as we see the passing away of religious dogma and institutions and the rise of DIY spirituality.

So with that said, what are some of the principal teachings of the Upanishads? Instead of giving you a whole treatise on the subject, I will rather give you a more subjective list of some of the more relevant upanishadic teachings for our purposes here. Most of these teachings, by the way, are to be found in the Upanishad that we will be looking more closely at, the Katha Upanishad, which dates back at least 2500 years ago (around the same time as the Bhagavad Gita and containing even some of the exact same teachings).

First and foremost, the Upanishads are the first to mention the word "yoga," generally defining it as both as the means to union with God, as well as the end state of Union. The Vedas do not use the term anywhere, although there are foreshadowings of things to come in those more ancient texts. The Katha Upanishad itself has the following definition of yoga:

"When the five senses, along with the mind, remain still and the intellect is not active, that is known as the highest state. They consider yoga to be firm restraint of the senses. Then one becomes un-distracted for yoga is the arising and the passing away" (6.10-11)

Here is one of the earliest definitions of yoga, that of restraint of the senses, or the practice of restraining the senses to arrive at undisturbed state of mind.

Why is this important? It's important because here we have the idea that there is a **path** and a **practice,** called **yoga,** that are key to inner peace and ultimately finding our way back to union with God, a union which is also termed **yoga**. And that one can even possibly quicken the way through the yogic preparations one makes, preparations such as cleansing the mind with mantras, breathing exercises, meditation, charitable works and spiritual study. Yet these preparations are no guarantee and who will wake up is still a mystery and still a matter of grace, God only knows. But somehow yoga or a yogic path is important in the process of awakening to one's essential nature (Brahman/God/Self/Oneness/Spirit).

As for God, the word that the Upanishads largely use is "Brahman" (not to be confused with "Brahma" or "brahmin" – also to be discussed). Brahman, the Upanishads tell us, is "One without a second" (*ekam advitiyam*). Brahman is actually the nameless, formless, unchanging, undying Ground of Being (we could call it "Gob") and essential Self of all things, both immanent and transcendent, meaning God is in all things and yet still beyond the world of impermanence.

For our purposes here, it is enough to have this idea of a One Reality that is "one without a second." Meaning, as the non-dualists like Shankara later picked up on, that God/Brahman (the Ultimate Reality) does not partake at all of the world of duality, of separateness, opposites, or otherness. Rather, God is a state of perfect oneness. And again, that oneness can be approached through yogic practices such as adherence to ethical principles, meditation, acts of charity, etc., but these practices do not necessarily grant access and when the individual soul (atman) realizes its essential oneness with Brahman is really anybody's guess.

And that's another point to be made and the flip side of what was just expressed: From our standpoint, we are each individual souls that are separate from each other and God. But waking up is just the realization that we are all one and that our seeming individuality is an illusion. Even the *atman* (individual soul) that seemingly reincarnates lifetime to lifetime is ultimately an illusion. In the end, the individual soul and, let's call it the Sole Soul for convenience, are one. Just as Jesus Christ was able to say "I and my father are one," so too are we ultimately one with the One.

Now, the one who realizes these truths while still in their body would be considered wise, and they would have attained what is called "Self-realization" and "*moksha*," the highest goal of life. Moksha is a Sanskrit word usually translated as "liberation." The idea is that in realizing their own true nature, the wise person realizes the Self (God, Brahman, Spirit) in all things. And in doing so, they are liberated from *samsara*, which is the seemingly endless cycle of birth and death and the pain and suffering that they entail. Such liberated beings no longer have to reincarnate, or come back into a body, because they have transcended the need for a body, which poses a limit to Self-awareness. But they can come back into a body for the purpose of helping others. (By the way, there are many terms for the same thing; the word, *nirvana*, for example, is no different than *moksha*.)

So the truly enlightened person is one who somehow attains moksha while still in the body. But how does one recognize such a truly wise person or sage? Another way of putting this is that how do we know who is a true guru? The Bhagavad Gita (which is also considered an Upanishad and which we will discuss later) actually goes into much detail about how to identify a person who has achieved God-consciousness. Perhaps the most telling characteristic is that such a person has no more fear and does not grieve or suffer. Again and again the Katha Upanishad says that the wise person has gone beyond all fear and does not grieve. For they have gone beyond their body (physicality) and realized their essential oneness with the One Spirit who does not know fear and is only Love. And only such a one is then qualified to help others reach the same place; in other words, that person is a guru.

About the guru, the Katha Upanishad in particular has much to say. In fact, the story (Katha means "story") can be seen as a transmission/initiation from guru to disciple. Only the guru in the story is Yama, the god of death (or Death incarnate), and the disciple is a young brahmin boy named Naciketas.

As the story goes, Naciketas calls his father out on the pitiful sacrificial offering he makes at a Vedic fire ceremony and his father basically tells the boy to go to hell. And so he does! Literally (though it's just a story). While in hell/underworld, Naciketas has to wait for Yama, who is Death incarnate, for 3 days while Yama is on other business, and because in the Hindu tradition the guest is like God, like a genie, Yama grants Naciketas 3 boons, meaning 3 wishes. He can ask for anything he wants.

Apparently Yama underestimates the young boy's power of choice, because after making his first 2 wishes, for the third he chooses to know what death is and what happens after the death of the body. In other words, Naciketas wants nothing less than for the entire mystery of life and death to be revealed to him – the whole shebang, all she wrote and nothing but the truth so help me God of Death, and thank you very much! Realizing that he underestimated the boy, Yama can only try to talk him out of it, promising him that he will give him anything else in heaven and earth that he could possibly ever want, if only he does not have to answer that question!

But Naciketas is no fool. No, he is like Solomon, Buddha, and Jesus who all also fought off temptation and gave up everything just to have the real prize, what we all are really seeking, which is to know who we truly are. So despite Yama's insistence that he will give him all the riches in the world, Naciketas basically says, "Nah, why would I want anything so flimsy as that, something that will not last?" And then Yama, realizing that the boy is sincere and ready for it (and that was really why Yama was delaying), proceeds to relate to him the most profound spiritual teachings.

Most of those teachings I have already noted above, but the one other that I left for this moment regards the spiritual seeker (aspirant) and the guru. Yama tells Naciketas in no uncertain terms that a guru or teacher/guide is essential for the spiritual path. Why? Because it is usually a quite challenging process, not an easy one! In perhaps what is the most famous passage in this Upanishad, Yama tells Naciketas:

Like the Razor's sharp edge is difficult to traverse,
The path to one's Self is difficult.

In other words, the path to God is like a razor's edge, it's difficult, edgy, even dangerous and deadly. Many have sought God climbing high mountain peaks, only to die trying. Or they went crazy. Or they suffered some other great loss and lost their courage.

Think of a peak like Mt. Everest. Many have lost their lives attempting to climb it. Relatively few have succeeded. Go it alone and good luck. Go with a Sherpa or other experienced guide and you have more of a chance of getting there, but no certainty. Why should the spiritual path be any different?

It isn't any different. In fact, it's harder. In a sense, only a fool would think they can get there on their own, and actually there have been holy fools who have! But most others apparently need some kind of guide, at least in the initial stages. Although some would say that a guide is necessary more towards the end when the going really gets tough. But I would say that if you have a good guide at some point along the way, you can get the rest of the way there yourself. It's like that old Lynyrd Skynyrd song, " I know a little 'bout love, and baby I can guess the rest."

For me, *A Course in Miracles* is the guide par excellence. Even beyond the Upanishads, the Gita, and the Yoga Sutras. Not that those weren't helpful to me at a certain point! But for me, ACIM goes beyond them because it really gets down to some fundamental issues that are not as central in the yogic texts. Such as... the person of Jesus and his core message of non-judgment and forgiveness, that we are not guilty sinners but are all as innocent in the eyes of God as he is, and that as we practice and share this, we experience it more and more. But also, ACIM provides a rather sophisticated understanding of the psyche, particularly in regard to what the ego is and why if we follow its "voice," we will search in vain for peace of mind. So for me, Jesus and his simple, gentle Course are my main guru and what I have turned to these past years for the greatest guidance on the path. And I do feel that I have gone the furthest in the shortest amount of time using ACIM as a guide, even to the point of having the experience of awakening from the dream of this world.

Would I have gotten there as quickly without the help of my Hindu gurus, the ancient yogic scriptures, the practice of yoga, ayahuasca, and ACIM? Highly doubtful. In fact, I might be dead right now without all of them. And I don't think that death would have been better than life, certainly not premature death. Not that I think death is real, it's not, but darned if I wasn't scared to death about it for a good spell there.

Right now I'm just opening to how to express these things more coherently and down-to-earth so that they can be better and more clearly understood. So far I don't feel like I've hit my stride. Maybe comedy is the way? Observing comedians like Key and Peele, Dave Chapelle, and Sacha Baron Cohen (recent favorites) remind me that this all doesn't have to be so serious, and that the end goal is learning how to laugh and make light of everything (at least in your mind), and ultimately to take nothing seriously. Yes, I've noted that the best comedians seem to have no bones about making fun of anything and everything, no sacred cow goes unmilked lest for we forget that we still *can* laugh at the seemingly unlaughable.

You think I'm just talking to myself here, and maybe I am, but it's all about breaking out of the box we're in, and the "books box" is just as much of a box as any other. So please allow me to try a little stream-of-unconscious "sit down" comedy here…

When I was 13-years-old I had a very filthy mouth. (But I only say that now for the sake of the story. Now I would say I was simply free in my expressions.) Every other word was "fuck" or "shit," just as it is for many other pre-teens and teens, of whatever generation. And one summer day when I was away at summer camp, I was in the canteen with a friend and we were playing pinball and cursing up a storm. Then some older folks, guests of the camp, came in and overheard us, but we didn't care, we just went on cursing away, maybe even more than before. Then, later that day, all of the boys in the upper camp got taken out to the basketball court for a serious meeting. And I bet you know for what. Yeah, it was that we all needed to watch our language and that our counselors (who cursed just as much as we did) would kick our asses if we didn't. So I guess we did, I don't remember. And you can bet I felt a little guilty about the whole thing.

But the point of the story is that not too long after that incident, I was at home with two of my brothers and I heard them talking and cursing. Something about it suddenly really disturbed me, and I essentially took a vow then and there that I was never going to curse again. And actually, I did keep that vow for most of my teens, twenties and even thirties. I never cursed. Really. I really watched my language, not just curse words. I took it upon myself to actually think before speaking. Even when listening to friends and even teachers who could really curse well, I was not tempted to jump back on that bandwagon.

In recent years, however, I've been feeling it's my bounden duty to start cursing again, if only because it will possibly help us all not take things, including words and whatever trip we're on, so seriously. And you know that I'm partially kidding because I still wouldn't use language that I thought might be hurtful to someone. But in retrospect, I probably stopped cursing not because I thought it was the wrong thing to do, but partly out of guilt and to feel better than my brothers and other people. In that sense, by cursing I am helping to correct an ego-driven mistake. But I will still choose to choose my words carefully :).

I will say, however, that there was a funny moment in one ayahuasca ceremony where amongst a flurry of "f" words I half told the above story about taking a vow not to curse, and then I added: "And tonight, I will make up for that vow!" People laughed, it was a hit. It brought out the natural born comedian in me a little more.

Listen y'all, I'm just preparing you for my next book. Here's a little taste…

> Into eternity, where all is one,
> there crept a tiny, mad idea,
> at which the Son of God
> remembered not to laugh.

(An Only Seeming Slight Digression) Great Moments in Ayahuasca Ceremony History

One night I did a mini aya ceremony with a friend in his bedroom. We both took about the same amount, maybe just an ounce or so. Suddenly I was on my back laughing and laughing and laughing. It was not just normal laughing, mind you, this was freakin' cosmic comic hilarity, the kind you only get from some deep deep place of Knowing within. I mean, I laughed so hard that my face became transfigured. I didn't see it, but I felt it. And while it was happening, there was a part of me that was still witnessing it all thinking: "Damn, I guess I really needed this!" And there was another part of me that realized why I was laughing, and it was because I got to a place so deep that I realized the absurdity of everything, especially the idea that there is anything truly outside of ourself (our Self). To think otherwise was actually very funny. And it occurred to me that this was a great correction for the "original sin" of forgetting to laugh at the absurd idea of a sin and separation from God.

Meanwhile, my friend got nothing. He just held loving space for me, and I think he got quite a kick out of it, too.

*

Another time, not too long after that, we had a ceremony at our place with about 18 people, maybe 2/3rds of whom were young people between the ages of 18-25 and who had never done ayahuasca. At first, everyone obeyed the rules and was quiet, kept to themselves and meditated with the medicine. But after the second round, all hell broke loose. I began playing the song "Christmas Presence" (the lyrics of which are included somewhere in this book) and the song somehow ended up morphing into a lovefest, don't ask me how. Suddenly, half the group was in the middle of the room in a huge "cuddle puddle," laughing and crying and screaming and hugging and caressing each other. Meanwhile, one young woman was puking her guts out and seemingly having a fine time of it.

One of the most interesting things about this for me was that there was an older couple with us that night for the first time, and what happened with them was very telling... These two had spent time in recent years with a prominent ACIM teacher, one who does not himself endorse or condone the use of psychedelics. But this pair clearly differed in that regard and had been exploring the use of ayahuasca in particular for help on their path.

Now, for the first part of the ceremony this couple had been sitting along the wall to my right, deep in their own inner work. But when the whole melee in the middle of the room happened, I looked over and they were no longer there. Uh-oh, I thought, this was all too much for them, it was just too loud and wild and crazy. I began to wonder whether I should try to bring everyone back into a more quiet and grounded space, and actually I did try that at one point, but to no avail. Then to my surprise I noticed that the male half of the couple was actually on the floor in the middle with the kids! And he was having a great old time! His partner also was okay, and she told me later that at first she found the noise and chaos challenging, but then she realized that the point of it all for her was just to surrender to what was happening, to accept it for what it was and not judge it.

As for the man, he told me that in light of the ayahuasca experience, *A Course in Miracles* makes total sense. From what he said, I gathered he had a very similar experience as I did many times with the medicine, the feeling of getting to the point of complete forgiveness and experiencing what the Course calls "the real world," and then going beyond that to the non-dual, transpersonal state. Although I didn't really need outside confirmation of what I had myself experienced by that point on more than several occasions, it was good to hear that, and maybe it will be an added confirmation for you, too.

Christmas Presence

The Sun Has Risen
Oh in my Heart & I shall listen to what
He shall impart

So pure and innocent
As a little lamb
My Christmas Present
To Know that Love I am

***

Now the Son also rises
In every sing-all Person & the surprise is
We shine in Unison

***

So Love thy neighbor
Oh 'tis the Season
Become thy Savior
In the light of Reason

We'll learn our lessons
Guided by your star
Our Christmas Presence
To Know that Love we are

**Into Christ's Presence will we enter now
serenely unaware of everything except
His shining face and perfect Love.**

You Are Forgiven 'n' on & on…

The Sun Has Risen
Oh in my Heart
Now I shall listen to what
He shall impart
So pure and innocent (you)
As a little lamb
Our Christmas presence
To know that love we are[31]

---

31   From the CD "Heart 'n' Hands: A Musical Celebration of A Course in Miracles."

That said, now I want to tell you about a few experiences that were a little bit more on the edge. This is to show that ayahuasca is not something to play with, nor is it appropriate for everyone at any given time, and that set, setting, and dosage are definite factors. But this is not scare anyone either, for in the end, everything turned out okay in all of these cases. In fact, I would go further and say that in general, the more challenging the experience, the more effective and beneficial it is – the more it has to reveal about deeper issues and blockages that are being worked through.

So on several occasions I've witnessed people basically go berserk with the medicine. I mean, they really needed strait jackets; but in lieu of that, they had to be physically pinned down so that they would not hurt themselves or anyone else, not to mention break things.

I'm thinking of one ceremony in particular in which one participant, a dear friend, was flipping out – quite literally, at moments. He would suddenly just go wild and jump and roll or even spin around in a rather spasmodic and violent way. At one point, he seemed to be calmed down and back to normal in front of the shaman-facilitator. Then all of a sudden, he was wild again and he jumped up, spilling the brew all over the floor and the shaman! On this occasion, I had the honor of pinning him to the floor, holding him there for at least an hour while he blissfully babbled on and on about how amazing this all was, somehow bringing Jim Carrey and Wayne Dyer into the mix, don't ask me how. When he finally came back to earth, he actually remembered some of what had happened, but much of it was gone from memory, only to be recalled in fragments over the coming weeks and months.

Now what was particularly interesting to me on this occasion was that while my friend had been ecstatically flying about the room, scaring all of us who thought he was really going to hurt himself, not once did he in fact hurt himself or anyone else. There was a certain protection about him, it seemed. I mean, you would have thought that he was going to kill himself the way he was moving! It was actually all quite funny in retrospect, but when it was happening, he had us all really concerned there. But we had no reason to worry, somehow someone was in charge of the whole thing and was watching out for him.

Laugh At Every Thing & Be Free

The point of all of this was to bring in a little humor and some stories to make this all a little bit more personal and down-to-earth. Even these ancient scriptures have humor, as with Naciketas' taunting his father in the early part of the Katha Upanishad until the father gets so angry he sends his son to hell. The deeper point is to not take things all so seriously, because ultimately they're not. This is not to downplay what happens in the world of form and not to be responsible in how we deal with life and the facts on the ground. Rather, it's about what we do in our minds in how we are thinking about everything. And if we are making anything so serious that we are getting upset about it, then (at least according to the Course) it is because we have chosen the ego as our teacher and are taking its view of things over that of Spirit. For Spirit, there is always another way of looking at our seeming "problems," and that is the simple (but maddening, I know) solution: **Nothing Happened**. Meaning that God Is and Love already won. The game is already over. Are we at least open to this good news? Or do we want to interminably delay and keep delaying our way back?

*

Okay one more "great moment" to share… I have been discussing the phenomenon of channeling and working with ayahuasca has given me deeper insight into how channeling works. It has also given me an understanding of how artists might profitably use ayahuasca to help them create even more intuitive and sublime works, as many are now already doing…

One night at a ceremony outside around a campfire, just as the medicine was peaking, I began to play a favorite Hindu bhajan (devotional song) of mine. This time, I was delighted to find how much *shakti* (energy) there was in it, it felt as if **this** – *this* was how the song could sound, if only I could get out of my own way. As the song worked its way to a heightened pitch of feverish intensity, I experienced what I can only describe as a timeless moment when I was no longer playing the song – *it was playing itself through me.* Really. It was as if I was no longer the player, I was being played. I was the instrument! And the result was pure magic, as was confirmed by the listeners afterwards. And you can bet that for me that alone was worth the price of admission. If I had lived only for that moment, it would have been enough. And just maybe I did…

For the Lunatic Fringe

You will go through many PHASES...
until you are no longer FAZED by anything

Takes One to Know One: (How) Grace Works

"The thing we tell of can never be found be seeking, yet only seekers find it."

~ Bayazid Bistami

"For it is by grace you have been saved, through faith—and this is not from yourselves, it is the gift of God— not by works, so that no one can boast."

~ Ephesians 2:8-9 New International Version (NIV)

"Be receptive to the grace of God."

~ Sri Dharma Mittra

There is one more element of the Katha Upanishad that, while it was already touched upon above, would be helpful to bring more to bear on this whole discussion, and that is this thing called "grace." Or should I say – "Grace" – with a capital G, as in the woman's name (and that U2 song). You will perhaps recall the discussion in section 2 about how Ayahuasca as "Mother" and the Holy Spirit might be understood as the same essential principle (content) acting in different contexts (forms). And here I will further propose that Grace is added to this honored group, it being the principle of compassionate giving above and beyond what has been earned, and this compassion again can be construed as symbolically feminine in nature.

To put this in very simple terms, Grace is the idea that there is no way that we could reach God without some help. And when I say "some," I really mean a whole helluva lot, because from our perspective, we are so imprisoned by our own minds that it would seem to take lifetimes or more to get out of the maze/hell we're in. Do what we will, practice and perform as many mantras and prayers and offerings and good deeds as we might, it would seem to be a mere drop in the bucket (to which we're going to hell in, thank you Dead & Co) with no seeming hope of finding our way home. But then Grace sweetly whispers: "Ok, you've done enough, I see that you really want this and so, here we go…"

My teacher, Sri Karunamayi, has a great way of putting this: "*If you take one step towards me, child, I will take one thousand steps towards you.*" The Course calls this the "little willingness" we need but have, and the Holy Spirit will do the rest. Grace is always working, but "She" needs our effort in the form of opening to Her in order to really work.

Of course, how this all works is really a mystery, and as I have noted before, why someone receives Grace and another does not seems to be beyond our comprehension. Yet again, I will suggest that one's desire for liberation must be the strongest desire – perhaps even the only desire – for Grace to reveal Herself. (At one point in the Course, Jesus uses the phrase "abundant willingness," shifting from his usual phrasing of "little willingness.")

Here is something Yama tells Naciketas in the Katha Upanishad:

> *They say yoga is this complete stillness*
> *In which one enters the unitive state,*
> *Never to become separate again.*
> *If one is not established in this state,*
> *The sense of unity will come and go…*
>
> *Only the one-pointed mind attains this state of unity.*
> *There is no one but the Self.*
> *Who sees multiplicity but not the one indivisible Self*
> *must wander on and on from death to death.*

This sounds a little discouraging, I know, but it gets better. Elsewhere, Yama informs Naciketas that…

> *The unitive state cannot be attained*
> *Through words or thoughts or through the eye.*
> *How can it be attained except through one*
> *Who is established in this state himself?*
> *Katha II.3.11-12*

Does this sound like a spiritual Catch-22 to you, too? It seems to be saying that in order to get to the One, you have to be one already (or, "takes One to know One"). How is this possible? But before you try to answer that, there is a similar passage which seems to make the situation even more confusing...

> *The Self cannot be known through study*
> *Of the scriptures, nor through the intellect,*
> *Nor through hearing learned discourses.*
> *The Self can be attained only by those*
> *Whom the Self chooses. Verily unto them*
> *Does the Self reveal himself.*
> *Katha I.2.23*

Some have noted that here for the first time in the yoga tradition we have the idea of "Grace," that somehow through one's deep longing to know God (the one-pointedness of the seeker), a way to God reveals itself. This one-pointedness of mind is in a sense both the means and the end itself; I would suggest that, as the Course puts it, once this one-pointedness is in place, "God takes the last step" so to speak, and brings you all the way there. In other words, Grace goes to work.

Yet the question still is: Why does one soul make that choice for God and only God in any given lifetime? In a passage that is very similar to what Krishna says in the Bhagavad Gita (there is a bit of overlap between the two scriptures), Yama tells Naciketas that it is actually very rare and fortunate to wake up (attain Self-realization)....

It is but few who hear about the Self.
Fewer still dedicate their lives to its
Realization. Wonderful is the one
Who speaks about the Self; rare are they
Who make it the supreme goal of their lives.
Blessed are they who, through an illumined
Teacher, attain to Self-realization.
I.2.7

What I am getting at here is a very essential question in spirituality, which is who can honestly lay claim to enlightenment (or Self-realization). I certainly would not do that (though in places in this book it might seem that I do). No, it would indeed seem that true enlightenment while still in the body (*jivanmukti*, in Sanskrit) is very rare, if not near impossible, as both the Course and the Upanishads concur. But perhaps it is also not completely necessary; perhaps it is enough to just humbly practice and embody lovingkindness and non-judgment based on our brief revelatory glimpses of the non-dual state.

Another, related issue that I will raise again here is that of who is a true guru, one qualified to lead another to realization of their true nature? How can we really tell? Particularly these days when almost every major guru has had a scandal surrounding them. I have noted that this is why I find ACIM so intriguing, because it appears to be able to serve as a guru in a post-guru world, or for those who, like me, are post-guru. The same with ayahuasca. Granted, ACIM still needs an interpreter, and ayahuasca, for most, still needs a shaman or guide, and these guides can also be fallible. But while we (or I) might point to the failings of the guru – and in fact *every* human-all-too-human teacher – all they need to do is point the way, they don't need to be perfect, just as we don't need to be perfect to find the way.

I will have more to say on these issues as we go on. Next we will be considering another Upanishad, and in fact the most famous one, the Bhagavad Gita, Krishna's love song to us about how to know that we are Love…

I AM LOVE

When you are afraid
Be still & know God is real

I'll Just Be Me, You Just Be You

Nowhere to go
Nothin' to do
No one to be
I'll just be me
& you just be you

Hare Krishna Hare Krishna
Krishna Krishna Hare Hare

Hare Rama Hare Rama
Rama Rama Hare Hare

I have no name
I have no shame
All praise & blame
It's all a game
& It's all the same

Hare Krishna Hare Krishna
Krishna Krishna Hare Hare

Hare Rama Hare Rama
Rama Rama Hare Hare

Make up your bed
Make up your mind
Make up, you've read
To make up is kind

'Cause It's all for free
It's all for love
It's all a dream
& you made it up

Hare Krishna Hare Krishna
Krishna Krishna Hare Hare

Hare Rama Hare Rama
Rama Rama Hare Hare

The Bhagavad Gita: A Very Brief Introduction

What is the Bhagavad Gita?
When was the Bhagavad Gita Written & by Whom?
Why is the Bhagavad Gita Considered Such an Important Text?
What does the Bhagavad Gita Teach Us About Yoga?
What Are Some of the Most Essential Teachings of the Bhagavad Gita?
How Might I Use These Teachings in My Life, Practice, and Teaching?

What is the Bhagavad Gita?

What, you don't know? What!?!?!?

It's only one of the greatest masterpieces of world spiritual literature, ranking up there with the Bible, Qur'an, & the Hobbit! It's only read and loved by millions and millions of people the world over, particularly the Hindu faithful in India. It's only one of the most profound presentations of yoga that we might ever find within the covers of one book! It's only the very scripture that Thoreau called "stupendous and cosmogonal philosophy," Hesse called it "a beautiful revelation of life's wisdom," and Gandhi called it a source of comfort form him in troubled moments! And you didn't know that yet?

What's up with dat?

Seriously, it's something definitely worth reading and exploring, which is why we're here, right?

If you haven't yet read the Gita (as it's affectionately called), I recommend the translation and commentary by Eknath Easwaran (click HERE) to start. Keep in mind that there are many translations of the Bhagavad Gita out there now, and some of them are better than others. The one that I'm currently using for putting together this section is

Winthrop Sargeant's "The Bhagavad Gita" (SUNY Press), because it's a more complete work intended for the serious student of the Gita.

Let's start with the basics…

First, the name. Bhagavan = Lord, God.

Gita = Song

Put the two together you get Bhagavad Gita,

the Song of God.

Why is it the Song of God?

Because in it, Krishna, who is considered to be God (an avatar/incarnation of Vishnu, the Preserver/Sustainer, but also the Supreme Godhead), gives the deeper teachings of Yoga to Arjuna, a great warrior who is about to fight a terrible battle against his own kinsmen.

What are some of those teachings?

Read on!

When Was the Bhagavad Gita Written, and By Whom?

Good question! Go figure! First, though, who is it that wants to know? What if this ancient scripture is really not so ancient? What if it's just a fairy tale, never really happened? What if the text was altered so much over time that the original message is now lost? If so, would that give us just the excuse we need to ignore its message? And what if I were to tell you that revelations such as this one are still occurring, even to this day, and that there are contemporary books that we can date with equally profound messages? It's important to transcend the illusion of time here. This is a timeless message. It is timeless, and yes, it was meant for a particular time and particular culture. The deeper message of the work is universal, applying in all times and places. Remember this saying: *"Just because it never happened doesn't mean it ain't true!"* (Another Yogi Berra-ism that he probably never said!)

Ok, that rant out of the way, tradition has it that the actual war about which the Gita relates started on February 20, 3102 B.C. Most academic scholars, on the other hand, say the date is more like 800 B.C (Georg Feuerstein suggested 1500 B.C.) Most scholars seem to think that the work itself was composed sometime between 500 and 200 B.C. (i.e., before the time of Jesus), with interpolations (additions) to the text added later by those with a stake in promoting a certain message.

Why is the Bhagavad Gita Considered So Important?

Another good question! Who really knows?

That said, generally what I have found is that when someone or something reaches let's call it global recognition, there's something very powerful about it, something of truly great quality that transcends the norm. Today, a song or artist will achieve such global status, for example, when their song or video goes "viral." You can't fool people in this regard – they will always be able to recognize greatness and celebrate it through that recognition. So the Bhagavad Gita is perhaps so popular because it is a work of such rare quality, such profundity that speaks on some of the most key issues regarding spiritual life.

There are other reasons, too, that this work has received both top critical and popular reviews.

First of all, it's dramatic and epic, and we all love that. It's a story, but it's really not a story – it's just a dialogue between the Godman Krishna and his friend/student, Arjuna. Yet in that dialogue is some very profound spiritual wisdom, stuff that still holds up to this very day. Universal issues like War & Peace, Duty, the Spiritual Path, Meditation, Devotion, Metaphysics, the Way to Wisdom and God-Realization…It's all in there, all in this small little book that might take a night to read but a lifetime to assimilate and truly understand.

Why do I personally find it to be so worth reading (and writing about)? Well, like any great work of art, it speaks on many levels. One is just the issue of war and peace, and how Krishna (God, remember) almost unbelievably counsels Arjuna to fight and kill others, in this case his own kinsmen.

Why would God do such a thing?

Krishna presents an argument for a "Just War," or why sometimes war IS justified. Yet on an even deeper level, the Bhagavad Gita teaches the way of the yogi, the evenmindedness or equanimity (*samatvam*) with which the true yogi sees and acts. According to Krishna's words to Arjuna, the true yogi views everything the same – pleasure and pain, "good" fortune, "bad" fortune, war, peace, friend, enemy, Brahmin, outcaste, pure, impure – it's all one, there's no difference, no separation. So this gives me a bit of a mirror or measure by which I can witness my own progress in transcending duality. Am I finding things of this world bothering me? Which of my buttons keep getting pushed, and why? Where is my practice going astray, what am I missing? What am I still attached to that needs to be let go of, where does my ego still have a stake firmly planted and is not budging? What are my personal demons that need to be slain, etc., etc. etc. Anyway, that's why it's helpful for me. And if you should need some more inspiration to take this all a bit more seriously and dive into it, here's what some wise guys have said about this work over the millennia…

"The Bhagavad-Gita is the most systematic statement of spiritual evolution of endowing value to mankind. It is one of the most clear and comprehensive summaries of perennial philosophy ever revealed; hence its enduring value is subject not only to India but to all of humanity." ~ Aldous Huxley

"In the morning I bathe my intellect in the stupendous and cosmogonal philosophy of the Bhagavad-Gita, in comparison with which our modern world and its literature seems puny and trivial." ~ Henry David Thoreau

"The Bhagavad-Gita is an empire of thought and in its philosophical teachings Krishna has all the attributes of the full-fledged monotheistic deity and at the same time the attributes of the Upanishadic absolute." ~ Ralph Waldo Emerson

"In order to approach a creation as sublime as the Bhagavad-Gita with full understanding it is necessary to attune our soul to it." ~ Rudolph Steiner

"From a clear knowledge of the Bhagavad-Gita all the goals of human existence become fulfilled. Bhagavad-Gita is the manifest quintessence of all the teachings of the Vedic scriptures." ~ Adi Sankara

Samatvam Yoga Ucyate
Yoga is Equanimity

**One short definition of yoga that Krishna offers
In the Bhagavad Gita, Chapter 2.
Yoga is *samatvam* – equal vision, seeing everything the same.
(Also, *samadarshana*.)**

The Bhagavad Gita
In Light of *A Course in Miracles*

"Of thousands of men, scarcely anyone strives for perfection [siddhaye/siddhi]; even of the striving and perfected [siddha], scarcely anyone knows Me in truth."

~ Bhagavad Gita, VII.3

After many births the wise seek refuge in me, seeing me everywhere and in everything. Such great souls are very rare.

~ Bhagavad Gita, VII.19

"Sometimes a teacher of God may have a brief experience of direct union with God. In this world, it is almost impossible that this endure. It can, perhaps, be won after much devotion and dedication, and then be maintained for much of the time on earth. But this is so rare that it cannot be considered a realistic goal. If it happens, so be it. If it does not happen, so be it as well."

~ *A Course in Miracles*, Manual for Teachers

"When doubts haunt me, when disappointments stare me in the face, and I see not one ray of hope on the horizon, I turn to Bhagavad-Gita and find a verse to comfort me; and I immediately begin to smile in the midst of overwhelming sorrow. Those who meditate on the Gita will derive fresh joy and new meanings from it every day."

~ Mahatma Gandhi

"Without your smile the world could not be saved."

~ A Course in Miracles

The Bhagavad Gita has been called the "New Testament" of India, it is perhaps its most revered and sacred scripture. It is actually just a small section of a much larger epic story from ancient India, the *Mahabharata*, which tells the tale of two warring factions of the same family in competition for the rulership of their Kingdom. But I am not here to give much factual information regarding the story and history of the Gita (as it is often abbreviated), which can be found elsewhere. I'm here more interested in merely providing just enough background so that we can open a comparative discussion of the Gita and ACIM, two writings that are on the surface rather different, yet are in essence the same.

Let's begin with a basic question: Why is the Bhagavad Gita so important, why is it so widely read and given the status of "classic"? I also don't presume to attempt to answer this question here, but rather just point to the fact that many brilliant minds east and west have found the Gita to be of great inspiration, among them Gandhi, Emerson, and Thoreau. While a thing's popularity is not necessarily a sign of its excellence, it is generally indicative of its noteworthiness. That is why I begin with it.

What has always been most interesting to me about the Gita is that it purports to be the word of the Godman (Avatar) Krishna to the great warrior, Arjuna, on the eve of an epic battle. Krishna is Arjuna's charioteer and also teacher, and Arjuna turns to Krishna for help. Arjuna is despondent to the point of tears over the fact that he is being called to battle with his own family members, a fight to the very death. In this state of poignant despair, at the last moment, Arjuna tearily lays down his weapon and tells Krishna that he will not fight, yet still remains open to what his teacher has to say. Instead of lauding Arjuna's pacifistic stance, however, as some might expect, Krishna instead smiles and gives Arjuna all of the reasons why he *must* fight this battle. And in the process, Krishna reveals to Arjuna the deeper teachings of yoga, what it is and what a real yogi looks like.

"Yoga is equanimity, perfect evenness of mind."

Now, there are some who do not read the story of the Gita literally. Mahatma Gandhi was one such interpreter. For Gandhi, the story is an allegory that speaks of the great war that goes on inside each and every one of us, the battle between man's lower and higher nature. Thus, Krishna was not asking Prince Arjuna to kill anything external to him, but rather, to vanquish the lower forces within himself, the inner demons of sloth, envy, ignorance, lust, pride, hatred, etc. As an adherent of *ahimsa* and complete pacifist himself, Gandhi could not accept that God would ever want us to kill anyone for any reason; rather, the Gita is a pre-eminent guide to the inner quest, and must be read metaphorically.

While I certainly appreciate Gandhi's approach, I would like to make a case for why not reading the Gita literally might lead to not receiving the full impact and blessing of its teaching. And the simple reason I say this is because when we do read the Gita literally, it helps us on both the inner and outer levels of our experience (until the realization that they are really one). But let's focus just on the outer for a moment, as that is what is in question here.

Essentially, Krishna in the Gita is giving us the crucial tools we need to navigate our world experience and return home to God. He is saying, as Christ did, that there is a way *to be in the world but not of the world*. And the way to do that is to do one's duty, one's *dharma*, and to do it just because it's the right thing to do at any given moment, not for any lesser, selfish reason. In other words, to release all expectations and sense of "I, me, mine" in our thoughts, words and deeds. And as we do this practice more and more and more, it won't be long before we feel better and better and better, until we are back in the best version of ourself (our Self), sitting pretty once again, so to speak.

In this sense, on a literal reading, the Gita is not presenting a completely pacifistic philosophy, or at least not in the commonly understood sense of pacifism. Because one's *dharma* (atonement path back home) might entail sometimes defending the truth if it is attacked and there is no other means to resolve the situation. If someone is coming to kill you, in other words, does it make sense to allow yourself to be killed rather than to try to defend yourself – even if it means a fight to the death? No, in most cases, to just allow that to happen is not truly serving anyone because it is condoning unconsciousness. Rather, defend yourself if you must, but do it from a place not of anger, hatred, revenge, or any negative frame of mind, but just because it is the right thing to do in that moment. It has to be done, that is all.

The problem is, how is that even possible? How is it possible to "love one's enemies" and not even feel upset or anger or any charge towards someone with ill intent? If I see a stranger hurting someone I love, for example, you bet I'm going to not just retaliate against them until they stop, but probably become mindlessly enraged in the process. So is it even possible to be loving while using violence? Krishna is saying *yes*, it is not only possible, but necessary if you want to fully awaken to the truth of what you are. Because all anger and upset and grievances need to be let go of as preconditions for awakening to one's true self (Self).

Now, most would be incredulous if you suggested to them that it is possible to live in this world and be relatively free of anger, greed, lust, jealousy, arrogance, vengeance, and all of the other grosser expressions of the egoic human condition. I say "relatively" because it is highly doubtful that even the more enlightened on earth are entirely free of the ego; rather, the ego is still there, it is just not taken seriously or given energy, with the effect being that it is *as if* the ego is not there. There is no more suffering. Krishna explains to Arjuna in so many words that this is indeed possible through yoga, but it is a lifelong practice and process requiring great dedication and devotion. Only by remaining "one-pointed" to the goal (as the Katha Upanishad also said, remember) does one arrive there, which is nowhere (Now Here).

Freeing oneself of the ego also generally requires someone who has already done this to come and tell us it is possible. Whether that someone is a person, a book, a substance or otherwise doesn't really matter in the end. What matters is that they inspire faith and devotion, providing motivation that sets in motion a consistent practice that results in awakening, ultimate freedom.

When *A Course in Miracles* came into my life, I recognized it to be the proverbial straw that broke the camel's back in my own spiritual journey. Above all, it gave me the final information and inspiration I needed to walk that final extra mile to the goal. But it wouldn't have happened if I hadn't taken seriously the idea that this was Jesus coming now telling me (or rather, all of us) what forgiveness really is and why it is the fast track to remembering my true identity as Love.

In other words, I needed something outside of myself, something seemingly external to me to show me that there is actually nothing truly external to me. "This is all y/our dream," said the master. "U made it all up, you just don't remember." Most people would say that's crazy talk, and again, that is where an external guide who inspires faith and devotion and who tells us no, actually it's really all true, comes in.

Recall that I mentioned earlier that at the beginning of the Gita we are told that Arjuna is crying in despair, meanwhile Krishna is smiling. This is very telling. We are told again and again both in the ancient Indian scriptures that "the wise do not grieve," for they know what is real and what is not real.

"Those who are seers of the truth have concluded that of the unreal there is no endurance, and of the real there is no cessation. This seers have concluded by studying the nature of both." ~ Bhagavad Gita 2.16

Krishna is telling Arjuna that once he learns to separate what is real (permanent) from what is unreal (impermanent), he will see as Krishna sees, and he, too, will no longer cry when faced with suffering in this "vale of tears," but smile as he does. The only tears he will shed will be tears of joy at the wonder and beauty of it all.

And Krishna is also saying that the way will be easier and quicker if Arjuna but follows his lead, his teachings. He has paved the way, cut the work out for him, so to speak, so it becomes more about humility and trust, faith, surrender. So, too, in the Course, Jesus tells us:

*"In this world you need not have tribulation,
because I have overcome the world.
This is why you should be of good cheer."*

> In this world you need not have tribulation,
> for I have overcome the world.
> This is why you should be of good cheer.

**This is very similar to the verse in the Gospel of John (16:33):
"*These things I have spoken unto you, that in me ye might have peace.
In the world ye shall have tribulation: but be of good cheer;
I have overcome the world.*"
The difference is that the Course is emphasizing that we can
be free of tribulation, even in this world, by taking Jesus
(or Krishna) as our model.**

In other words, the work is already done, already accomplished. Love has already won. Even more than that, *Nothing Happened* to begin with. The only real program left is to *get with de-program* and follow the master's lead. If he tells you "love holds no grievances" and "anger is never justified," (as do two famous Course lessons) rather than argue with that, it is wiser to surrender to it. And you can do it now, or do it later, it's up to you. The good news is that once you are at the point where you can even be open to seeing this, you are already almost on the other side of it.

But to even get to this point is not at all easy. Let's not underestimate or be in denial about the power of denial, which is the power of the ego, the power of illusion. As Jesus in the Course says, it is powerful enough to make up an entire world and pull the wool over all of our eyes (so to speak). As one gets closer to the goal, there is an obvious recognition that it is all really just a simple choice between love and fear, but the clouds of denial, guilt, anger, judgment, etc., will obscure the obviousness of that for a seemingly long time yet. (If you've ever seen the movie The Truman Show, it's getting at the very same thing.)

Which brings me to one final consideration, and one that I have been harping upon in this book: Why do some seem to get this and others not? Or rather, why do very few seem to wake up and realize who they really are, whereas most do not? This is the question that you're not supposed to talk about because it sounds arrogant, but let's do it for that very reason. I began this section with the following passages from the Gita:

"Of thousands of men, scarcely anyone strives for perfection [siddhaye/siddhi]; even of the striving and perfected [siddha], scarcely anyone knows Me in truth."

~ Bhagavad Gita, VII.3

"After many births the wise seek refuge in me, seeing me everywhere and in everything. Such great souls are very rare."

~ Bhagavad Gita, VII.19

I have already answered the question of why only a few get this in a number of places above, but it bears repeating. The simple answer is FEAR (**f**alse **e**vidence **a**ppearing **r**eal) and the power of the illusion (*maya*). Maya is just sooo powerful that it requires someone who is beyond *maya* (like Mother Aya) to come and tells us that the world is *maya*, it's an illusion. Very few would ever come to that understanding on their own, because it flies in the face of our sensory experience and egoic human conditioning. What do you mean the world (universe) isn't real? That it's all a huge conspiracy, a cosmic hoax? What do you mean that, being a part of its makeup, I also am made up? Yes, all made up and nowhere to go…

Jesus in the Course says it is not arrogant to think this way, to say "I Am Love" – nothing more, but also nothing less. What is arrogant is in thinking otherwise, because following the ego, we think of ourselves as "special." Whereas the one who awakens from the dream knows that they are nothing special, because if they had thought they were special, they wouldn't have woken up in the first place (pun intended)! Indeed, the one who awakens learned not to separate themselves from anything in any way, to the point that there was nothing in it for them anymore. It was no longer about me, but about WE. Which is why the "good teacher" learns that true teaching, true giving, means to give it all away. To hold back is to create more separation, entrenching oneself deeper in the ego, in self propaganda (the ego's "prop agenda").

As Yeshua put it very simply and clearly so long ago now (but wasn't fully understood by most):

"And you shall love the Lord thy God with all thy heart, with all thy soul and with all thy might...and thy neighbor as thyself."

So why do some wake up and others don't in any given apparent lifetime? Go figure, but what we *can* say is that the one who wakes up is the one who made the choice only for God, only for Love, nothing else.

But why one person makes that choice and not another is a mystery. As Jesus says in the Course, correcting a quote from Matthew…

*"'Many are called but few are chosen' should be:
All are called, but few choose to listen."*

This is also a correction for the much-maligned notion of the Jews as the chosen people. As one poet sardonically put it:

*How odd of God/
To choose the Jews.*

To which another poet gave the more enlightened response:

*Not so odd/
the Jews chose God.*

This reminds me of the best answer I ever heard to the question of where was God during the Holocaust. This is one that many Jews and thoughtful people around the world have asked, and one that was much the topic of discussion at a yeshiva (Orthodox school) in Jerusalem I lived at for a while in my early twenties. As we all know, many lose their faith when they see bad things happening to good people, feeling as if God has abandoned them, or is even punishing them. Even Yeshua is thought to have asked this question on the cross: "*My God, My God! Why hast thou forsaken me?*" (A Course in Miracles would say that Jesus would not have said something like this because he was not feeling pain or suffering. However, his body might have done it. Or perhaps he did say it, in which case he might have been merely quoting Psalm 22, which begins with those very words.)

But again, the more enlightened answer to the question of where was God during the Holocaust (or any apparent tragedy), is:

Where was *man*? Where was *humanity*?

Right? Why was it necessarily God's problem? And what we are getting at here is that maybe, as that old Jimmy Buffet song goes, it's nobody's fault. Or if it's anybody's fault, it's everybody's fault. But if we need someone to blame, well, go ahead and blame God – apparently the only one who can take it! And maybe this is why God is the only one who gets the Cosmic Joke – He's the only one who can take it. (So to speak! ;)

And so the choice for God alone must be by the only one who can make it. For it takes One to know One. Which is a way of saying that we are already God, we have just allowed "Twoness" to get in the way.

And in making that choice only for God, said person woke up to realize that there was never an *other* anyway, so the question is meaningless. But asking the question was important somehow. At the very least, the idea that very few wake up was motivating, because it helped them to recognize that the ego is extremely crafty and one can suffer under the illusion of a false sense of security and final accomplishment for quite a long time. In my own experience, one's forgiveness lessons become damn near impossible as one approaches the experience of awakening, it is almost too much to take. Until one realizes that, actually, you can just not take it… seriously. Lol.

***

I would like to conclude this section by making a rather bold claim, yet one that has already been made by others: Krishna and Christ are getting at the self-same thing, and the Gita and ACIM are have essentially the same message. And that message is to realize the essential "sameness" of everything and thereby return to our essential "*sane*-ness." In other words, where we now see an inessential separation due to following the ego, we will learn how to see the essential unity everywhere. And in learning to do that more and more, we will begin experiencing more and more and more peace and joy and harmony everywhere, until the point that we realize the world of bodies and separation is unreal, made up, and we find ourselves back home in our spiritual reality once again.

My point in this book has been to show that the *experience* of this truth is available to us here and now, if we want it, though the fuller realization of this might not occur until we lovingly let the body go at the time of "death."

The Yoga Sutras, ACIM and Psychic Powers

"These experiences resulting from samyama are obstacles to samadhi, but appear to be attainments or powers to the outgoing or worldly mind." (*te samadhau upasargah vyutthane siddhayah*)

~ Yoga Sutras 3.38

*

"As his awareness increases, he may well develop abilities that seem quite startling to him. Yet nothing he can do can compare even in the slightest with the glorious surprise of remembering

Who he is. Let all his learning and all his efforts be directed toward this one great final surprise, and he will not be content to be delayed by the little ones that may come to him on the way."

~ *A Course in Miracles*, Manual for Teachers #25

*

"The use of miracles as spectacles to induce belief is a misunderstanding of their purpose."

~ *A Course in Miracles*, Miracle Principle #10

This will be one of the book's briefest comparisons as we will focus here just on one little point of similarity, although there are many that could be brought to light. One reason I will be narrowing in on "psychic powers" is because I devoted an entire chapter of my first book (*Who Am I?*) to a deep discussion of *siddhis* (psychic or yogic powers) that might come through psychedelic experience. The discussion was inconclusive, but it did establish a few things: 1) Yogic powers are definitely a thing – an entire chapter of the Yoga Sutras are dedicated to them, or roughly a quarter of the text; 2) The Yoga Sutras say that while *siddhis* can come from plants (which most commentators maintain are psychoactive in nature, though there is no agreement as to what they are), the real and true and staying powers come from disciplined meditation practice; 3) Yogic powers, in any case, are not to be sought as ends in themselves for those who are seeking liberation.

This last point is the one I want to discuss here, though it was not one I spent much time on in the first book. The interest here is in how much agreement the Course and the Yoga Sutras have in regard to these powers. It is to these point of agreement that we will turn now.

Let us first remember that the use of the word "miracle" in *A Course in Miracles* is radically different than our usual understanding of the term, and certainly when we think of the signs and wonders that Jesus was said to have worked during his lifetime. For the Course, a miracle is when we remember to see our brother as ourselves and forgive him (or her, or it) for what they have not done to us (because "nothing happened"). A student of the Course doesn't do this for any ulterior motive other than because it is the truth and in line with our true nature. We don't, for example, *try* to move mountains, to heal the sick or raise the dead, or even cure our cold, because that is thinking that we know what we need. Perhaps our highest good is better served by having a certain illness or dis-ease? We don't know. But rather, the focus is always on getting out of the way and letting Spirit move through us. So this is why, as already quoted, one of the miracle principles states that…

"The use of miracles as spectacles to induce belief is a misunderstanding of their purpose."

Jesus elaborates on this in the Manual for Teachers under the title: "Are "Psychic" Powers Desirable?"[32] Here we are talking about the same thing – powers that develop during the course of one's spiritual journey that some might consider "miraculous" in nature, such as extrasensory perception. We will remember that such powers became to Helen Schucman in the months prior to her receiving the first words of the Course, after she and Bill had agreed to find "another way." So as we might guess, Jesus does not say that such powers are "bad," for clearly they were an important part of Helen's journey and played a key role in her ability to serve as the conduit for the Course's message. But neither does Jesus say they are "good." Rather, as with everything else in the world, they are neutral and can be used to serve the purposes of the ego or the Holy Spirit, depending on the purpose with which they are used.

"'Psychic' abilities have been used to call upon the devil, which merely means to strengthen the ego. Yet here is also a great channel of hope and healing in the Holy Spirit's service."

If they are used in service of Spirit, which means if they are used to assist in one's awakening from the dream, then they are indeed useful; otherwise, they will only serve to strengthen the ego and thus become obstacles on the path to awakening.

"Let all his learning and all his efforts be directed toward this one great final surprise, and he will not be content to be delayed by the little ones that may come to him on the way."

---

32   Question #25 in the Manual. The quotations that follow are from this section.

Likewise, for the Yoga Sutras, the *siddhis*, or what we might call "miraculous powers," are not necessarily a bad thing, and actually the YS seems to view them as milestones along the path – evidence that one's practice is bearing fruit. And, too, they seem to even be viewed as incentives to practice, as most worldly minded individuals would not even practice if there weren't some worldly incentive involved. Indeed, I related in my first book that developing such powers was certainly part of my mindset when I first was introduced to yoga, as I wanted some evidence that my practice was bearing fruit, at least to silence my critics (family)! And indeed, I did begin to develop such powers, though they were not consistently available to me.

So the Yoga Sutras does seem to almost promote such powers, as we would readily suggest were it not for sutra 3.38 which says that for the one seeking samadhi (and ultimately Self-realization), these powers can be obstacles:

"These experiences resulting from samyama are obstacles to samadhi, but appear to be attainments or powers to the outgoing or worldly mind." (*te samadhau upasargah vyutthane siddhayah*)

One only needs to read a book like Yogananda's classic *Autobiography of a Yogi* to see how master teachers such as he viewed trafficking in such powers as generally missing the point and leading people astray. Yet it's never that simple because we do not necessarily know what the motivation of such a person is. This is why, for example, someone like Sathya Sai Baba, who called miracles his "calling cards," is not so easily dismissed, despite the scandal surrounding him. In fact, it seems that by the end of his life, Sai Baba's movement was split between those who think he is God, and those who maintain he is a demonic charlatan.

But better than getting mired in thinking about and discussing such controversies, we can forget the messenger and work with the actual message. Does it work for us? Does it add to our peace of mind and those around us?

And we can also see that there is agreement in these scriptures about such powers. They are not an end in themselves, nor are they absolutely good or absolutely bad. They can be fruitfully used in the service of awakening, and they can also take us on one big ego trip that leaves us trapped in illusion indefinitely.

I will be talking more about channeling, but I will just note here that this is just another psychic power that can be used to serve the ego and lead unwary minds astray. For example, if the "entity" being channeled is attacking other teachers or entities, we might rightfully "reconsider the source" and question the motives of said channeled entity, not to mention the channeler themselves.

Ultimately, what we are getting at here is to the point of complete non-attachment (holding onto nothing, as the Course says), where there is no investment in anything, whether gross or subtle, and thus no need to defend or attack anything. Rather, there is an acceptance of what is, with not mental interference blocking the way to the full appreciation of the eternal moment – the All That Is.

Hold Onto Nothing

Simply do this…

Be still
and lay aside all thoughts of what you are
and what God is;
all concepts you have learned about the world;
all images you hold about yourself.

Empty your mind
of everything it thinks is either true or false,
or good or bad,
of every thought it judges worthy,
and all the ideas of which it is ashamed.

Hold onto nothing.

Do not bring with you one thought the past has taught,
nor one belief you ever learned before from anything.

Forget this world, forget this Course,
and come with wholly empty hands
unto your God.

~ A Course in Miracles[33]

---

33   From Workbook Lesson #189.

Shankara in Light of ACIM

"The Soul **appears to be finite because of ignorance.**
When ignorance is destroyed, the Self, which does not admit of any multiplicity, truly reveals itself by itself,
like the Sun **when the clouds pass away."**

~ Shankara, *Atma Bodha*

Legends and myths abound about the man. Centuries after his holy feet walked the earth, stories of his life and times proliferated in the country of his birth. Over time, he became a larger-than-life figure, a god to some. He was claimed to have worked miracles that brought him considerable fame. He also put to shame the religious authorities of his day, showing them the error of their thinking. By the time of his death at the young age of 33, he had profoundly impacted the religiosity of the country of his birth, perhaps more than any had ever before or since.

No, his name was not Jesus Christ, it was Adi Shankarcharya, and we really need to talk about this dude…

Shankara (as his name is often shortened) is of particular interest here, not only because his life parallels that of Jesus in some interesting ways, but because he was such a prolific, vociferous, and non-compromising exponent of Advaita Vedanta, which is India's high philosophy of radical non-dualism. As I have already stated, and will now again, to discover that there are such strong ancient traditions of such radical non-dualism is to lend credence to the contemporary teaching of radical non-dualism under review here, namely, *A Course in Miracles*. And, too, to learn about one system is to help shed light on the other, and vice versa. Simply put, for our purposes here, examining some of the essential teachings of Shankara can help us to understand ACIM better, and to appreciate and trust it more.

What are some of those teachings?

Perhaps the summary teaching of Shankara's entire philosophy is the oft-quoted Sanskrit phrase:

Brahma satyan jagat mithya, jivo brahmaiva naparah

One translation of this is:
*Brahman (God) the Absolute alone is real;
this world is transient, but the jiva or the individual soul
is not different from Brahman.*

God alone is real. ~ *Shankara*

In other words, what is impermanent has no ultimate reality, only what is everlasting can bear the title "Real." The Course is in full accord with this, even though much of it is written in dualistic language – at the level we believe we are. Only less occasionally does the Course present us with the radically dualistic language that is regularly expressed in the yogic scriptures – the language of God as "One without a second."

And what is the nature of Brahman (the Real, God, Spirit, Oneness, Ground of Being, etc.)? Truly no words can express what God is, which is why for ages philosophers, including Hindu philosophers, have generally only spoken of apophatically as what God is not: Unchanging, Undying, Ineffable, Infinite (not finite), and so on. But in the yogic texts we do also find more positive descriptive words for God, the most famous being "*satchidananda*" – Existence, Consciousness, Bliss. And yet, God is beyond words, beyond intellectual comprehension, so these words can really only be at best approximations or pointers to what must lay beyond all language and symbols. And the Course (and also some Hindu philosophers) would even disagree with this use of words, too, because they are still dualistic. For example, "consciousness" requires something to be conscious of, and "bliss" is likewise in relation to something else. Even if we add "pure" (as in "Pure Consciousness"), we still are only pointing at the thing, while the actual reality is *something else*.

Shankara himself used the words "*satyam-jnanam-anantam*," usually translated as Truth, Knowledge, Infinity. This is actually closer to what the Course says – God is Truth without any falsity, and Knowledge that is free of perception (subject-object dichotomy), and Infinite in the sense of being unending, forever One.

Shankara also gets at the idea that it is only due to Maya (Cosmic Illusion) and the *avidya*, or ignorance, due to it that results in our bondage. Ignorance is not a sin, but it is a mistake, and one that must be corrected in order to attain liberation (*mukti* or *moksha*) from bondage. The way is through attaining Self-knowledge, and that is through the experiential knowledge (*gnosis, jnanam*) that the individual soul (*atman*) is one with the supreme Soul (Brahman). While nothing we can do can prepare us for this experience, nor can we know when it will happen, yogic practices and selfless action can help purify the mind so that it is ready to receive the revelation of the Divine.

Now, while there is in yogic philosophy the idea of *ahamkara*, usually translated as "ego," perhaps the notion of Maya is closer to the Ego-at-Large, as the idea of Maya is getting at an Illusion just so *so* BIG that it completely permeates every aspect of our existence. This is what we have become "conditioned" to, over seemingly countless ages. It's damn near impossible to *not* be influenced by Ego/Maya, it's just so part and parcel of everything here. And once this is recognized, one begins to get an idea of the excruciating enormity of the task at hand. But the good news and the paradox is that *once this is recognized*, the mind is already well on its way to being ready for Grace to reveal that Ego and Maya, as Great as they seem, are really nothing. A tempest in a teacup, as Shakespeare put it. Or a tiny mouse that would rule the universe, as the Course phrases it in one place.

But to get back to Shankara the man… It is tempting to compare him with Jesus, and I do feel that the passion and conviction with which he defended the radically non-dualistic message of Advaita Vedanta in his short life should, at the very least, give us pause. We might also look at the massive influence Shankara has had on Hindu religious life and wonder if maybe, just maybe, he really knew something and wasn't just talking out of his asana.

***

PS. Legend has it that when as a wee lad of 8 years, Shankara was asked "Who Are You?", he answered with the following 6 stanzas…

The Atma Shatakam of Shankara

I am not mind, nor intellect, nor ego,
nor the reflections of inner self.
I am not the five senses, beyond that I am.
I am not the five elements: neither ether,
nor earth, wind, or fire.
I am indeed That eternal knowing and bliss,
eternal love, pure consciousness.

Neither can I be named as energy alone,
nor the five types of breath,
nor the seven material essences,
nor the five coverings.
Neither am I the five instruments of elimination,
procreation, motion, grasping, or speaking.
I am indeed That eternal knowing and bliss
unchanging love, one consciousness.

I have no hatred or dislike,
nor affiliation or liking,
nor greed, nor delusion,
nor pride or haughtiness,
nor feelings of envy or jealousy.
I have no care, nor any wealth,
nor any desire I am,
nor even liberation.
I am indeed That eternal knowing and bliss,
boundless love, pure awareness.

I have neither merit, nor demerit
I am not bound by sins or good deeds,
nor by happiness or sorrow,
not pain or pleasure.
I am free from mantras, holy places,
scriptures, rituals or sacrifices.
I am none of the triad of
observer, act of observing or the object itself.
I am indeed, That eternal knowing and bliss, Shiva,
pure love, flawless consciousness.

No fear of death I have,
I have no separation from my true self,
no doubt about my existence,
nor have I discrimination on the basis of birth.
I have no father or mother, nor did I have a birth.
I am not the relative, nor the friend,
nor the guru, nor the disciple.
I am indeed, That eternal knowing and bliss,
immaculate love, fully awake.

I am all embracing,
without any attributes, without any form.
I have neither attachment to the world,
nor to liberation.
I have no wishes for anything
because I am everything,
everywhere, every time,
always in equilibrium.
I am indeed, That eternal knowing and bliss,
That unfathomable grace.

Only One Well, Dig?
(a story – only slightly digressive)

Has this ever happened to you?

There was once a young lady who wanted to dig a well to find water for her family. Not knowing much about digging wells, she consulted someone who knew about such things and they told her to dig in such and such a spot. Her intuition also told her that this was the right spot to dig in.

So on the appointed day, the young woman went to the spot with a big shovel and began digging. And she dug and dug for hours, but she only managed to dig about 10 feet down as the ground was very rough.

She began to despair. There was no sign of water anywhere. Maybe this wasn't the right place to dig after all?

Just then, a man came over and surveyed the situation…

"Dear lady, I admire your efforts, but you will never find water here, it's impossible. But! I do happen to know for sure that if you walk about 800 meters north of here you will find water for sure. Come, I will take you there."

And so our young well digger followed the man to the new spot.

"Right here," he declared with infectious confidence. "Dig here and I guarantee you will find water in no time."

So once again the young woman began digging.

And digging.

And digging…

It was hours later and once again she had nothing to show for her efforts but blisters on her hands and some muscles in her arms. And had still dug only about 10 feet down. Once again she began to lose hope. "That guy seemed so sure, but he must not have known what he was talking about," she thought.

And just then another man walks over. He asks her what she's doing and she tells him the whole story about how she began digging one hole and then a man told her to dig here, promising that she would find something…

"That fella didn't know what he was talking about at all," this man said. "There's no water over here, this land is as parched as can be. But come with me and I will show you where, without the slightest doubt, you will find more water than you could ever wish for, come…"

And the young woman again abandoned her small hole to follow the promise of a new and better place to dig her well.

And as you might guess, once again the same thing happened.

And it happened repeatedly again and again that day until she had a dozen different holes she has dug in different places.

It was now late at night and the young girl finally sat down, discouraged and near tears. "Why is this happening?!?" she wondered.

And just then a toothless old woman with a hunchback hobbled by and saw her with her head in her hands.

"What's the matter young lady?"

"Oh, I'm so upset!" she cried, tears rolling down her cheeks. "I dug one hole, then another, and another… and now I have nothing to show for all of my hard work!"

"Well, you know," said the old woman solemnly, but with a gleam in her eye," If you had just stuck with that first hole, you would have eventually found water. But now you have many shallow holes and no water. All you ever have to do is dig one well and dig it well."

And the young woman went home, resolving to begin again another day and dig only one well, and dig it well.

The Beginning

You and I are the same.
What I have done is surely possible for all.
You are the Self now and can never be anything else.
Throw your worries to the wind,
turn within and find peace.

Who Am I?
Sri Ramana Maharishi's Gospel

Question: *What is the purpose of creation?*

Ramana Maharshi: *It is to give rise to this question, and finally abide in the supreme or rather the primal source of all, the Self. The investigation will resolve itself into a quest for the Self and it will cease only after the non-Self is sifted away and Self realized in its purity and glory.*

If Shankara is the most revered Hindu sage of the last 2000 years, then Ramana Maharishi might just be the most celebrated of the last hundred. Like Shankara, no discussion such as this would be complete without mention of him, and like Shankara, we see many parallels between Ramana's teachings and that of ACIM. Again, these parallels are drawn with the caveat that similarity does not mean sameness – while uncannily similar, these are all unique teachings that, at best, help to mutually reinforce and shed light on each other, increasing our faith and trust in a process that is anything but easy.

But before delving into Ramana's teachings, I would like to relate a personal story that might be helpful in making this all a bit more relevant and relatable…

When I first met my Hindu guru, Sri Karunamayi, in 1996 (in a synagogue in Philadelphia designed by Frank Lloyd Wright, of all places), I didn't quite know what to make of her. She was very soft-spoken and did not have a big retinue, nor a presence or message that was remarkably remarkable. Yet, as I got to know Karunamayi (Compassionate Mother, in Sanskrit), I began to get a sense of who she really was. I myself was at that time just a green young kid and serious seeker who had by now been on the path for only some months, a recent convert who showed all of the signs of being one, from my blissed-out giddiness to my missionizing zeal.

While in a sense you could say that I was making all of the typical rookie mistakes, I was also doing so with a sense that I was truly on the path to enlightenment and that it was definitely going to happen (and maybe sooner than later, for all I knew). This was confirmed at one early private meeting with Karunamayi when she said to me with complete seriousness and conviction that this was to be my last lifetime. Meaning that I would be liberated from *samsara* (the cycle of suffering characterized by continual rebirth into a body), that I would be enlightened. I took this as good news indeed, and it definitely bolstered my newfound faith, not to mention adding to my cockiness, which I did my best to contain (it took awhile to fully get that this whole process is about become selfless).

A couple of years later, I was in Bangalore to visit Karunamayi at her *mandir* (temple) there, where I again was granted a private audience with her. This time I was led into a private chamber where Karunamayi gave me mantra *diksha* (initiation – she wrote my mantra with honey on my tongue), and told me some more nice things about myself. Among many other things, she said that I was from "one of the highest Hindu families" (in a past life) and while that gave me a head start, I should "dig only one well," meaning stay true to one path and not get side-tracked. Earlier that week a Nadi astrologer had given me a similar message, telling me that my work was to essentially teach Vedanta (what is here under consideration), and that my liberation would come through doing that. (Not that I completely believed all of this unquestioningly, mind you, I did have my doubts.)

Sitting there in Karunamayi's inner sanctum, I couldn't help but notice some of the pictures she had up on the walls. One, I recall, was of Ramana Maharishi. I wondered what was her connection to the sage? Later, I was to learn that Karunamayi's mother was a devotee of Ramana and had gone to visit the sage at his South Indian ashram sometime in the '50s. During that visit, he had informed her that she was going to give birth to "Thai," meaning the Divine Mother, an avatar with a special mission for global healing. Not long after, Karunamayi was born. I met her when she was in her early '40s and had just recently come out of seclusion in a remote forest in South India where she had meditated for some 12 years (!)

This all resonated greatly with me as I was already a budding devotee of Ramana myself. Not that I understood much of what he was talking about at that point – most of what he said would take me years to more fully comprehend and appreciate. But I had heard from a number of sources that Ramana was *the man*, a truly wise man from whom we all had much to learn. And clearly his approval rating in South India was very high and continues so to this day. So I tried to learn more about how he came to be the enlightened being he was widely considered to be.

What I learned from checking out certain sources was that Ramana was first "touched" when one day, at the tender age of 16, he suddenly experienced a great fear of dying. At that moment, he was guided to lie down in the Corpse Pose (*Shavasana*) and visualize his own death. As he described later, upon doing this, he got in touch with his true s/Self (what he later called "Ishwara" or "Jnani"). This was a transformative moment, a taste of enlightenment, and his life was forever changed. He soon left his home and traveled to the city of Tiruvannamalai, and specifically the sacred mountain, Arunachala, where he was to live for the rest of his life. For many years, he lived as a solitary yogi in a cave of the mountain, and in later years he came down from the mountain and an ashram was built for him, attracting God-thirsty seekers from around the world. He was a true *muni*, a silent sage practiced in *mauna* (silence), and he spoke but little, yet there are books of his teachings available, many of them in question and answer format, as this is the way he generally taught.

Now, all of this alone is quite mind-blowing stuff, but Ramana's teachings are equally so. Essentially, Ramana, like Shankara, was teaching in the same tradition we have been considering, that of Jnana Yoga, the path of Self-inquiry (*atma vichara*), and Advaita Vedanta, the philosophy of radical non-dualism. This is a high, abstruse philosophy and its esoteric nature is why I, like many others, found what Ramana was getting at so difficult to fathom. Actually, I doubt many people would know what he was talking about without having an experience of it first – again, the paradox of spiritual seeking. And Ramana understood this, which is why he, like Shankara, acknowledged that many souls would need an easier path to start with as preparation for the most radical of all teachings. Just as the Course itself suggests, while it is true that the world the senses perceive is an elaborate sham (smokescreen, illusion, hoax, etc.), it will not help to just affirm this intellectually without climbing the ladder of spirituality and fulfilling the conditions necessary to fully realize this truth.

If I may digress slightly and say that in my personal life the truth of this was born out on more than a few occasions when the reality of where I thought I was and where I really was in my spiritual development was painfully brought to my attention. And many times it had to do with love interests and the degree to which I would become obsessed and not able to think or act rationally or keep my turbulent emotions from overcoming me. Not that there's anything really wrong with that (if you know the ego is an illusion and can just be laughed at), but at the time I was still in deep shame and self-judgment, otherwise perhaps I wouldn't even have needed to encounter those situations and learn those lessons, see those reflections.

Which is why (it bears repeating for the umpteenth time), that this is all a process, and usually quite a gradual one. Why, even Ramana, after that transformative moment in Shavasasna, didn't just declare himself enlightened and go out and teach. No, he recognized that what he had experienced was so profound that he was going to need to sit with it and integrate it all for a bit. And isn't it true that sometimes in life we experience things that are just so shocking or beyond us that we spend the rest of our lives just processing it all. That's what we're talking about here.

If Your Faith Is Strong, You Will Not Get Upset About What I Am About to Say

"As all living beings desire to be happy always, without misery, as in the case of everyone there is observed supreme love for one's self, and as happiness alone is the cause for love, in order to gain that happiness which is one's nature and which is experienced in the state of deep sleep where there is no mind, one should know one's self. For that, the path of knowledge, the inquiry of the form "Who am I?", is the principal means."

~ Ramana Maharishi

A running theme of this book is that Truth needs no defense. If it did, it would not be the truth. Similarly, those who are here to embody truth also realize that they do not need to defend Truth because, God knows, it does not need any help from anybody. Truth, or God, just is. That said, in the world of perception and form, it would seem that certain correction is yet possible when truth is attacked. In such cases, a defense of truth might be made, yet all the while relinquishing any attachment to such a defense. It is in this spirit that I tell the following story…

I recently met a man in his mid-30s of Indian descent, born and bred here in the United States. His father is Hindu, but has a Sikh guru, meaning he practices a form of yoga that is specifically Sikh (3HO Kundalini Yoga is the most well-known example of this today).

It turned out that this brother was interested in my yoga teacher training program, so we connected by phone about that. When we did, I learned that he had gotten into some trouble with the law, did some jail time, and was now on parole and trying to get his life back together. He was hoping that yoga would help him to do just that, as well as to quit smoking. But it also turned out that in the process of serving time, he had also become a disciple of Christ. He was attending a church in the area, but he didn't see any disconnect between his church attendance and his yoga study and practice. So I invited him to join our yoga teacher training program at a very reduced rate to help him out.

Also attending the training was a 71-year-old man, a former pilot who in recent years had developed a great appreciation for yoga and desired to learn to teach it. He was coming from a solid Christian background and was also happily married for 50 years at that point. Unlike the relatively young man (half his age) who had been paroled, he felt perhaps just slightly more that there is some tension between his Christian upbringing and the path of yoga. Yet he was very open to learning about the deeper philosophy and spiritual teachings of yoga. And from day one, he really applied himself to his studies.

By the end of the training, the younger man had dropped out of the program (for various reasons, he was still interested and would continue later – we'll get to that), and the older man completed the program feeling like he had learned much about his own Christian faith through the lens of the teachings of yoga. He told me that he felt that learning yoga actually helped him become a better Christian and person. I have heard this before, and I myself experienced this phenomenon (in regard to Judaism), so I was not surprised. Nor was I surprised when I heard from another student that what was being presented was too Christian (I was bringing in the ACIM teachings), and she felt inclined to drop out. I actually have witnessed the whole gamut over the years, and interestedly noted leaps from one camp to another – fundamentalist or traditional Christians becoming yogis, and yogis disavowing yoga and becoming born-again Christians, plus many shades in between the extremes. I also recall in my first year in Southwest Florida going to a church to see if they would be open to a yoga class and being told in no uncertain terms that they do not allow yoga there.

And just the other day it happened again… I had re-connected with the young man on parole who was still interested in pursuing his yoga studies, with the intention of eventually teaching yoga. But one of the pastors at his church was not at all in favor of him doing that, telling him it was the worship of other gods. What was interesting was that he insisted on having me meet this pastor, and then having her open her church's sanctuary for us so that I could take a look…

I could tell that at first she was reluctant to speak with me, but she did cordially say hello and shake my hand. On the way to the sanctuary, the young man asked her what her issue with yoga is? She said it wasn't her issue, it's the Bible. The Bible is the word of God and says clearly that yoga falls under the category of forbidden things (she didn't say what, but I understood it is things such as soothsaying, necromancy, idol worship, serving gods other than Yahweh, etc).

"Well, but it's really good exercise," he countered.

"If you need exercise, you can go take a walk on the beach," she curtly and sardonically replied.

All the while she said nothing to me, and I was also saying nothing.

I found the whole sanctuary quite impressive, there was clearly a lot of love and labor that went into it all. When we came back to where the pastor was, she was nicer. She asked me my name and said it was nice to meet me. I said the same. It felt like she was wanting to redeem herself a bit, to show that she hated the sin, but could love the sinner. But can you really love someone if you are judging them at such a core level? I mean, disrespecting their person by denying their entire belief system? Isn't love about non-judgment and acceptance? Isn't it the willingness to even say, "You know, I don't really know, I might be wrong and maybe there's something that I can learn from you. I would like to hear about what you believe, and I will listen with as open a mind as I possibly can." But – and this is what this book is getting at – most of us are not ready to do this yet, because it would be too threatening. So we use things like religion as a defense against what we are not ready to see yet. And so it becomes, to be right, others must be wrong.

Don't get me wrong, I'm not making her wrong. I can also see how the dedication to her belief system (no matter how close-minded it might appear, and appearances are often deceiving) is its own path that will surely lead her home. But in the end, my sources (Source) tells me that we will all come to kindness and learn not just to tolerate the beliefs of others, but to respect them; and even more than that, to recognize our brother (however much we think they have gone astray) as ourselves. And the golden rule, expressed in the negative ("do not do unto others what you would not have done to you"), applies to all of us in the sense not to judge the other as we do not want to be judged, even and especially in the name of Jesus.

Jesus. As we walked out from the sanctuary and away from the pastor, my young friend was asking me why someone can't believe in Jesus and practice yoga? Aren't we all still believing in one God, we just have different ways of getting there? These were rhetorical questions on his part, mind you, though I could sense a part of him that was a bit troubled by the pastor's dismissive reaction. I, too, was a bit troubled, but I replied without hesitancy that yes, God/Truth is one, and there are different ways to get there, one not necessarily better than the other. And yes, I firmly believe that it is possible to have a personal relationship with Jesus and practice yoga, and in fact, even many yogis do.

*

This may have all seemed like quite a bit of a digression from a discussion of the revered modern Hindu sage Ramana Maharishi, but not if it is understood that to truly understand what Ramana was getting at we would need to really be open to what he has to say. And to do that we must go beyond the realm of spiritual/religious warfare and recognize that, just maybe, he was pointing to a universal experience and reality that is beyond color, caste, and creed. Even more than that, we would need to be open to the possibility that demonic spirits or other gods are not truly the problem, but rather it is our own mental projections taking the form of fear (ego) and judgments that are in the way. To put it simply: Hell is our own doing, and salvation, likewise, is our undoing.

Ramana's Path of Self-Inquiry

> *"The mind should not be allowed to wander towards worldly objects and what concerns other people. However bad other people may be, one should bear no hatred for them. Both desire and hatred should be eschewed. All that one gives to others one gives to one's self. If this truth is understood who will not give to others? When one's self arises all arises; when one's self becomes quiescent all becomes quiescent. To the extent we behave with humility, to that extent there will result good. If the mind is rendered quiescent, one may live anywhere."*
>
> ~ *Ramana Maharishi, Who Am I?*

I mentioned that Ramana seldom spoke, especially in the early years, and when he did speak and teach, it was generally in Q & A format. One of the earliest existing documents that encapsulates Ramana's teaching style and his essential message is from 1902 and is called *Nan Yar?*, or *Who Am I?* in Ramana's mother tongue, Tamil. This brief text is a great entré into Ramana's message, as well as being well-representative of the non-dual literature.

The text can be found in a number of places online. I could easily include it here as it is so short, but I would rather offer an even more succinct re-phrasing of it for the modern western reader (probably you)…

Ramana begins by affirming that all beings desire to be happy and free of suffering, because that is their true nature. In order to arrive at this, there is a practice known as "Self-inquiry" which involves asking the essential question: *Who Am I?*

To get at who I am requires a sifting away of who I am not.

Who am I not? I am not this body, nor even this mind.

When I have inquired and seen this is so through a process of elimination, I will arrive at the fundamental "I Am."

This "I Am" is of the nature of *sat-chit-ananda*, or Being-Consciousness-Bliss.

I will realize this when I have gone completely beyond the world of perception.

While the world is still seen and taken to be real, I will not have this experience/realization.

Why? Because the two cannot be experienced at the same time.

The world will disappear when the mind becomes completely quiet (quiescent) through the practice of Self-inquiry; otherwise, it will still be experienced.

The mind is composed of thoughts; when thoughts subside/disappear, there is no more world.

The thought of "I" is the first thought that arises in the mind, and all other thoughts follow. When one inquires where this "I" thought comes from, one finds it emanates from the heart.

My mind will become quiet as I continue to ask where the thoughts come from, as I continue to ask "Who Am I?" In doing this, I will go back to the root source, and as I keep doing it, eventually my mind will stay rooted in Source-consciousness.

This practice of Self-inquiry is the best and most adequate path as it goes directly to the root source of things. Other paths are only preparations for this practice of Self-inquiry. Meditation can be very useful as a preparation for this, making the practice of Self-inquiry much easier. So, too, can adherence to a diet of pure food (sattvic diet).

It is also helpful to not let the mind wander and project judgments of good or bad onto others or oneself.

One should persist in the practice of Self-inquiry uninterruptedly, continually going to the source of the "I" thought.

In truth, all that truly exists is the Self, and the Self is where there is no longer any "I" thought.

The best devotee/practitioner is the one who practices continually and lets go of all worry.

The Guru can help point the way, but in the end, one must make the necessary effort to attain Self-realization. Spiritual books also cannot lead one to Self-realization, they can only point to the practice of making the mind quiet.

One does not need to analyze the error to know it is a dream, but rather to practice Self-inquiry, that will be sufficient.

Happiness is abidance in the Self, and that is also wisdom. No object in the world can bring true happiness, and life in the world is really misery/suffering.

Spiritual powers are real, but they are not the goal, which is total abidance in the Self of all. This is also wisdom, which also means having no desire whatsoever for worldly objects, or complete non-attachment.

***

So that was a summary and paraphrasing of Sri Ramana's "Who Am I?" Now let's just go over a few of the most pertinent parallels between it and ACIM, keeping in mind that for all of their similarities, they are still quite unique paths...

First, it seems clear that both Ramana (and non-dual sources before him) and ACIM are presenting a radical dualism, one that asserts that the world is unreal, and that only God (Self, Brahman, etc.) is truly real.

And both suggest that as long as thought persists, and as long as the world is experienced, God will not be experienced. It's either one or the other, but never both at the same time. One way the Course phrases this is by saying that unless forgiveness is *complete*, or as long as one illusion still persists, the revelation of the oneness of the Son and God will not be forthcoming. But however we term it (and the Course is rife with symbol and poetic allusion), it comes down to the total dissolution of the ego-mind.

Although for Ramana, the practice of Self-inquiry is a solitary practice that does not require others (even a Guru – he did not have one), he does mention that one should not harbor any ill feelings towards anyone, because "all that one gives to others one gives to oneself." This is essentially the same as one of the ACIM Workbook Lesson (#126), which says, *"All that I give is given to myself."* So if I have hateful or hurtful thoughts towards others, I hold that against myself and it detracts from my peace of mind. And if I share peace and forgiveness with others, all of our minds become more at ease. Of course, for the Course, the practice of forgiveness is also an individual practice that does not necessarily require any other person to practice. What it does require is to get to the root cause of what is at issue, which Ramana's practice is also aiming at. And that root cause is only in the mind, not outside of it in the world or in the body or *any*body.

So letting go of judgment is crucial to the process, and this means stepping outside the bounds of conventional moral standards of right and wrong – at least in one's own mind. And Ramana adds, which is also true of the Course, that analysis of the problem is not necessary, practice is. Metaphysical principles can be helpful to a point, but they can also serve as a diversion and delaying maneuver of the ego.

Finally, and this is one of the biggest sticking points for many, both Jesus in the Course and Ramana (and the other non-dual sources) do not give life in the world high marks. Essentially, life in duality is suffering, no matter how you spin it or cosmetically enhance it. Waking up is the only game in town. Or put otherwise, there are many games in town, and awakening is the game to end all games. And it's the only game worthy of the name. There's nothing happening here of any lasting importance, besides Love in the abstract. And Love is all there is in reality. Because (did I mention?), Nothing Happened.

And now, some answers to those questions we posed at the start…

Questions for the Yoga Quest

What is yoga? Where did yoga come from? How old is it?

The academic response is that yoga is about 5,000 years old, but its origins are no doubt far more ancient. No one really has a definitive answer to this question, at best there are traditions and educated conjectures.

For our purposes, we can say that yoga is eternal. The name for the Hindu tradition is Sanatana Dharma, meaning Eternal Religion, or Eternal Law. Put simply, if we understand yoga to be the name for our natural state of Love, our eternal reality, then yoga is and has always been. Where it is from is irrelevant. It is ageless, eternal, beyond time and space. Those who are in tune discover it in every age.

Yoga is often defined as "Union." What exactly does this mean? How does the practice of yoga bring one to this seemingly exalted state?

Yoga means "union" in the sense of the realization that the small self (the individual soul, atman) is really one with the Great Self (Brahman). In other words, we who think we are separate from God are really not. When we realize this, we have attained yoga and we are free. The irony, if you want to call it that, is that yoga (union with God) is our natural state which we have forgotten. The yoga tradition offers different pathways back to this awareness, or remembering. The one that I have been focusing on in this book is the path of Jnana Yoga, which we can say is the method of separating what is real from what is unreal, or what is true from what is false. We can also say, with Ramana Maharishi and A Course in Miracles, that Jnana Yoga (this discerning/discriminative method) is potentially the quickest path, though quickest does not mean easiest.

What do the most ancient yogic texts from India, the Vedas and the Upanishads (which includes the Bhagavad Gita), say about yoga and what it means to be liberated?

The main points I have been making throughout this book is that there is a commonality found in yoga, A Course in Miracles, and ayahuasca, and it is this: All of the ancient texts suggest that *moksha*, or liberation from suffering, is a process of moving from darkness or ignorance to the light of Knowledge (gnosis), from illusion to Truth, and from fear to Love. This is by no means an easy process and it apparently takes lifetimes to happen, but it is simple because Love is our natural state. The ancient texts also stress again and again the need to have a qualified teacher or guide, someone who has already made the journey and can inspire faith in this most challenging process of awakening. This generally is a human teacher, but as we have seen with ACIM and ayahuasca, is not always the case. There is a specific path for each individual soul, though the goal for each is the same, and each one who truly seeks will find.

What is Vedanta? And what are the various forms of Vedanta? In particular, what is Advaita Vedanta? Why is "Advaita" generally considered to be the highest philosophy of India?

For our purposes, Vedanta is the highest teaching of the Vedas and is found first in the Upanishads, which are considered part of the Vedas. Over the millennia since the earliest Upanishads were composed (most likely through the kind of "channeling" we have been discussing), there have been various forms of Vedanta that have been expressed. Our concern here has been primarily what is known as Advaita Vedanta, which has been called "radical non-dualism." The essential teaching of Vedanta, particularly Advaita Vedanta, is that there is only one reality disguised as many (called "One Without a Second"), and the true goal of life is to realize this, to awaken from the world dream. To do so is to go beyond all fear and grief and return home to our natural state.

Shankara, who some consider to be the greatest exponent of Advaita Vedanta, encapsulated the essence of Advaita in the statement *"Brahman satyam, jagat mithya jivo brahmaiva napara.*" Only Brahman is real, the world is an illusion, and the individual soul is no different than Brahman.

Or, as I have put it here, only Love is real and Love is beyond the dualistic world of separate bodies and interests.

What are some of the most important Advaita scriptures? What is the provenance of these scriptures, meaning who wrote them?

Hinduism (whose real name is Sanatana Dhama – Eternal Religion) is interesting because it does not have one founder figure like Buddha, Moses, or Jesus. Rather, it is attributed to the work of many named and nameless sages who over the ages have contributed to its flowering. Names like Vyasa, Valmiki, Vashista, Patanjali, Panini, Shankara, and so on and on. So, too, there are many many scriptures in the Hindu "canon" of literature, and numerous works of Advaita Vedanta alone. The list includes the following:

Mandukya Upanishad, Mandukya Karika, Sri Atma Gita, Avadhuta Gita, Ashtavakra Gita/Samhita, Atmabodha, Brahma Sutras, Viveka Chudamani, Yoga Vashishta, and *Ribhu Gita.*

To name but a few of the more important works.

Who were/are some of the great exponents of Advaita Vedanta?

As this book has attempted to show, Advaita Vedanta essentially began with the Upanishads, though not in fully fleshed out form. The figures who have had the greatest impact are as follows: Badarayana, Shankara, Gaudapada, Ramana Maharishi, Vivekananda, Nisargadatta, to name some of the most well-known and influential exponents. I this book, I have made a very fledgling attempt at looking at Shankara and Ramana Maharishi in particular, especially as they relate to the non-dual message of A Course in Miracles. All of these thinkers/sages deserve much more in-depth study and treatment than what I have done here, but these can be found in plentiful supply elsewhere, including online where a lot of the original texts in English translation can be read for free.

What is "Neo-Advaita"?

This is a term that is actually old but has recently been applied to some contemporary popular teachers of non-dualism, such as Eckhart Tolle, Adyashanti, and Gangaji, as well as many who are not so well-known. Critics of Neo-Advaita say that some of these teachers make non-dual awareness seem too easy when for most of us it's actually quite a long and arduous journey. This was my initial reaction to some of these teachers, that they made it seem too easy. Later, ACIM helped me to understand that most of us are quite attached and resistant to the simple truth of Oneness (Oneness Without a Second), and so we need to be honest and gentle with where we are at, wherever we are on the ladder back Home. Denial and repression of the body and the world ultimately don't work; rather, we must gently and gradually free ourselves of our attachments with the simple but studied recognition that they do not offer lasting happiness and so we do not really want them, we only want the Peace of our true nature.

What is the path of Jnana Yoga and how can it best be practiced?

Jnana Yoga can be simply stated to be the practice of separating what is true from what is false, or the real from the unreal. For this, most of us need a guide to help us understand what is actually true/real and what is false/unreal, otherwise we would too easily be tempted to continually be entrapped in the false self. Ramana Maharishi, like the Course, maintained that this is actually the quickest path, but it really is only for those who are ready for it. If not, other paths will serve better as preparations, but in the end there is no getting around that the return to Truth means letting go of all that is false. Or as the Course says, everyone must come to the complete forgiveness of all illusions before their return to Love is complete. Ultimately, what great sages like Ramana Maharishi have been pointing to is no different than what the Course points to, it is just cloaked in different language.

How do Jnana Yoga and Advaita Vedanta relate to A Course in Miracles? Do Advaita and the Course really point to the same thing?

As has been expressed, Jnana Yoga is a direct path to the non-dual truth through a process of separating what is false from what is true.

A Course in Miracles presents a form of Jnana Yoga (a "Christian Vedanta" as Bill Thetford called it), clearly describing what the ego (false self) is, so that we may more clearly realize what God, our true reality/Self, is. Yes, Advaita Vedanta and the Course do essentially point to the self-same Reality and also offer very similar ways to get there. Perhaps the one difference is that the Course emphasizes the undoing of guilt through "forgiveness" more than the eastern traditions seem to do. But in the end, what the Course means by forgiveness is really just the "witness" consciousness that we find in the non-dual traditions. It means watching the ego without being at all affected by it one way or the other.

What is Maya? What is Moksha? Is it possible to attain moksha, or liberation, while still in one's body?

Maya is the power of illusion. The Course would say it is the part of the mind (the "ego") which wants to believe in separation and is essentially programmed to do everything to maintain the belief in separation. Though ultimately an illusion, it's an extremely powerful and persistent one. The Course warns us not to underestimate the power of the mind – after all, it's what got us into this to begin with – and so it can also get us out, if we could only become aware of its power. Moksha, or liberation, would be when the ego-mind is seen for what it truly is – nothing – and the return to our "right mind" is complete.

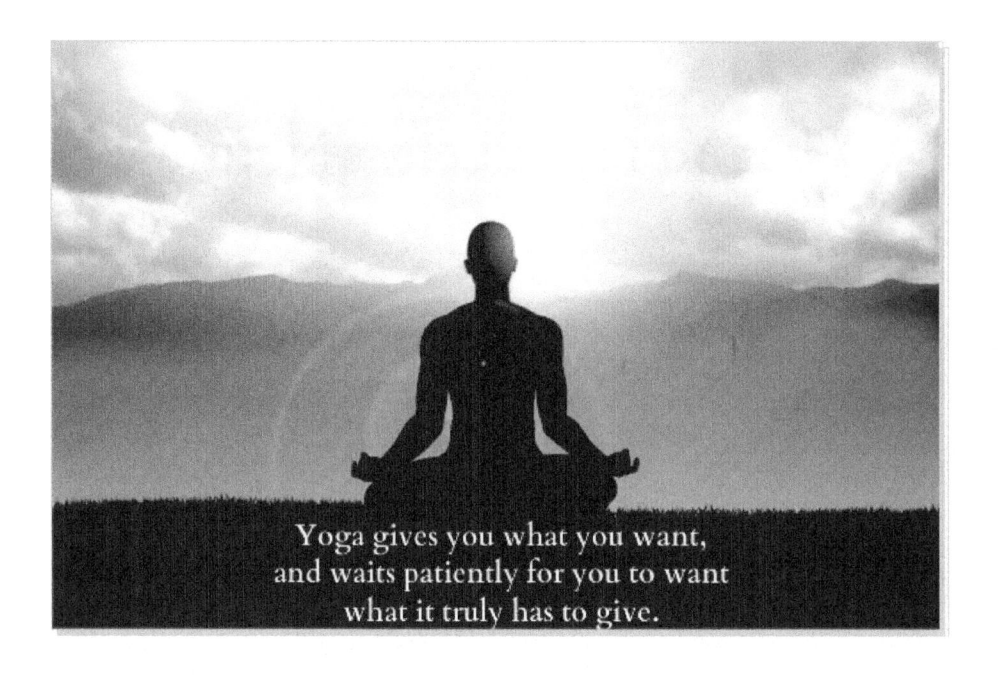

I Am Love

> Yoga gives you what you want,
> and waits patiently for you to want
> what it truly has to give.

Synthesis

What You Got Left...Nothing!

"What Is Truth?"

~ Pontius Pilate

"Do the thing you fear most, and the death of fear is certain."

~ Mark Twain

"God is a comedian playing to an audience too afraid to laugh."

~ Voltaire

"To take offense is to give offense."

~ Helen Schucman

"The truth will set you free, but first it will piss you off."

~ Gloria Steinem

"First they ignore you, then they laugh at you, then they fight you, then you win."

~ Gandhi (not an exact quote)

Synthesis

Make Light of Every Thing

WARNING: Please do not read the following if you feel you cannot take a joke. Actually, here's a joke about that...

Knock Knock
Who's there?
The Cosmic Joker
The Cosmic Joker who?

The Cosmic Joker who no one gets because no one can take the Joke.

Earlier I brought up the idea that Truth needs no defense. If it did, it would not be the truth. Yet perhaps (and I say this with tongue-firmly-in-cheek) the truth needs some *offense* for those who are on the fence, and when it comes down to it, most all of us on the fence when it comes to matters of faith, truth and trust. So I will here make a little offense, and I hope that it is just offensive enough to help those of you on the (de) fence...

Let me first re-affirm that I Am Love.

And now I also want to affirm that YOU, dear reader, are not.

How's that for an offensive? Were you offended?

Good. Now go fuck yourself.

And to add insult to injury, I offer no refunds, just in case you're now thinking you want your money back.

But seriously, folks, here's what I really meant...

Various teachers have gone on record as declaring, "I am God." But if they were true teachers, they would also add: "Yes, I am God, but so are you. The only difference between you and me is that I have realized this, and you have not – *yet*. And by the way, here's some tools and methods to help you get there..."

So when I affirmed that I am Love but you are not, it's along those lines. The truth, of course, is that we are all one in Spirit, and so it's in a way more true and inclusive to say "*We* are Love." And any apparent differences are not real differences anyway, because of our old friend, Nothing Happened (what a badass ;)

That said, if you are still in the process of finding your way back to your Self, then our new friend "Go Fuck Yourself" is just an added nudge of inspiration/motivation, kind of like "Onward. Inward. *Godward!*" It's a way of seductively saying, well, get on with it and get it on, just like the *ouroborous*, the snake swallowing its own tail, the spiritual quest is ultimately bringing us to the realization that there's only one of us here. There's only one egomind, and there's only one Spirit and we're all it. (And I want to give props to Norman Allen in the yoga documentary "Enlighten Up!" who used just that phrase – the "go f*** yourself" one – and explanation in that film.)

So I hope that made amends for my quote-unquote bad language. But either way, I still am not in the business of offering any refunds, mainly because the way this book is turning out, it might be read by about as many people read academic dissertations – usually reckoned at something like "2-and-a-half"!

"Discomfort is aroused only to bring the need for correction into awareness."

— A Course In Miracles

Don't Stand on Ceremony

(Don't Stand, Don't Stand…)

Yes, I have no illusions that this book will reach more than a few people, and most of them won't even need it. For the rest of us, our egoic defense systems are just too strong for any such foreign, radical ideas to find a quiet landing spot. Even longtime Course students and teachers will probably find this presentation problematic, mainly because it seems to condone the use of a psychedelic drug for help in understanding ACIM, which it does. Well, it does condone it, but does not necessarily encourage it, which is different. Not everybody is ready yet for ayahuasca, just as not everybody is ready for yoga or ACIM. But the trends suggest that all of these modalities for non-duality will find greater and greater acceptance with the slow march of time.

Still, I would like to go down as saying the following: **I will be the first person to tell you that you don't need ayahuasca… and the last person to tell you not to use it if you feel it might be helpful to you.**

Yes, I will be the first person to tell you that you don't need it because, if not ayahuasca, some other (less scary and risky) means for going home will reveal itself to you; all that is needed is your own decision to wake up. Once you are clear that you want to do that, the way will present itself to you.

And I will be the last person to tell you not to use ayahuasca because hey, I used it and it seemed to be helpful to *me*. Why would I tell anybody else they shouldn't use it? That would be hypocritical and dishonest. But I will say that if you do, ask for inner guidance and confirmation as to whether it is truly right for you, and do your due diligence before embarking on any perilous journeys.

In either case, if asked if ayahuasca is okay to use, I will only say: "**Just say 'Know'.**" I will not "stand on ceremony" (ayahuasca or otherwise), and I trust that you won't either.

SYNTHESIS

The Jew Will Bother You At Last

I see ACIM (and this book, too) as a document of the future. One day it will be read by more than a few who will understand that it speaks to all of us and is coming from a grounded place of experiential Knowing. Until that time, it will be ignored, then mocked, then hated and laughed at, and finally accepted as the obvious truth – just like Gandhi said (though not exactly), and just like happened with Jesus.

"And then you win."

Actually, Truth has already won, Love already won (One), most of us just didn't get the memo yet, we're still getting up to speed and on the same musical page to read the cosmic Note to Self. At the risk of obnoxious repetition, let me not refrain from the refrain that this is all a process, and it will require time and patient practice and perseverance, even unto death (seeming death – nothing truly dies). But in the end, all will find peace and go home, it's just a matter of time.

On that note…

Working with ACIM has allowed me to re-examine my relationship with Jesus. When I was in graduate school studying religion, I took some courses on Jesus and Christianity that were formative. One course was specifically on the topic of who Jesus was exactly? A prophet, philosopher, sage, zealot, myth, mystic, messiah, god/Son of God, cosmic rock superstar etc., or what? Everyone, it seems, has a different understanding based on the perceptual lens through which they see the world, and in particular, this guy Jesus. Over the centuries, scholars have presented some very persuasive pictures of the man, but they always seem to come up short, not fully taking into account the whole picture. There is even a school of thought gaining currency that says that Jesus never existed, that the entire story is a myth.

For all intents and purposes, Jesus could be a myth – it doesn't really matter. What matters in the end is the message. Even ACIM could be just a new myth of who Jesus was and what he had to share, a new fairy tale drama where Jesus and God are wholly loving characters who come to sing us a lullabye about how there is no sin and there was nothing ever to forgive. Again, it doesn't matter. What matters is whether the message of non-judgment and forgiveness of self brings you to peace (even if it's not the perfect peace which "passeth understanding"). The problem, however, is that before it brings you to peace, it will first (as Gloria Steinem noted) no doubt piss you off mightily. Why?

So here's a funny little story to talk about what for some might be very serious, but which doesn't have to be…

Way back there in my twenties I had a little stint as a substitute teacher in an Orthodox Jewish day school. While I had not grown up remarkably aware of or even much interested in my Jewish identity, that had changed when I spent two years in Israel after university. During that time I had really engaged deeply with the traditional Jewish religious texts (Torah, Mishna, Talmud, Midrash), learned Hebrew, and even became Orthodox myself for a bit. That's how I got the gig at the day school.

What I didn't know when I took that job was that I was taking over the class with the problem kids – about 8 teenage boys, all about 15-16 years old, who did not appear to have much spiritual/religious sensibility at all. No, they were just like any other cocky teenage boys, maybe worse. All I can remember now is getting so infuriated by their rudeness that on more than several occasions over the couple months that I taught, my face turned red and I raised my voice much more than I ever thought I would.

Finally, feeling somewhat guilty about this and wanting the kids to like me (or *me* to like me), I tried to come up with some ideas to make class time more fun, while still learning something. What came to me was what I thought was a brilliant idea: throw out the lesson plan and just have the dudes translate classic rock songs into Hebrew. I don't recall all the songs I chose now, but I will never forget the day we tried translating Stairway to Heaven…

Actually, they translated it, I just gave it to them as a homework assignment. The first thing that was curious to me was that some of them actually did it, or attempted to at least. That told me I was on to something. What I found even more interesting when we read the lyrics in English together in class was not only did the kids all know the song pretty well, but they had alternative lyrics (or misheard lyrics) for some of the lines. This is understandable, of course, as this was in the days before you could find almost any song's lyrics on any number of websites that provide them, and the last verse of Stairway is notoriously hard to decipher – you know, the one that begins *"And every wind on down the road..."*

So I was interested to hear that these yarmulke-wearing hooligans had their own song lyric traditions in place. And the one tradition they had that I thought was particularly hilarious was for the line, *"And if you listen very hard/the tune will come to you at last."*

Again, if you don't actually *listen very hard* to the song (or have the lyrics), you probably would have no idea what Robert Plant is singing there. I know I didn't have a clue for years (not that I thought to think about it, either). And even if you do listen very hard, the words are nearly impossible to make out. But these young kids all seemed to be in agreement that the words there, get this, are: *"The Jew will bother you at last."* Mind you, there wasn't just consensus on this, there was insistence – they insisted that this was the only way to hear the song, what the song actually says. The kids were so insistent, in fact, that for a moment there I thought that maybe they were right, just maybe they had access to some secret knowledge about the song to which I myself had not been privy. Because after all, the song is mysterious (and if played backwards, spooky), and that particular line is especially indistinct. Who's to say that the official lyrics are what Plant was really singing?

But nah, when it came down to it, I knew that the official lyrics and story behind how they were written is probably pretty accurate. Robert Plant claims that the words came to him one evening as he was staring at the fire (in the fireplace) at the band's mansion and contemplating "spiritual perfection." I have no reason to doubt that story, just as I have no reason to seriously entertain the theory that Led Zeppelin made a pact with the devil to become famous rock stars and intentionally planted satanic messages into their music, and Stairway in particular. (Now, perhaps that happened unintentionally and unconsciously, but that's another theory for another day.)

So I asked the kids what they thought that meant, the "Jew will bother you at last" thing? As far as I can recall, they had no real good answer to that, otherwise I probably would have remembered it. But while they didn't have something, I do, and I want to try it out on you right now...

That last verse of the song is what I would call the "redemptive verse" of the song. It's where the "lady" in the first part of the song, the one who we are told is "buying a stairway to heaven" (she is heavily in thrall to materialism), now either becomes or has the chance to become this other "Lady," the one who "*shines white light and wants to show/that everything still turns to gold.*" Now this other Lady, following a thread that I have been weaving throughout this book, we could call "Divine Mother" (or Holy Spirit), who is the still small voice reminding us of who we really are, which is Spirit. "*And if you listen very hard, the tune will come to you at last.*" That is, if you listen very hard to the inner voice of the heart (again, what the Course calls "The Holy Spirit" and what I am also calling "Divine Mother"), you will find your way home. Back to where "all is one and one is all."

So how does the "Jew will bother you at last" fit into this? Well, the Jew in this case would be Jesus, who has been a symbol of love and forgiveness, but who has also been a symbol of all that is wrong with religion. Or better put, all that is wrong with religion has sometimes been impugned to Jesus, but this is often a red herring deflecting us from really deeply considering who Jesus was and what he came to teach us, particularly all that crazy stuff about non-judgment and forgiveness. In other words, we look at how fucked up Christianity is (or how we choose to see it), and we say, "To hell with it all. To hell with Jesus. I don't need him and I don't need no religion! I can't be bothered." But what we're really saying, especially in light of the Course, is: "I find it really hard to love my neighbor as myself. I want to hold onto my anger and judgment and grievances, I'm not quite ready yet to let all that shit go."

But Jesus (at least in the Course) is just saying to us that we're going to have to let those things go at some point (because the return home to God/Spirit is inevitable for all of us) so why not sooner rather than later? Again, we have a deep resistance to this, even though intellectually we might think it's a good idea and worth doing. But when it comes down to it? We'd rather see our "neighbor" (think of anyone you don't like) lying dead in a pool of blood than to treat them as we ourselves would like to be treated. And we'd sooner kill ourselves than learn true forgiveness, because the ego (which we have allied with) is not going to go quietly. No, once it knows that you have intentions of "undoing" it, it's going to throw a pissy fit and kick and scream bloody murder. In other words, it will *greatly* bother you.

So you might think it is Jesus who is bothering you, but Jesus is really just coming to help you to discover the Truth for yourself (the pissy-offy Truth). He will not coerce or force you to do anything, because Love doesn't need to. He will only say, quietly and with conviction: "This is how it is, and you can either wake up now, or wake up later, it's your choice." So when it comes down to it, it's not Jesus who is the bother – he is our true friend – it is our own ego that gets all riled up by all of this spiritual talk. But in the sense that Jesus is the catalyst for what is generally a long, involved process of letting go of all that is false within ourselves (removing the blocks to the awareness of Love's presence), of going through hell before getting to heaven, then yes, Jesus ("oh brother!") is quite a bit of a bother.

But the good news is, we can take our time, and with each baby step forward (or inward, upward), we feel lighter, happier, and life gets easier. And over time, things will just bother you less and less. You see each brother (seemingly separate self) no longer as a *bother*, but truly as a brother that is helping you on your journey home. Sure, you will still continue to get pissed off (and pooped out) at times by Jesus' message, but you will keep trust and faith in the end goal, which is the actual Knowing that I Am Love.

Change the Channel

One night during an aya ceremony I was in a half-dream state, the kind where you are almost lucid, but not completely conscious either. And in that state, I was being told by a voice of some sort that it (or she – felt like a she) was going to take over my body and live through my body as if it were me. Now, for those of us who have seen movies like *Invasion of the Body Snatchers*, or more recently, Jordan Peele's *Get Out*, the idea that a foreign entity would non-consensually take over your body and live as you is horrific beyond belief. In fact, those movies are merely picking up on a great collective fear deeply embedded in our unconscious of not being in control and of not being our self (egoic personality).

Yet I will say that for a moment in that lazy, hazy, half-dreaming state, it did not seem too threatening. Yet the moment that my rational, egomind came back, fear came over me and I inwardly nixed that idea in the bud as quickly as possible. Like: *"No you won't be taking over my body, thank you very much!"*

And you might say that this was a kind of victory on my part, that I had somehow fended off some malevolent entity, guarded myself against some potentially demonic force. And perhaps that is, in a sense, true.

Yet the way I see it now, in light of the Course and non-dual teachings, I actually feel as if I was being presented with a test and that I failed the test. I will explain…

> **"There is nothing outside of you.** *This is what you ultimately must learn, because it is in this realization that your Oneness with God is restored to your awareness."*
>
> *-A Course in Miracles*

There is nothing outside of you… So if there is indeed nothing outside of the mind, this means that all seemingly "outside" forces are actually all part of this one dream that we are collectively dreaming. And so, as threatening and potentially horrific as that possession proposal sounded (to take over my body), I understand that it was actually just another part of myself (my higher self, perhaps) that was essentially asking me: *"Are you ready yet?"* Meaning, are you ready to go beyond your body and your personal mind? And when I got scared, I was in effect saying: *"No. I'm not ready yet. I'm still too scared."* And that ended that, because my higher self wasn't going to force the issue, it was there just to bring to awareness that there was still fear there and I wasn't quite ready to give up the thought of being a body. I wasn't quite ready to be a channel.

In later sessions with ayahuasca, however, I did succeed in overcoming the fear and let the spirit move me to a certain extent. And I began to understand more clearly how Helen could have been the channel (in the truest sense) for the brilliant message of the Course.

I think it's worth mentioning here that the shaman that I worked with (and which I wrote about in both this and my first book) is currently a channel for an ancient yogic sage. Though I don't know the full story, I would guess that he began to channel that particular identity through working with ayahuasca.

However, I do want to now make the point that, like all of us fallible humans, perhaps not all channeled entities are themselves channeling the highest truth. In fact, being a discarnate spirit does not necessarily mean that you are all-knowing or are presenting the truth and nothing but – in fact, such entities have been known to purposely delude the unwitting, and most of us would fall into that category.

I raise this point because in the 45-odd years since the Course came into being, there have been other channeled writings that have claimed to be extensions or additions to the Course, and there have also been channeled entities who have disparaged the Course or its founding figures. This just is what it is, and those with eyes to see will see, but it is just a caution to those who are working with this material not to get waylaid, so to speak, by those who might have an investment in their own system.

Again, the truth needs no defense, and the Course itself has nary a word to say about any other thought system or teacher, and in doing so, it truly lives up to its own message. There is never a need to attack another (and attack can be done in the most subtlest of ways) in order to establish your own validity or superiority.

As Ken Wapnick made it a point to say: We are all channels all of the time. In every moment, we have a choice, either to listen to the voice for God (the Holy Spirit), or to listen to the voice of the ego. Choose the former, and we go home quicker; choose the latter, and we delay our return indefinitely. And as we practice this again and again in our daily life, after a while turning off the voice of the ego becomes as easy as changing the channel on our TV.

And finally, given what was just said, I would like to suggest here that the book before you is a channeled/scribed work – channeled through an entity/personality named "Allowah." Again, this doesn't necessarily more or less true to the truth than anything else, especially because we can say that everything is channeled, just that perhaps we can expand our definition of what channeling is. That said, I will also affirm that this book comes from a grounded, experiential place of knowing, and also that said "Allowah" has done his best to get out of the way and let the ideas speak for themselves.

***

Synthesis

I Am Love ~ A Synopsis

This is what I might have said in the Introduction, had I fully known where the book was going at that point...

What I was aiming to get at with this here book is that here we have this brilliant "channeled" scripture (ACIM) whose message is confirmed by the eastern non-dual traditions, particularly that of Advaita Vedanta. Not only that, but there is a movement in the world of shamanic plant medicine such as ayahuasca towards approaching the plants from a non-dualistic perspective, for they certainly are capable of granting access to the experience of oneness to those who are open and ready for it (such as yoga and ACIM practitioners). I would even make a case, based on my own experience, that ayahuasca in particular has the potential of bringing one to the radical non-dual experience which ACIM is pointing to, if used cautiously in conjunction with it.

For me personally, exploring plant medicine was one big piece of my getting outside of my own box and over my judgments of people who use substances for recreational and/or spiritual purposes. I make a point in one place in the book to question the idea floating about in the ACIM world (and elsewhere) that things like ayahuasca are a no-no and are not in keeping with the practice of ACIM. I feel this position to be dishonest and hypocritical, though understandable (because it's based in fear), or perhaps just a mis-reading of the Course. To my understanding, the Course is not telling us what to do or not do, but rather, it's asking us to look at the purpose with which we do whatever we do. And if somehow ayahuasca feels useful to one's atonement process (journey home), then that's all the confirmation one needs. (Of course, one might still be doing this from ego, but that won't make it a sin, just a mistake that can be corrected.)

Even more than this, I do not think I would have ever understood the Course at a deeper level, not to mention even be interested in it, had it not been for my "ayahuasquatic" experiences, and that is because ayahuasca tends to reveal the unconscious – the shadow self that we resist looking at. And this has made all of the difference as it gave me the faith that there really is light at the end of the dark night of the soul's tunnel. And that faith, and the practice based on that faith, I strongly sense is what made possible the experiences in "wonderland" – or, my momentary experiences of Oneness – with the revelation that I (We) truly are Love.

SYNTHESIS

The I AM LOVE Manifesto

Love is.

Love is Now.

Love is Now Here.

Love is the Eternal NowHere.

Yet if Love is our eternal reality,

Why do we not live in Love now all of the time?

Because we have chosen to be and see what is not Love.

Because we have chosen to identify with what is not of Love.

Because we have willfully chosen to be a separate, autonomous, and seemingly free individual being, and in so choosing, we have chosen to hide our true identity from ourselves.

And now we find ourselves subject to guilt, fear, uncertainty, lack, sickness, judgment, betrayal, doubt, confusion, shakiness, false identities and identifications, etc., and a world that constantly reinforces these things.

In other words, we have chosen to not know who we truly are because since we have identified with the ego (the body, the world), we are afraid of losing our separate existence which looks and feels so real.

The ego is just the mistaken thought that it could be possible to live apart from Love (God, Spirit), to somehow be separate from the whole, and that we could truly want this more than our true HOME, the Universe – an eternal Song sung in uniSon to the One, to the All in All.

And now, if you want it, the only way out is through…

Through the body, through world, and through forgiveness of the body and the world.

And this means learning to accept what is and not judge, to not think that we know what is best, because we do not.

Yet in our heart of hearts we do know what is best.

And what is best is what is in our heart of hearts, which is the knowing that the only thing that really matters in the end is the Truth – the truth of what we are.

And the truth of what we are is Love. And in Love there are no grievances and thus there is no grief. No more fears and no more tears. Only the Perfect Love that We Are – that We All Are.

So to affirm "I Am Love" and to keep this in the forefront of our awareness is to bring us closer and closer to our true identity, which is that "Me" and "We" are no different. And thus to say "I Am Love" is no different than to say "We Are Love."

But the work is by no means easy and resistance to it will be great. Faith and trust in the process are our greatest needs and also our greatest challenges.

Indeed, we all have major trust issues, but at least please trust that the resonance you feel with these words is because deep down you know that the words point to a Reality that you still remember somewhere deep within yourself.

And let that trustful knowing lead you to begin to practice the undoing of fear through forgiveness more and more and more, until all fear is past and Love is your ever-present experience.

Yes, this is a difficult process, but just trust that in the end, it's all you really want.

And how you get there is up to you, but all ways will always lead to forgiveness in the end, until even forgiveness is no longer seen to be needed and Truth in its Fullness is revealed.

And that Fullness is just the last shedding of anything that still separates you from anything else.

And that Fullness is simply the Knowing, without a shadow of a doubt, that I AM LOVE.

Each of us is a Miracle of Love

The Key to the Universe

Ah so you want the key to the Universe?

Yes, well I have some good news
and some bad news for ya.

I'll give you the bad news first so you have
something to look forward to…

The bad news is there actually is no key to the Universe.

Yep, sorry Charlie.

But now for the good news…

The good news is

The Door was never locked

Actually, there is no Door.

Actually, *you* are the Door.

I mean, you and Jim Morrison.

The Beginning.

And Now, Some Final, Practical Considerations

5 ways Yoga complements Plant Medicine

1) **Prepares One for a More Easeful & Useful Process** – The first and perhaps most important way that yoga practice can help in the context of a plant medicine journey (such as mushrooms, ayahuasca, San Pedro, etc.) is also the most general: Yoga practice can prepare the body and mind for what is often a challenging process. And not just that, but yoga theory and practice can be a great aid in getting more out of the plant medicine experience. This will be touched upon in what follows…

2) **Finding the True Undying Self Requires Stillness** – In general, those who come to plant medicine without a physical and mental discipline like yoga will find it more challenging to handle the rigors of the psychedelic experience. Learning to gain mastery over the mind and body so as to sit still with eyes closed and turn one's gaze inward is a skill that often requires a fair amount of cultivation prior to said experience. Most importantly, the ability to "witness" the mind as opposed to identifying with thought forms is one of the most important tools one possesses during a psychedelic journey. The more one is practiced in this, the less likely it is that one will get trapped in negative thought patterns.

3) **Breath, the Great Ally** – Yoga stresses the breath, particularly breathing deeply and being mindful of the breath, and this can be one of the most useful tools or allies during a plant medicine journey. When a challenging moment comes, full deep breathing can be very effective

in mitigating the effects of it. Deep breathing can also prevent purging and thus help keep the medicine in one's system longer so that it can optimally do its work. It can also help to amplify the experience for those who want to go even deeper. Yoga practice prior to a psychedelic journey can thus be a very useful aid to the process.

4) **The Value of Sitting Up With Spine Straight** - While it is true that there are traditions that recommend lying down for a plant medicine journey, there is much to be said for treating one's session like a meditation and sitting up straight with erect spine for as much of the time as possible. The first shaman with whom I worked is trained in both the Peruvian ayahuasca tradition and the yoga tradition, and he encourages all his ceremony participants to sit up straight and keep as still as possible. He would actually go around and gently but firmly ask those lying down or moving to sit up and sit still. I tend to agree with this methodology, because it does emphasize that there is work to be done in these sessions beyond just being a passive observer (though of course being in "witness" mode is definitely a key ingredient!) It is quite easy to get far afield if one does not remain in a calm, focused and centered state, and sitting up does in general seem to be more conducive to this than does lying down.

5) **Plant Medicine Informs Yoga, and Yoga Informs Plant Medicine** - It is difficult to fully understand what terms such as God, ego, non-duality, maya (illusion), forgiveness, compassion, Love, and so on, mean except through direct experience. While some are able to receive such experience through meditation alone, for others, plant medicine provides the means to access these concepts experientially. And conversely, using plant medicine alone without a spiritual tradition or discipline to help guide the process is generally misguided and will lead to a useless expenditure of time and energy. In short, the entire awakening process seems to work better when the two disciplines – yoga and plant medicine – are used in conjunction with each other.

5 Ways Plant Medicine Complements Work with A Course in Miracles

1) **Access to Other States of Consciousness** ~ Very generally speaking and to state the obvious, Plant Medicine grants access to states of consciousness that are generally inaccessible to normal waking consciousness. For many, including myself, access to these states of awareness are very difficult to achieve through meditation and other spiritual practices alone. Many who study ACIM find it difficult to understand, to say the least, and it is my understanding that this is due to not having access to these states. In my own experience, plant medicine (particularly ayahuasca) prepared me for ACIM, and ACIM has since informed the ayahuasca experience for me. To me this is invaluable help on the spiritual journey.

2) **More specifically, Plant Medicine Helps to Reveal the Ego (Shadow)** ~ A Course in Miracles says over and over again, sometimes directly and sometimes by implication, that it is offering a way out of fear back to our true essence, which is Love. Many do not engage with plant medicine due to fear, and even those who do sometimes stop out of fear. One example that comes to mind is John Lennon's saying that he literally took LSD a thousand times, but stopped when he began to have very terrifying ego death experiences with it. The same thing almost happened to me with ayahuasca, but ACIM really helped me to make sense of it all as the Course really highlights what the ego is. My understanding now is that Plant Medicines like ayahuasca merely help reveal the extent to which our minds are still in throes of the ego (or Shadow). To the extent that we are is the extent to which we might have difficult and even traumatic experiences using these substances.

3) **Plant Medicine Highlights the Need for Surrender** ~ Many who use plant medicines, perhaps especially ayahuasca, have noted that the call to "surrender" looms large in the process. Generally this takes the form of surrendering to what the plant spirit has to teach. Interestingly, the term "surrender" is not used anywhere in A Course

in Miracles, and the reason is perhaps because the Course is wanting to highlight the idea that there is nothing outside of you calling for you to surrender; rather, it is our own decision for dissolving the ego through recognizing our resistance to God (Love, Oneness) that is the key component to our return Home again. In a sense, indeed, this is a form of surrender, but the point is that there is not some force outside of you to which you need to surrender; rather, it is more of a letting go of what we are not, and an acceptance of what we truly are and have always been. It is also true that in the ACIM process, one is surrendering, or giving up, one's selfish interests, need to be right and judge, and also one's trust in one's own judgment. Again, it is very difficult to recognize the need for such surrender without the help of a plant medicine. And I know of no better guide than ACIM in helping to explain and expose the whole process to full awareness.

4) **Plant Medicine Makes Forgiveness More Possible** ~ The simple reason for this is because plant medicines can help highlight how our judgments affect ourselves and those around us. Until we can really see and feel the pain – the deep existential pain – that holding on to our past hurts and judgments are causing us, we will remain enmeshed in the samsaric cyclical wheel of suffering. Or, otherwise put: we will not yet awaken from the dream. So plant medicines make forgiveness more possible, and even a little forgiveness is better than no forgiveness; and yet, only complete forgiveness (which is the idea that "nothing happened," the Atonement) will fully return us to the place we never really left. And, as the next point makes clear, plant medicines do afford a glimpse of what that looks and feels like…

5) **Plant Medicine Can Grant a Glimpse of Enlightenment** ~ Many psychonauts and explorers of plant medicine have reported getting a glimpse of what it feels like to be enlightened, or one with God (Spirit, Source, Self, Universe, etc). This is no small gift, and yet such experiences rarely if ever fully stick. As one shaman put it to me, sometimes with these medicines we feel that we've gone from Point A to Point Z, but when the dust settles and the experience wears off, we discover we've really only gone from Point A to Point B. Again,

this is nothing to sneeze at! Yet there is no getting around that there is inner work that must be done to completely dissolve the ego (shadow, or false self) and thus make this mere glimpse a more enduring, permanent state. ACIM says that this is nearly impossible while in a body, though apparently there are degrees of realization. I want to add a personal note here to say that I've had the experience of waking up a number of times now with ayahuasca, and the experiences have certainly validated ACIM for me. But the extent of my own realization remains an open question...

5 ways ACIM complements Yoga – and Yoga complements ACIM

1) **Yoga and ACIM Both Offer a Process of Learning How to Let Go** – Yoga is a process of de-conditioning or de-programming from the egoic reactive mindset we have conditioned ourselves to accept as our reality. A Course in Miracles similarly presents one of the most in-depth program of how this deprogramming can be accomplished. It presents a kind of **Jnana Yoga**, which is essentially the process of discriminating between the real (Spirit, God, Love) and what is unreal (the egoic thought system). As we continue with this process, we will discover that we more and more become our true self, and "others" will be inspired by our mere presence.

2) **God Is Perfect Oneness** – Yoga means "Union" and this is the purpose and goal of all yoga – Oneness with the Divine. And the goal of A Course in Miracles is likewise to know the "Self" (it actually uses this terminology) through the process of "undoing" or dissolving the egomind through witnessing. The Heart of Yoga and ACIM is a radical non-dualism. In the Yoga tradition, **Advaita Vedanta** espouses the idea that God is quite literally "One without a second." In other words, in God there is only perfect oneness, and anything that is of duality or separation is not ultimately real. It is illusion, or Maya, which can be quite persuasive in its agenda of keeping the Truth hidden, utilizing

Synthesis

much smoke and mirrors. Learning to peel away the layers of illusion (like the proverbial onion) will return us to the original Union, which we never truly left.

3) **All Is Within** ~ Both ACIM and Yoga aim to put you in touch with your own inner teacher, the proverbial Guru within. The essential idea is that there is nothing outside of us, all is within, and so there is nothing outside of us that can save us, or deprave us, make us happy or sad. This is always a choice that we make in our own mind. Nothing can make us sick or angry or upset unless we have already chosen that. In other words, both ACIM and Yoga are attempting to help us get in touch with the power of our minds, and particularly the power of our minds to choose our destiny. No one can do this for us, any external Guru can only bring the horse to the water, but they can't make it drink. That is a choice that only each individual can make. For many today who are wary both of traditional religion and of gurus, this is liberating knowledge indeed, for it does mean that one does not necessarily need an external teacher. That said, the Course itself is an external teacher, and many do actually need such a teacher to at the very least get them started on their path.

4) **Getting Beyond the Body** ~ Ultimately, both Yoga and ACIM help us to get beyond identification with the body. The difficulty these days is that it is not so easy to just transcend the body, and most such attempts generally become exercises in denial and repression. A well-known tantric idea is "the only way out is through" and in this case, it would mean that only through **not** denying the body (including other bodies) and the world, but rather showing them love and appreciation, can we generally begin to get beyond identification with the body.

5) **Turning the World Upside Down** ~ *A Course in Miracles* teaches that the thought system upon which the world is based is antithetical to spiritual awakening, and so the way to genuine awakening must come through reversing the egoic thought system upon which the world is based. When this is accomplished, the "real world" will be revealed in all its glory, and it will be a world in which there is no more judgment,

no more separation. Likewise, the headstand (*shirshasana*) – a yoga posture – symbolizes this movement toward turning things on their head in order to bring things into right perspective. The true yogi is ultimately able to be "in the world, but not of the world" in that s/he is no longer disturbed by the play of opposites, but sees everything of one piece and thus is at peace.

For more about the connection between yoga and ACIM, please see the following:

https://allowah.com/2015/10/02/a-course-in-miracles-in-light-of-the-yoga-tradition-part-i/

http://realitysandwich.com/221023/yoga-ayahuasca-a-course-in-miracles-long-reads-short-roads-home/

(The Last But Not Least Brief Digression…)
From Grief to Grrr8full
(or: From Groan to All Grown Up)

There are certain sounds that seem to be universal. Take sighing, for example. How 'bout laughing. The "oh" of surprise. The "wow" of amazement. The "ah" of delight or discovery.

Well, the universal sound that I would like to consider today is similarly universal, but not as talked about.

It is the sound "grrr" that comes from the pit of the stomach when we're feeling stress, anger, or just about any upset. While it might not always be a "grrr," and maybe sometimes more of an "ugh", for our purposes today, let's talk about the "grrr" sound as it directly connects with a point to be made about grief and grievances.

Did you ever notice how many words we have in English that use this "grrr" sound? And most of them are negative words. Consider the following list…

groan
grief
grievance
grievous
gross
grody
greedy
grimy
grumble
grotesque
grisly
grasping
grating

grave
grind
gruesome
grueling
grungy
grunt
gray
grouchy
grumpy
gruff
growl
angry

Taking the last word first (the only one not beginning with "gr"), you will note that most of these words have to do with anger, disgruntlement, or some sort of grief or grievance. Most would call these natural or instinctual responses to things that appear offensive. It's somewhat counterintuitive to think that the "grrr" we feel way down in our bowels when we're angry or grossed out is something that we have any control over. Or when we feel loss, as with the word "grief."

I wouldn't have thought that either. But it does seem to be possible to not feel these negative emotions so much, or even at all – or if we do, to not take them so seriously. I am even beginning to see how it may even be possible to become completely free of what we might call "the old grind." Imagine that. To not even be aggrieved by those gruesome grievous feelings in your *kishkes*, meaning your belly (Yiddish, folks), which can only lead to a grotesque kind of self-aggrandizement.

And what is the way to get to that? Well, it's through another "gr" word actually, but this one not so grave. I mean the word "grateful." Yes, through the attitude of gratitude we can make our way free of all grief, because gratitude means acceptance of what is, and that is great wisdom. So next time you've got a plate full of grisly grody gruesomeness, remember to be grateful. (Please don't groan.) It can make all the difference.

SYNTHESIS

When you want only love
you will see nothing else.
A Course in Miracles

Radical Forgiveness Yoga

The word "radical" means root. Radical Forgiveness Yoga is the practice of going to the radical root of any and all dis-ease we have, re-minding ourselves that, as A Course in Miracles teaches, there really is only one root problem, and one root solution.

The "problem" is that deep down we believe we are separate from God, alone in the universe, unloved and unlovable. As such, we feel guilty, ashamed, unworthy, fearful, and essentially doomed and damned. No matter how hard we try, we think, there's no way out.

Yet the solution is very simply the affirmation that all of that is not true. For if we go even deeper down, we will recognize the Light of Spirit within us that has never died out. Our mission is thus to seek that light, and to let go of identification with the ego, or false self, which would deny that Light. This is a continual, step by step, moment to moment practice, and it happens on the level of the mind, not the body.

As such, this form of Yoga is essentially a form of Jnana Yoga, which seeks to discriminate between what is Real and what is unreal. In each and every moment, we have an opportunity to choose light over darkness, Spirit over ego, Love over fear, Forgiveness over judgment. We do this by looking at any and all "dis-ease" that is in our mind, and dis-identifying with it as we remember that our essential nature is Love.

Radical Forgiveness Yoga is also a form of Bhakti Yoga in the sense that we put our full faith in Jesus (or any other enlightened master) who have with 100% conviction told us that our reality is only Love. Jesus, or our "ideal" teacher, is our guide back to Source, and we devote ourselves to them by being faithful to their lessons.

Radical Forgiveness Yoga Practices...

Jesus in his Course in Miracles teaches us that we are not our bodies, that our bodies were made by the ego as an attack on its own mistaken conception of God. Yet the Holy Spirit re-interprets the body as a learning device for bringing us home. As such, we are asked neither to condemn nor to glorify the body, but to find a balance in which we see the body as a tool and temple to fulfill our true function here, which is forgiveness.

The first and primary practice of this form of Yoga has already been described: Jnana Yoga, which is a yoga of the mind, seeking unification by denying any and all identification with separation.

The next important practice of RFY is breathwork. Breathwork is a way of silencing the "monkey mind," and bringing both body and mind into a deeper state of stillness and presence.

The physical positions (asanas) and exercises of RFY also serve the same purpose of preparing oneself for a deeper release. For when one feels clear, calm, and relaxed, one is in a more conducive state to look within and to release even deeper identifications that are not serving.

Song and chant also serve to open the heart and reinforce the lessons.

Finally, it should be noted that intention (Sanskrit: *sankalpa*) is very much essential to this process. We are asked to continually look at our inner motivation in our practice, to insure that we are always practicing with an intention of non-harm, non-comparison, and non-judgment.

Some Relevant Course Quotes...

Forgiveness is the healing of the perception of separation.

The body is the ego's idol; the belief in sin made flesh and then projected outward.

The body was not made by love. Yet love does not condemn it and can use it lovingly, respecting what the Son of God has made and using it to save him from illusions.

"The Holy Spirit interprets the body only as a means of communication… Healing is the result of using the body solely for communication… The Holy Spirit teaches you to use your body only to reach your brothers, so He can teach His message through you. This will heal them and therefore heal you."

"When you equate yourself with a body, you will always experience depression.

"If you use the body for attack, it is harmful to you. If you use it only to reach the minds of those who believe they are bodies, and teach them through the body that this is not so, you will understand the power of the mind that is in you."

"I am not a body, I am free, I am still as God created me."

"The reality of everything is totally harmless, because total harmlessness is the condition of its reality. It is also the condition of your awareness of its reality. You do not have to seek reality. It will seek you and find you when you meet its conditions."

"When you limit yourself we are not of one mind, and that is sickness. Yet sickness is not of the body, but of the mind. All forms of sickness are signs that the mind is split, and does not accept a unified purpose."

Radical Forgiveness Breathwork

Guidelines

The session is approximately 2 1/2 hours.
Participants gather in a circle.
The first 15 minutes are explanatory: What it is. Q & A.
The next 15 minutes is intention setting, aloud in the circle.

The next 20-30 minutes is warm-up with ecstatic dance.

Then the breathing begins, first standing, then kneeling, then sitting, and finally lying on one's back. This takes approximately 1 hour, possibly a little more or a little less.

For the next 15 minutes, the group rests in Shavasana, in silence or with relaxing music. At least a few minutes of silence is recommended.

The final 15 minutes is a closing circle where participants share about their experience.

Radical Forgiveness Breathwork

What It Is…

The intention behind Radical Forgiveness Breathwork is simply to provide a vehicle for deep healing via the medium of the breath and communal support. In this safe and loving setting, participants are allowed to let go of all that is no longer serving them, and to be "reborn" into a truer, more authentic version of themselves.

The main practice of RFB is deep, connected breathing through the mouth for a period of an hour or more. This can be intense and does give new meaning to the word "work" in "breathwork." Yet it pays off in deep releases that occur if sustained for a period of time. These releases can include crying, laughing, ecstatic states, kundalini, release of stored memories, etc. None of these are to be denied, and all of them are welcome in the group. They are deep traumas and/or blockages that are being cleared, and as such are to be embraced.

In reality, the deeper practice of this form of breathwork is the mind's firm decision for healing. As A Course in Miracles teaches, getting to the "radical root" of the "problem" means recognizing that it is not the body that needs healing, but the mind. Yet our belief in the body is yet so strong that these practices can indeed feel very helpful. Still, let us not lose sight of the fact that the only thing that really needs healing is our investment in the belief that we are separate from God. This is what is meant by "radical forgiveness." In this forgiveness, we re-mind ourselves that there is no need for forgiveness, because the separation from God never happened.

Radical Forgiveness Breathwork

What It Does & What Might Happen…

Radical Forgiveness Breathwork is akin to shamanic practices and has the potential of bringing about an altered state. This state might include blissed out breathlessness (Samadhi), a Kundalini awakening, and even a full awakening to one's essential nature, among other things.

On occasion, intense fear might come up, and this is nothing to be afraid of. The Facilitator/Space Holder will insure that you are safe and feel protected at all times. He/She might also assist you in the process through some comforting thought, word, or action. The music that is played throughout will also be uplifting, inspirational, and supportive of your journey.

Some people experience something called "tetany" when they do this form of breathing. Symptoms of this include a curling in of the hands, sometimes feet, and sometimes a change in facial expression. Again, this is nothing to be afraid of, but comes with the territory. In fact, it's a sure sign that you have been successful in your breathing!

In physiological terms, you are introducing a very increased amount to the upper respiratory system. This often induces feelings of heat, increased heart rate, shaking and trembling. Again, all of these are signs that you are well on your way!

SYNTHESIS

Affirmations

Forgiveness is my only function here.

I remember my function with each breath.

Inspiration: I breathe in the guidance of Spirit.

Expiration: I let go of all false images that hide the Light of Spirit.

I Breathe in Love

I Breathe out Fear

I Breathe in Forgiveness

I Let Go of All Judgment

Inhale Love

Exhale Fear

Inhale Love

Exhale Peace to All

Inhale Joy

Exhale All that Does Not Serve

Afterword

Question Everything
An Introduction to Yoga Quest University

*Do not believe in anything simply because you have heard it.
Do not believe in anything simply because it is spoken
and rumored by many.
Do not believe in anything simply because it is found
written in your religious books.
Do not believe in anything merely on the authority
of your teachers and elders.
Do not believe in traditions because they have been
handed down for many generations.
But after observation and analysis, when you find that anything
agrees with reason and is conducive to the good and benefit of one
and all, then accept it and live up to it.*

~ Siddhartha Gautama Buddha

"*The important thing is to not stop questioning.*"

~ Einstein

"*The unexamined life is not worth living.*"

~ Socrates

"*Your task is not to seek for love, but merely to seek and find all the barriers within yourself that you have built against it.*"

~ Rumi

"*I didn't say everything I said.*"

~ Yogi Berra

"*Questioning illusions is the first step in undoing them.*"

~ A Course in Miracles

For a while, I was calling my yoga school Yoga University, with the idea that it would provide a well-rounded education in the art and science that is yoga. But when I saw that there were at least several other Yoga Universities out there, I felt it would be important to distinguish my school from others, if only for the purposes of identification. All along I've been playing with the idea of the "quest," as in the "spiritual quest," or more specifically, the *yoga* quest (although I don't make a hard and fast distinction between yoga and spirituality, to me they are essentially the same).

For me, this quest is all about *question*ing, and the questioning begins first and foremost with the basic existential questions: *Who am I? Why am I here? How should I live? What should I do? What happens when we die? Is there a God?* etc. From early on, these questions were all-important to me and motivated me to spend much of my adult life seeking answers, both in the world of academia and in more experiential ways such as yoga practice. One of my earliest heroes was Socrates, who said neat things like "philosophy begins in wonder" and "the unexamined life is not worth living." Socrates was the master of questioning, and what is now called the Socratic Method is his method of seeking clarity about a thing through separating what it is from what it is not (a form of Jnana Yoga).

Socrates' approach is all about being unafraid to ask the more challenging questions, and not being satisfied with easy answers or persuasive arguments for or against anything; it means questioning until there is nothing more to question, until, in fact, there is "no question." This is true philosophy, and this was truly Socrates' approach and the cornerstone of the Socratic Method. Apparently, it was also Buddha's approach to some extent, as is evidenced by the quote about questioning everything with which I began this piece, one that I have placed at the front of each of my yoga training manuals. The funny thing is, and one that I share with my students now: that is not a direct quote from the historical Buddha (who is still something of a mystery), but rather somewhat of a poetic rendering of a teaching that is attributable to him. That teaching is found in the Kalama Sutta and runs like this:

"Now, Kalamas, don't go by reports, by legends, by traditions, by scripture, by logical conjecture, by inference, by analogies, by agreement through

pondering views, by probability, or by the thought, 'This contemplative is our teacher.' When you know for yourselves that, 'These qualities are skillful; these qualities are blameless; these qualities are praised by the wise; these qualities, when adopted & carried out, lead to welfare & to happiness' — *then you should enter & remain in them.*

Granted, the distinction between the fake Buddha quote and the original might not be all that important, though the real quote does seem to stress that one should actually not even rely so much on one's own reasoning abilities, but rather on one's own lived experience. In other words, you can only know if something is valid and valuable by practice and its fruits. This is actually the hallmark of the yoga philosophy, that it is ultimately a *practical* philosophy based in experiment and experience, not mere analysis or theory.

Which reminds me of a fake Yogi Berra-ism, something Yogi Berra definitely didn't say: *"In theory, there is no difference between theory and practice; but in practice, there is."*

Yogi Berra is especially interesting to bring in here, because for one thing, he wasn't a yogi (per se), and because there have been many "Berra-isms" attributed to him over the years that he went on record to say he never said. One of these that I saw awhile back and have used ever since in my talks on history and mythology is:

"Just because it never happened doesn't mean it ain't true."

You will note the connection here with the "nothing happened" subtitle/theme of this book, which we could now reformulate along these lines to read: "Just because nothing happened doesn't mean it ain't true (on some level, just not the ultimate level)."

> Your task is not to seek for love,
> but merely to seek and find
> all of the barriers within yourself
> that you have built against it.
>
> ~ A Course in Miracles

Similarly, there are all kinds of quotes floating around out there in cyberspace that are mis-attributed to famous people. Some are clearly off base, others are not so clearly so. One such case is the quote attributed to the 14th century Persian Sufi poet, Rumi, with which I began this piece: *"Our task is not to seek for love..."* The problem with giving Rumi credit for this quote is that it's also found verbatim in the Text of A Course in Miracles(!) Now, many who are not familiar with the Course seem to just assume that the person who wrote the Course took it from Rumi. It seems that not many consider that maybe someone took it from the Course and attributed to Rumi as something the mystic poet probably might have or would have said. If so, it seems to have worked – most people now think the quote is from Rumi and couldn't be original to ACIM. While it is indeed possible that Jesus, the alleged author of ACIM, quoted the historical Rumi (who didn't speak English, btw), it's more reasonable to suggest that someone borrowed it from the Course and put it in Rumi's name.

The point, once again, is to question everything, certainly everything you read, and even more so everything you read on the internet(!) An even deeper point to all of this, and one which ACIM highlights, is the extent to which we form beliefs and then take them to be the gospel truth, no longer open to question. We do this because beliefs and a belief system generally make us feel safe, secure, stable. Indeed, questioning can be unsettling and upsetting, especially when it comes to examining our own most deeply held beliefs and values. But questioning our conditioned beliefs, and especially the ones that are keeping us in perpetual suffering, seems to be the first step in freeing ourselves from the prison of our own minds. As the Course says,

"Questioning illusions is the first step in undoing them."

And the one basic illusion that we all have deeply ingrained is the idea that our very individual personhood, with all of its needs and desires, hopes and dreams, is the be all and end all of everything. This is one of the cardinal egoic principles that is not open to question. We may in theory be open to another possibility, but in practice we generally go about living as if our small self is god, and we take our way of seeing things (beliefs, values, judgments, etc. – and the guilt that accompanies them) *very* seriously.

So this path of questioning is really leading to opening ourselves to lighten up more and more about everything. To stop making and taking things all so seriously. On this note, one of my favorite all-time book titles is former #1 tennis player John Mcenroe's very candid tell-all memoir, *You Cannot Be Serious*. The reason this title is so good and clever is because in his youth on the tennis court, Mcenroe was notorious for his brash badboy attitude, and one of the things he often yelled at the line judge when contesting a point was just that: *"You cannot be serious!"* Sometimes a ball or racket would also be thrown in for effect. This actually all made great theater, as I can attest having had the pleasure of watching Mac play live back in the '70s. So to use that as the title of his autobiography was not only funny, it showed that he had lightened up a bit over the years. (Of course, a lot of that was an act that Mac was well-paid for, but it doesn't affect my point.)

And to me this is one of the only things not really open to question anymore, that you cannot take seriously your egoic defense system and hope to understand yourself clearly and live and die in peace. On the spiritual quest, the ego is decidedly *not* your amigo, and to follow its dictates unquestioningly is to damn yourself and those around you to a hell of your own making. I know that was a serious sounding statement, but I don't take it too seriously (because *"nothing happened"* remember), I only say it to attempt to meet those who find themselves in serious straits and are seeking a way out. Well, this is the way, or at least, it is one way. But I do sense that in the end, all pathways will take us to a confrontation with the ego, and that confrontation will end with our realization that it is really nothing and that "nothing happened."

And when we wake up, even for a moment, we will find ourselves in a place where all questions have been resolved and only Love remains. Where we finally Know though direct experience that Love is all and Love is the answer, and the only question left (if there is one) is:

And what was the question...?

Love is the Answer

—What was the Question?

SYNTHESIS

Post-Script: Questioning Everything

Now, just for the sake of friendly argument and to play devil's advocate for a moment, let's indeed *question everything* here....

So ahem...

Just because something is ancient doesn't make it true. There are many ancient things we would be better off without, and we are. Other things, like religious dogma, die harder. If we can question the ultimate authority of the Bible to completely dictate my life, and I do, why not other scriptures? Who is to say that the Upanishads or the Bhagavad Gita are any less of a mixed bag that we would be wise to *not* take as gospel? And if we can question that, we can then bring into question all of the later scriptures and commentaries that were influenced by the earlier texts. Perhaps revered sages like Shankara just latched onto certain earlier ideas and became so enamored of them, for whatever reason, that they then "experienced" the truth of them for themselves and then proclaimed them to be the absolute truth. But they were only seeing what they were primed to see, it all became a self-fulfilling prophecy. And it became so ingrained in the culture of the east that it became the lens through which everyone growing up in that culture sees reality, or what they think is reality. But it is all off-base...

Similarly, with ayahuasca, you see with ayahuasca what you are prepared to see, what you want to see. And you might also see a lot of things you don't want to see, too, but you will also have rare experiences that go beyond the personal where the subject-object dichotomy no longer holds. But who is to say *that* is any more real than what is experienced in so-called duality? Okay, so you feel free of fear, worry, anxiety, what we have been calling "ego." But why is that any more or less real than the state in which all these things are felt? Why privilege one over the other? Why is one necessarily better than the other? Why become so absorbed in dissolving the ego when we could... just live our life?

As for A Course in Miracles, who is to say that the alleged voice of "Jesus" that Helen Schucman heard was not that of some departed Hindu sage trying to foist its non-dualistic message on the masses, for purposes of fucking with people's mind, or worse. And/or maybe it was a spirit engaging in spiritual warfare against the "Christian" worldview, as a way of trying to bring Yahweh and his minions down and raising up the eastern non-dualistic flag? Or by a spirit out to purposely confuse people, as many people are when they engage with ACIM?...

*

Yes, such are some of the thoughts one might have, and which I have had personally, and there is something to them, for sure. But such questioning also seems to me to be a slippery slope down to nihilism and inaction. Which I think is where most of us without a spiritual practice are at, because we already have such basic trust issues that it's damn near impossible to even begin to take the initial steps on the journey back home.

For myself, I will say that non-judgment and forgiveness based in the idea that we are all one on some fundamental level is crucial to living a happier life that is free of suffering. And that is what the modalities in question have the potential to offer us. So for me they are beyond question, really, because I feel like I am a more peaceful and happier person for having engaged with them – and have had those glimpses beyond the veil. And that is why I am here commending them to you.

Which brings me to my last joke, for now...

Yoga is for every body!

But not everybody is for yoga.

Why not?

Too much of a stretch.

Synthesis

Yoga Trainings with A Course In Miracles

Many people all over the world have by now experienced the "feel good" power of yoga, though for the most part what they have experienced is mainly the power of asana practice, and maybe a little breathwork, meditation, chanting, etc. Yoga, however, wants to take us deeper. It wants to give us everything, and it is just waiting until we are ready to receive that from it. In fact, I have a saying that I have found gets the message across succinctly: "Yoga gives you what you want… and waits patiently for you to truly want what it truly has to give."

And what does it have to give? Well, itself. Yoga means "union" or "oneness." The goal of yoga is to finally wake up and realize that we are one with everything, and that we have always been and will forever be just that. This is what is called "moksha" in Sanskrit. Anything short of that goal is yoga trying to get to Yoga.

The thing is, the way that yoga is taught and perceived these days, this basic, fundamental message is getting lost. Don't get me wrong: Feeling good in one's body and experiencing greater health and well-being is not a small gift. And yet, it is ultimately not enough. For that, we need stronger medicine than merely physical practice. As Einstein said, a problem cannot be solved at the level at which it was created. He also said, by the way, that the world of separation is a mass delusion of consciousness, and that our real work is to free ourselves from this delusion/illusion.

This is exactly what Yoga is getting at. And to understand this better, it is really helpful to dig into the traditional sources of the Hindu yoga tradition, sources such as the Vedas, Upanishads, Bhagavad Gita, and the Yoga Sutras. It is also helpful to explore other scriptures from sister traditions like Buddhism and Taoism. And I have found one more recent "scripture" to be very helpful in my practice and teaching, one that has been growing in popularity the world over: A Course in Miracles (ACIM).

The Course, as it is commonly referred to, is slowly being understood to be one of the best resources for those seeking spiritual liberation/enlightenment. In many ways, it is not only simpler than many traditional yogic paths, but also quicker. I feel that in combination with yogic wisdom (eastern philosophy), it can work wonders—or maybe rather, miracles. Some have questioned why I have seemed to have suddenly changed "course" and been bringing awareness to ACIM. I can only say that I have been looking all of my life for something like this. Why would I not share it?

Again, though, the Course really does not say anything too much different than what the highest Yogic wisdom is also getting at. The only difference is that it's in English and has a way of getting its message across in a way that seems to be a little more accessible for many today. As regards its validity, some of the top spiritual figures today have endorsed it, including Eckhart Tolle, Wayne Dyer, and Alan Cohen.

I have already been bringing ACIM in to my classes, retreats, and trainings. I am only now just more officially announcing the intention to bring ACIM teachings more into the yoga world via my offerings. And also I feel sure that this will be a trend that we will be seeing more and more in the wide world of yoga.

Synthesis

Supplement
A Guide To Radical Self-Inquiry

(or: Great Questions for the Quest)

Hey You!

Even if you are the inquisitive sort, the following questions might seem like something of an Inquisition, or at least an imposition, yet i humbly assure you they will put you in position to sort out what appears to be the most essential of all inquiries, the *maha* (great) question "Who Am I?"

The following self-interrogation checklist (if you will) is designed to be used for any question, issue, or even thought that arises in the mind's I, but especially for deeply held/entrenched beliefs. As you will note, most of the questions here are getting at the same beloved query from different vantage points, that question being: "What's my stake in this whole bloody thing, and why?" Or put more simply:

"What's it to ya, sweetheart?"

It is recommended that you bring these questions to bear on your most deeply held belief. Yes, you read that right in the singular: Belief. It doesn't have to be all of your deeply held beliefs, just one will do. You see, what this in intended to do is to spark an inward quest to the root of things, again one that will ultimately bring you to the ultimate question, "**Who Am I?**" Before that, you will get to the question: "What can I really believe with 100% certainty?" And after that: "What Can/Do I Really Know?"

& now without further about nothing ado...

Some Great Questions for *YOU*...

What's it to me?

What's in it for me?

What's at stake here for me?

What is my investment in this being true or not?

What do I stand to gain or lose from choosing one side or the other? (or simply: What do I have to lose?)

Am I able to "handle the truth" in regard to this?

Do I care what people (family, friends, colleagues, spouse, children, God, guru, etc) will think of me if I believe/think this or not? Why or why not?

Would I rather choose "the truth" or the censure or approval of others in regard to this issue?

Who/what would I be if it turned out I was dead wrong about this? Am I ready and willing to be that?

Would I be perfectly fine if I were wrong or not completely right in regard to this issue/belief/thought, etc.?

[switching pronouns from "I" to "you" now...]

Is there an emotional charge attached to this thought/belief/idea? If so, where is that emotional charge coming from, and would you label it good, bad, indifferent, or something else? (Please elaborate on your label, if you choose one.)

Do you feel angry when you think about this idea, thought, belief, issue, etc, or about people who think differently than you? If so, why?

Or, is your belief/thought/opinion, etc., coming from a place of fear? If so, what are you afraid of?

Was there a historical moment that you can remember where you took your current stance on this idea, belief, thought, issue, etc.? What prompted your decision at that time? Was it truly your own decision, or was it influenced by something or someone else?

Do you find it easy to dismiss those who think differently than you in regard to this particular issue, idea, belief, thought, etc.?

Are you able to listen with an open mind and heart to all sides of this particular point, thought, issue, controversy, etc.?

Do you actively seek out alternative perspectives on what you believe/think to possibly alter your position if there is evidence, reasoning, etc. that might put your thinking in question? If so, would you say (and let's be completely honest here, if possible) that even though you seek out alternative perspectives that might challenge your own, you really do so to look openminded, but in reality you were going to hold fast to your position anyway to the bitter end (you diehard, you ;)?

If you do look at alternative perspectives, would you say your search is exhaustive, or do you merely satisfy yourself with those that are easiest to demolish and stop there?

And even if you do come to a place where you see that it is truly difficult, if not impossible, to in all honesty choose one perspective or the other(s), do you still hold fast to your original perspective? If so, why?

Would you say your current beliefs are unshakeable? If so, and your beliefs have changed over the course of your lifetime, what is to make you think that they won't change again?

Is that your final answer?
(Do you hate me?)
(Is that your final answer?)

ok, Mr Smiley, by whom this work is being chaneled (one "n" – the perfume), suggested one more question with the suggestion that if not already doing so, to please sit down before you take a stand one way or the other:

Is it more important to you to stand for something…or sit for nothing?

[maniacal chaneled laughter]

I am not a body, I am free
I am still as God created me

SYNTHESIS

Come Home

"Listen to the story of the prodigal son, and learn what God's treasure is and YOURS: This son of a loving father left his home and thought he squandered everything for nothing of any value, although he did not know its worthlessness at the time. He was ashamed to return to his father, because he thought he had hurt him. Yet when he came home, the father welcomed him with joy because only the son himself WAS his father's treasure. He WANTED nothing else. God wants only His Son because His Son is His only treasure."

~ A Course in Miracles

Come Home (Shalom)

Forever Have I Loved You
Forever Have I Longed for You
Forever Have I Missed You
Forever Have I Called to You
Forever
Forever
COME HOME

*

"There is no death because the Son of God is like his Father.
Nothing you can do can change Eternal Love.
Forget your dreams of sin and guilt, and come with me instead
to share the resurrection of God's Son.
And bring with you all those whom He has sent to you
to care for as I care for you."

*

Thank you, Jesus,
Thank you, Friend
Thank you, Jesus
Thank you, again & again
Thank you, Jesus
Thank you, our Friend
Thank you, Amen
*

Forever Have I Loved You...
COME HOME
Well?...COME HOME...

Welcome Home
Welcome Home
Welcome Home

SYNTHESIS

Know yourself in the One Light
where the miracle that is you is perfectly clear.

Recommended Resources

Truly Helpful Course Resources

Websites

Official ACIM Website: ACIM.org

Facim.org ~ The Foundation for A Course In Miracles Website, containing much valuable info about the Course, such as a Glossary, very extensive Q & A, and many of Ken Wapnick's writings, plus the full Course.

UnderstandACIM.com ~ This is my own website, with essays (see below), plus daily readings and workbook lessons.

Videos

Ken Wapnick Videos

"What Is A Course in Miracles? ACIM Explained in 17 mins" by Kenneth Bok

Jon Mundy's Tribute to Ken Wapnick

The Story of A Course in Miracles

Books

The Disappearance of the Universe

Living with Miracles

Understanding A Course in Miracles

The Most Commonly Asked Questions About 'A Course in Miracles'

Articles

What is ACIM?

Other Resources

Glossary for ACIM

ACIM Q & A Service

The Theory of ACIM

ACIM Archives

See ACIM.org for this

Recommended Resources

Some of the Best Known Course Teachers

Alan Cohen

David Hoffmeister

Carol Howe

Gerold Jampolsky

R Patrick Miller

Michael Mirdad

Jon Mundy

Robert Perry

Gary Renard

Nouk Sanchez

Amy Torres

Ken Wapnick

Marianne Williamson

Some Pieces That I've Written As Aids For Understanding ACIM

(on UnderstandACIM.com)

10 Reasons Why Its Challenging to Understand A Course in Miracles + Keys to Understanding

10 Key Course Concepts I Learned from Ken Wapnick

100 Great Course Quotes

Who Wrote A Course in Miracles?

Some Thoughts on Leela, the Play of God

Yoga, Ayahuasca, and A Course in Miracles

13 Especially Remarkable Course Passages

22 Core Teachings of A Course in Miracles (And Compared to Yogic Wisdom)

A Course in Miracles ~ Select Bibliography

Books

Cohen, Alan. *A Course in Miracles Made Easy.* Hay House, Inc. 2015.

Hoffmeister, David. *Unwind Your Mind Back to God.* Living Miracles Publications, 2014.

Howe, Carol M. *Never Forget to Laugh: Personal Recollections of Bill Thetford, Co-Scribe of A Course in Miracles.* Waterfront Digital Press, 2016.

Jampolsky, Gerald G. *Love is Letting Go of Fear.* Third Edition. Celestial Arts, 2010. Carlos Santana wrote the Foreword for the third edition.

Marchand, Alexander. *The Universe is a Dream: The Secrets of Existence Revealed.* Inspired Arts Press, 2011.

Miller, D. Patrick. *Living With Miracles: A Common-Sense Guide to A Course in Miracles.* New York: Jeremy P. Tarcher, 2011.

Mirdad, Michael. *The Heart of A Course in Miracles: Understanding and Applying the 12 Primary Concepts of the Course.* Sedona: Grail Press, 2016.

Mundy, Jon. *Living A Course in Miracles: An Essential Guide to the Classic Text.* Sterling Ethos, 2012.

Renard, Gary. *The Disappearance of the Universe.* Hay House, Inc. 2004.

Skutch, Robert. *Journey Without Distance: The Story Behind A Course in Miracles.* Berkley: Celestial Arts, 1984.

Wapnick, Kenneth. His entire oeuvre. Read and learn.

Williamson, Marianne. *A Return to Love.* HarperOne, 1996.

Ayahuasca & Psychedelics

Books

Campos, Don Jose. *The Shaman and Ayahuasca.* Divine Arts Media, 2011.

Fadiman, James. *The Psychedelic Explorers Guide.* Park Street Press, 2011.

Kilham, Christopher. *The Ayahuasca Test Pilots Handbook.* North Atlantic Books, 2014.

Metzner, Ralph. *The Ayahuasca Experience.* Park Street Press, 2014.

Web

Alexander George Ward ~ www.Wardyworks.art

Maps

Kaphi

Film

The Last Shaman.

Metamorphosis.

Neurons to Nirvana

The Shaman and Ayahuasca.

Vine of the Soul.

Yoga Philosophy

Books

Primary Sources

Upanishads (Mandukya Upanishad)

Katha Upanishad

The Bhagavad Gita

Brahma Sutras

Yoga Vasistha

Viveka Chudamani

Ashtavakra Gita

Avadhuta Gita

Ribhu Gita

Secondary Sources

Feuerstein, Georg. *The Yoga Tradition.* Hohm Press.

Freeman, Richard. *The Mirror of Yoga.*

Prabhavananda, Swami. *The sermon on the Mount According to Vedanta.* Hollywood, California: Vedanta Press, 1963, 1992.

Ibid. *The Spiritual Heritage of India: A Clear Summary of Indian Philosophy and Religion.* Hollywood, California: Vedanta Press, 1963, 1979.

Ram Dass. All of his oeuvre. Read and learn.

Stone, Michael. *The Inner Tradition of Yoga.* Shambhala, 2008.

White, Ganga. *Yoga Beyond Belief.*

Web

Swamij.com

Ochsonline.org

Film

Yoga Unveiled

Enlighten Up!

Fierce Grace

Appendices

Appendix A

Is *A Course In Miracles* An Insidious Cia Mind Control Experiment?

https://truthinreality.com/2012/09/08/a-course-in-miracles-and-mk-ultra-mind-control/

http://www.eldontaylor.com/blog/2015/10/21/spirituality-as-a-tool-for-mind-control/

https://inpursuitofhappiness.wordpress.com/2013/12/19/a-course-in-miracles-a-cia-exercise-in-mind-control/

I am writing this piece today to help us separate fact from fiction. Recently two friends whose opinions I respect sent me the links above which claim that A Course in Miracles (ACIM) is none other than a CIA mind control experiment. This has led both of my friends to have doubts about ACIM and question my involvement with it.

First, I want to say that these claims against ACIM are nothing new, nor do they particularly disturb me. Nor am I much bothered that my friends have a bad taste in their mouth now in regard to ACIM. So why am I writing this? I could definitely simply ignore these (and other) claims, which is what many in the ACIM community do, because they are pretty far-fetched and maybe don't even deserve comment. But in this case, and actually in most cases, I do feel that it is appropriate to defend the truth when it is being attacked, though from a space of non-judgment and one of wanting to be "truly helpful." As a yoga and ACIM student, I am by now very familiar with separating truth from untruth in my own mind, and this piece is just a kind of extension of that, if you will.

Perhaps the most important thing I will say here is this: It is just so easy to write something and sound like you know what you're talking about, but in reality have not much of a clue about the thing you're criticizing. As we know, talk is cheap, and opinions are even cheaper. In this case, someone might claim to be an CIA-member, or have been an ACIM student for years, but so what? If your "facts" are off, they're off, no matter what your alleged level of experience is.

Conspiracy theories are a cottage industry these days, they clearly are proliferating on the internet (not to mention our feverish ego-conspired imaginations!). Which is not to say that they are all bogus, there is no doubt at least some truth to some of them. And in this particular case, there is indeed some validity to the claims being made (for example, that Dr. William Thetford worked for the CIA, this is an established fact). Yet anyone who is more familiar with ACIM would see these claims as just so much speculation and conjecture.

We can also rightly ask from the very outset: why are these anti-ACIM pieces being written? Is there a bias, some stake in things turning out one way or another? Clearly there is a fundamentalist Christian bias against ACIM, and I am leaving aside for now all of the arguments against ACIM from a fundamentalist biblical perspective, just focusing on this one topic at hand.

Turning this question back on myself, do I have an investment in this matter? Sure I do, but not enough to not be willing to change my point of view in the presence of real evidence to the contrary. Yes, if someone could convincingly prove that ACIM is none other than a mind control experiment that somehow the CIA concocted as a way to control the masses, or even as a mass personality study, I would gladly accept such news. Yet as we will see, there is (as yet) only conjecture and speculation, no convincing proof...

I really don't sense that those making these claims against ACIM are really informed about it or aware of certain materials that might help them to understand the context in which it came to be. It is not my purpose to go into all of those details here, but merely to provide some primary sources for you to educate yourself more about ACIM. What follows are just a few such sources.

These sources make it clear that Helen Schucman was the scribe of the Course. Was the "voice" that came to her conspiratorially implanted somehow by Bill or someone in the MK Ultra project? Anything is possible, of course, but very highly improbable. Bill didn't even start working for MK Ultra until 1971, and the scribing of the Course began in 1965. The entire Course was nearly complete by 1971.

Why not believe what Helen Schucman and Bill Thetford and Ken Wapnick all say about the origins of the Course, instead of concluding that they all were either victims of mind control, or that Bill Thetford somehow sinisterly implanted the entire Course into Helen Schulman's brain? Are these people not rational, sensible people, just like you and me? Why not give them the benefit of the doubt? If and when you do, you just might find yourself more and more at peace, and *that*, I maintain, is what A Course in Miracles is aiming at, and what we are all truly seeking.

Please Check Out the Following & Then Draw Your Conclusions

Helen Schucman INTERVIEW – Her Account of Scribing ACIM, 1976

http://acim-archives.org/Scribes/interviews/Helen-Aug1976.html

Full Version:

https://soundcloud.com/onefeather-journal/a-rare-interview-with-helen-schucman

Bill Thetford Talks About His Life & A Course in Miracles

https://www.youtube.com/watch?v=AuTThT2hht0&t=132s

The Story of A Course in Miracles COMPLETE

http://acim-archives.org/Media/articles/film-intro.html

Never Forget to Laugh: Personal Recollections of Bill Thetford, Co-Scribe of A Course in Miracles, by Carol M. Howe.

Finally, read this:

Ken Wapnick on the ACIM Manuscript History & Controversy

http://www.facimoutreach.org/qa/questions/ACIM_Manuscript_History.pdf

Thank you for listening!
    Ps. After posting the above piece to my ACIM Wordpress blogsite, Understandacim.com, I received the following noteworthy response:
    "Thank you for this article. I also absorbed the information when it came across my consciousness. I looked at it with an open mind, but it struck me as disingenuous considering the people who are making such claims seem to have never read the Course. In the meantime, science seems to be validating some of the major themes of the course which fly in the face of people claiming it is mind control. The nature of our illusionary universe, how our mind creates our reality, and how things in the "past" can be changed by events of the future. NOTE: In practicing true forgiveness, the Holy Spirit collapses space and time as we forgive. I like to call it "quantum forgiveness".

https://phys.org/news/2017-01-reveals-substantial-evidence-holographic-universe.html

https://www.scienceandnon-duality.com/experiment-shows-future-events-affect-the-past/

http://www.collective-evolution.com/2014/11/11/consciousness-creates-reality-physicists-admit-the-universe-is-immaterial-mental-spiritual/

Why would the CIA set up a mind control system that brings practitioners a deep loving internal peace, that betters their lives in so many ways? When I'm at peace I don't overreact, I'm discerning and focused. The CIA loves chaos, they don't want people who will think calmly and rationally in situations they want to control. Anyone who looks at their documented history of mind control programs will see this. Nice try Ego!"

Appendix B

A Response To The Circle Of Atonement's Interpretation Of A Course In Miracles

I would like to keep this short and sweet. Not, mind you, because this is not complicated – it is, or so it seems – but because I feel there is a way of seeing these issues in a way that will make simple sense of it all.

I assume that most reading this are already familiar with the work of the Circle and their arguments for a different interpretation of ACIM than that put forth by Ken Wapnick (as set forth in their book *One Course, Two Visions*, as well as on their website). I would not go so far as to assume, however, that you have read this entire book that sits before you right now, though if you have, you probably already can presume what my thoughts on this might be.

Essentially what I will say is that everybody's right. It's like that old joke (already noted above) about the wise-foolish judge who is presiding over a case...

The prosecution makes their case and rests. The judge jumps up and says, *"You know, you are so right!"*

Then the defense makes their case and rests. Again the judge jumps up and exclaims, *"You know what? You're right, too!"*

And finally, the judge's wife hits him over the head with his gavel and says, *"You fool! They can't both be right!"*

The judge just nods thoughtfully and says:
"And you know, dear, you're right, too!"

So... Ken Wapnick was right on when he said that the Course is at essence a radical non-dualistic teaching that uses dualistic and often poetic/metaphorical language to compassionately and gently lead us out of the hell that our identification with the ego has led us into. As such, the

Course is not to be taken literally in most places, it's rich with metaphor, rife with poetically pregnant allusion. You know that Guns 'N' Roses album, *Use Your Illusion*? Well, Jesus is not only telling us in so many words to use our **illusion**, but he is using his ***allusion*** with all get out to get his pointed and poignant point across. And as I said earlier, it is my strong sense that Ken understood all of this not only intellectually, but through his direct experience.

And Robert Perry et al are correct in questioning one very basic point: In Heaven, will there be any sense of individuality, because the Course does seem to suggest this in various places? In other words, is there any sense of "personhood" that is yet still persistent, even in Heaven?

Now, in one sense, and it is this sense that I believe Ken was correct, the answer to this question is a categorical **NOT!!** How can there be any sense of individuality in a non-dual Heaven? When everything is one, it's one, and so *so long* and bye bye separate selfhood. And the one who wants to have their proverbial heavenly cake and eat it, too, is just one who is still afraid of losing his prized individuality – he has an authority problem!

But perhaps there is something to the idea that it could be, paradoxically, both: That waking up from the dream means both realizing that separate selfhood is an illusion/delusion, and that somehow, just somehow, everything is still right there! Everything, that is, minus the pain, hatred, fear, shame, guilt, separate interests, etc. Perhaps it truly is a state of "one in many, and many in one," or of "all in one, one in all"?

Now, don't get me wrong (or, as Yogi Berra said, *right* :), I do take the Course literally when it says that God does not have a body, and that there are no bodies (nobody) in Heaven. It's just that the great I AM might also somehow be a *We Are*…

In short, I'm trying to make a case for a "both/and" perspective (however helpful or not, I don't know), and I'm doing this on the basis of my own direct experience, my own revelations of the Reality beyond the veil of illusion. And those revelations have suggested that the state of Union somehow includes All in the One and One in the All. And this makes sense if you consider that if there truly is no cruelty in God (a metaphor!), that one does not at all need to be "cruel to be kind," then God would not will (another metaphor!) that you just completely "disappear" into an abstract Oneness at the end of your journey (yet another metaphor!).

Of course, and this is a point that Ken has made time and again, because the ego is being gently undone, by the time you get there, you will be well-prepared for the "surprise" (as Jesus calls it in the Course) that awaits. You will not fear that final dissolution/dis-illusion, because you will have already loosened all of your ties to this world and to the wanting to be "special" and your own authority – how we got here in the first place!

So to make a possibly long theological discussion shorter and sweeter, let's just say that the jury's still out on this one, as it is with all theological/philosophical debates. Seek within and ye shall find the answer waiting there.

And my final word: Stick with the Source – the Course – and Ken Wapnick as the most reliable guide. And a funny one, too! :)

Ps. An Addendum…

I trust the following statement will be "truly helpful" to some of you…

The Course is a unique and complete spiritual teaching, one that cannot be found anywhere else. Yes, there are similarities and parallels in other teachings, but they are still not the Course. The Course is the Course.

So we need only stay "on course" here to get to the experience that the Course in pointing to, the Holy Instant, which is the recognition that what Jesus is sharing with us is, in fact, the truth.

This means that we need not seek elsewhere, and in fact, mixing the Course with other teachings can confuse things. And this includes the teachings of ACIM teachers themselves, or books based on the Course, including other "channeled" messages that claim to be the further revelations of Jesus or the Holy Spirit.

I have been sharing that the one teacher of the Course that I would start with and continually defer to in your own process, is Ken Wapnick. Was Ken always right? Maybe, maybe not. Is he the easiest to listen to? Perhaps not always so. Are there some in the Course community who sometimes radically disagree with him? There are, yes. Nonetheless, Ken understood and was able to convey the Course like no one else, and there is most certainly a very good reason why he was the one chosen to do the great work that he did.

So to keep this short, the message here is that if you've been drawn to the Course, please consider really doing just the Course exclusively and thoroughly, and just see what that does for you. I realize we all have a fear of doing this, of doing just one thing to the exclusion of others, but remember that the Course is here to help us get beyond all fear. And this is possible, as Jesus tells us again and again, we need but take his hand.

Thank you for listening, and trusting…

Thought it also might be helpful to add that what I wrote is not to in any way negate any other teacher or teaching, but just to highlight the fact that we have before us a master teaching that is sufficient unto itself. All prior teachings on our spiritual journey brought us to this point, and so gratitude for those other teachings is in order. At this point, however, we can lovingly let go of any and all other paths, beautiful and wise as they might be. It would only be the desire to be delayed and waylaid that would keep us from going all the way, with the Course as our guide.

Appendix C

22 Core Teachings of A Course in Miracles

[Please Note: What follows is a blog piece I wrote early on in my study of the Course some 5 years ago. Even then, I was attempting to draw parallels between the Course and eastern wisdom, particularly that of the Hindu yoga tradition. I've decided to include it here mainly because it represents what I thought was most important early on in my exploration of ACIM, so perhaps other newcomers will find it helpful, too.]

This is not the Course, not even close. The Course presents a whole system of practical metaphysics that requires repeated application to truly be effective and undo the ego.

These quotes really must be read in context to get the bigger picture and fullness of what's being expressed.

Yet they will still be helpful as a reminder for some and perhaps as an inspiration for others to actually begin to take a deeper look at the Course.

Personally, I would not have taken A Course in Miracles that seriously if I hadn't first read Gary Renard's *Disappearance of the Universe*, which really helps to clarify and simplify its message.

I still don't know how I feel about how Gary's book came about, yet as of now I have decided that it doesn't matter, it's the message that counts, and more important even, the practical application of the message.

So how is all of this connected to Yoga? Well, Yoga means "Union," and the highest philosophy of India, Advaita Vedanta, is the philosophy of Non-duality, which is essentially what the Course teaches, though with the added teaching of "true forgiveness" as given by Christ.

My teachers all held Jesus to be a great avatar (ascended master come to earth), perhaps the greatest ever.

I can see this now.

In any case, great minds think alike, and after all, as the Course says, there is only one mind anyway.

So let's not get caught up in superficial differences of "oh, that's Christian" and "that's Hindu," because it's really all one.

*

∞∞∞∞∞∞∞∞

Separating The Real From The Unreal

1) *"Nothing real can be threatened.*
Nothing unreal exists.
Herein lies the peace of God."

(Main message of the Course, from the Introduction)
[Compare with Shankarcharya's classic statement of Advaita Vedanta:
brahma satyam jagan mithya
jivo brahmaiva napara
Brahman [God] is the Reality, the universe is an illusion,
The living being is Brahman [God] alone, none else.

OM ASATOMA SADGAMAYA ~ *"Lead us from the unreal to the real."*
(ancient Sanskrit mantra)

The Course is a form of Jnana Yoga, which is the path of mentally separating the eternal from the non-eternal, until all that is left is eternity, the eternal peace of God.
"To mean you want the peace of God is to renounce all dreams." ~ *ACIM*
The Gospel of Rock: http://www.youtube.com/watch?v=oP6W1MaxJLI

APPENDICES

Removing The Barriers To Love

2) * *"The search for love is but the honest searching out of everything that interferes with love."* *

*"The course does not aim at teaching the meaning of love, for that is beyond what can be taught.
It does aim, however, at removing the blocks to the awareness of love's presence, which is your natural inheritance."*
(ACIM, from the Introduction)
"Your task is not to seek for love, but merely to seek and find all the barriers within yourself that you have built against it." ~ ACIM (not Rumi)
Commentary: This is all the process of yoga is – Peeling the onion, going back to union, to the One Love that we are… what we call "God." The Course calls this "undoing the ego."
http://www.undoing-the-ego.org/index-ute.html
The Gospel of Rock: http://www.youtube.com/watch?v=Kb9P8BLipqo

The World Is An Illusion

3)* *"There is no world!
This is the central thought the course attempts to teach.
Not everyone is ready to accept it, and each one must go as far as he can let himself be led along the road to truth…"* *

"The world you see is an illusion of a world. God did not create it, for what He creates must be eternal as Himself. Yet there is nothing in the world you see that will endure forever." ~ ACIM
"No one can escape from illusions unless he looks at them, for not looking is the way they are protected." ~ ACIM
"There is nothing outside you." ~ ACIM
Einstein: A human being is a part of a whole, called by us _universe_, a part limited in time and space. He experiences himself, his thoughts and

feelings as something separated from the rest... a kind of optical delusion of his consciousness.
This delusion is a kind of prison for us, restricting us to our personal desires and to affection for a few persons nearest to us.
Our task must be to free ourselves from this prison by widening our circle of compassion to embrace all living creatures and the whole of nature in its beauty."
***Will you bring truth to your illusions,
or your illusions to truth?***

Row Row Row Your Boat...Life is but a dream.
The Gospel of Rock: http://www.youtube.com/watch?v=ZW8TlrYhBxk

A Course In Mind Training

*4) * "This is a course in mind training.
An untrained mind can accomplish nothing." **

"One of the goals of the Course is to train your mind so the time will come when instead of judging automatically, you will forgive automatically."
~ *The Disappearance of the Universe*

But for most of us, this is a long, difficult and quite involved process!...
***"And now he must attain a state that may remain impossible to reach for a long, long time.
He must learn to lay all judgment aside, and ask only what he really wants in every circumstance."*** ~ ACIM

Commentary: The Yoga Sutras recommends constant practice and non attachment as the way to stilling the mind and awakening from the dream. It also says that we can get there faster with more intense practice. The paradox is that time is an illusion and that whenever we get there, in whatever dream lifetime, is at a time beyond time anyway! More Yoga Wisdom: "Make the mind your servant and not your master."
"The truth is simple, but it's not easy."

"Get with De-program."
The Gospel of Rock: http://www.youtube.com/watch?v=TSIajKGHZRk

Getting To The Root Of The Problem

5) * *"This is a course in cause and not effect.
Therefore, seek not to change the world,
but choose to change your mind about the world."* *

"The ego made the world as it perceives it, but the Holy Spirit, the reinterpreter of what the ego made, **sees the world as a teaching device for bringing you home.»** ~ *ACIM*
Compare: "You can't change the world, you can only change yourself."
"Be the change you wish to see in the world." ~ Gandhi
"Your own Self-realization is the greatest service you can render the world." ~ Sri Ramana Maharishi
Commentary: Putting yourself at "Cause" means that you take 100% responsibility for everything. There is no more allowance for blame or victimhood. Cosmetic or band-aid approaches will only work for a time; what we are really seeking is Cosmic Change, and that can only come from going to the root cause of the problem in our own mind and choosing to see it as Spirit sees it, which is that it is nothing.
Gospel of Rock: http://www.youtube.com/watch?v=vS-16m1OhtA

Our Only Choice: Fear, Or Love

6) * *"Fear and love are the only emotions of which you are capable."* *
"Fear binds the world. Forgiveness sets it free." ~ *ACIM*
"The presence of fear is a sure sign that you are trusting in your own strength." ~ *ACIM*
"Perfect love casts out fear." ~ *Jesus (Bible and ACIM)*
If fear exists, then there is not perfect love." ~ *ACIM*
"It is but your thoughts that bring you fear." ~ *ACIM*

"There is nothing to fear." ~ *ACIM*
"You cannot serve two masters." ~ *Jesus*
Ram Dass: "Live from your soul, not your ego."
Roosevelt: "There is nothing to fear but fear itself." –> and even that's **NOTHING** to fear!]
The Gospel of Rock: http://www.youtube.com/watch?v=o4fWN6VvgKQ

Guilt & Suffering Are Unreal

8) * *"The guiltless mind cannot suffer."* *

Commentary: According to Jesus' message in the Course, he was crucified, but did not suffer. He realized that he was guiltless and so were his apparent persecutors. He also realized he was not his body. So looking at our guilt and really seeing it for what it is, is a crucial part of the Course's practice.

A similar process of releasing our "stuff" happens in yoga. At first the practice of yoga can be very challenging, even torturous. Over time, it becomes easier and easier as blockages are released from the body-mind and self-love comes more naturally and consistently. For me personally, yoga and exercise in general have become nearly effortless and fun. Self-love is more of a constant whereas before guilt and self-hatred were more the norm.

Compare: **Buddha's 4 Noble Truths:**
The four noble truths are:[a]
The truth of *dukkha* (suffering, anxiety, dissatisfaction)
The truth of the origin of *dukkha*
The truth of the cessation of *dukkha*
The truth of the path leading to the cessation of *dukkha*.

The Course presents but one path among many that lead one from suffering (the world as a "vale of tears") to the end of all fears and all tears.

The Gospel of Rock: http://www.last.fm/music/Bob+Dylan/_/Watching+The+River+Flow

The Illusion Of Separation

9) * "A sense of separation from God is the only lack you really need correct."
*

"The truth about you is so lofty that nothing unworthy of God is worthy of you.
Choose, then, what you want in these terms, and accept nothing that you would not offer to God as wholly fitting for Him." ~ ACIM
"You dwell not here, but in eternity." ~ ACIM
"We are here to awaken from the illusion of separation." ~ Ram Dass (and other spiritual teachers)
The Golden Rule: *"Whatever you wish that others would do to you, do also to them, for this is the Law and the Prophets." ~ Jesus*
Commentary: The word "individuality" has the word "duality" in it.
The Gospel of Rock: http://www.youtube.com/watch?v=_tiOMu_Bf8Q

Forgiveness

10) * "Forgiveness is the healing of the perception of separation." *

Commentary: Ultimately, forgiveness is an illusion, because we're forgiving something that's not there…It's purpose is to lead you to God, but it's not of God.
Unlike all other illusions, it leads you away from separation and not towards it. The Course calls it a "happy fiction."
"This is not a course in philosophical speculation, nor is it concerned with precise terminology.
It is concerned only with Atonement, or the correction of perception.
The means of the Atonement is forgiveness." ~ ACIM
"He who would not forgive must judge, for he must justify his failure to forgive." ~ ACIM
"There is a simple way to find the door to true forgiveness, and perceive it open wide in welcome.

When you feel you are tempted to accuse someone of sin in any form, do not allow your mind to dwell on what you think he did, for that is self-deception. Ask instead, "Would I accuse myself of doing this?" ~ ACIM
"Forgiveness allows love to return to my awareness." ~ ACIM
"God does not forgive for he has never condemned." ~ ACIM
Jesus: "Judge not lest ye be judged."
"Let he who is without sin cast the first stone."
"That which is hateful to you do not do to your fellow man." etc.
[**Commentary** : All is forgiven – AND there is *nothing* to forgive!]
The Gospel of Rock: http://www.youtube.com/watch?v=Xezg3z5IE8I

Non-Judgment

*11) * "The ego cannot survive without judgment." **

"You have no idea of the tremendous release and deep peace that comes from meeting yourself and your brother totally without judgement." ~ ACIM
"Judgment and love are opposites. From the one comes all the sorrows of the world. From the other comes the peace of God.
Judgment will bind my eyes and make me blind." ~ ACIM
The Golden Rule: "Whatever you wish that others would do to you, do also to them, for this is the Law and the Prophets." ~ Jesus
'Truly, I say to you, as you did it to one of the least of these my brothers, you did it to me.'" ~ Jesus
"Judge not, that you be not judged. For with the judgment you pronounce you will be judged, and with the measure you use it will be measured to you. Why do you see the speck that is in your brother's eye, but do not notice the log that is in your own eye? Or how can you say to your brother, 'Let me take the speck out of your eye,' when there is the log in your own eye?" ~ Jesus
"Fire the Judge and hire the Witness."
("As God is my Witness." :)

"Non-judgment day is at hand!" ~ Swami Beyondananda

Commentary: Again, taking the Golden Rule to its most absurd conclusion: Loving our brother/sister as ourself because they are ourSelf!

The Gospel of Rock: http://www.youtube.com/watch?v=SwbGjzF3mB0

...and it's all in your mind!

Total Peace Of Mind

*12) * "There are no small upsets." *
They are all equally disturbing to my peace of mind."*

Commentary: Having a bad hair day is just as needing of forgiveness as having a bad hair life! Or if you're bald, a bald hair day! Forgive it all! All is Forgiven…AND There Was Nothing Ever to Forgive.
[Mr. Smiley's Recommended Mantra ~ "It just doesn't matter, it just doesn't matter, it just doesn't matter…"]
The Gospel of Rock: http://www.youtube.com/watch?v=-cTYhY3NUWE

The Master Teacher Leads By Example

*13) * "To teach is to demonstrate." **

"As you teach, so shall you learn." ~ ACIM
"I am among the ministers of God." ~ ACIM
"The ego does not want to teach everyone all it has learned, because that would defeat its purpose." ~ ACIM
"There is nothing you say that contradicts what you think or do; no thought opposes any other thought;

no act belies your word; and no word lacks agreement with another. Such are the truly honest." ~ ACIM

"Be the Change." "Lead by example." "Walk your talk." "Practice what you preach." – And forgive yourself if you don't! Because you probably won't! Gandhi ~ "Happiness is when what you think, what you say, and what you do are in Harmony…Always aim at complete harmony of thought and word and deed."

The Gospel of Rock: http://www.youtube.com/watch?v=-4GZFbCqx18

Okay, that was a joke, try this one instead:

http://www.youtube.com/watch?v=1Qd-fAnHjPg

Miracles Come As Fear Is Undone

14) * *"Each (of us is) a miracle of love."* *

"Miracles arise from a miraculous state of mind, or a state of miracle-readiness." ~ ACIM
"There is nothing my holiness cannot do." ~ ACIM
"Miracles mirror God's eternal love." ~ ACIM
"The miracle is the only device in your immediate disposal for controlling time…
The miracle substitutes for learning that might have taken thousands of years." ~ ACIM

[**Commentary:** Ram Dass' book about his guru, Neem Karoli Baba, is called "Miracle of Love."

The Gospel of Rock: http://www.youtube.com/watch?v=g26e89xV1HU

Health & Sickness Start In The Mind

15) * *"Sickness is of the mind and has nothing to do with the body."* *

*"Sickness is but another name for sin.
Healing is but another name for God.
The miracle is thus a call to Him."* ~ ACIM

«*The acceptance of sickness as a decision of the mind, for a purpose for which it would use the body, is the basis of healing. And this is so for healing in all forms.*» ~ ACIM

The Gospel of Rock: http://www.youtube.com/watch?v=Oy625sZAHN8

Real Abundance Is Not Of This World

16) * *"You have sought first the Kingdom of Heaven, and all else has indeed been given you."* *

"For what does it profit a man to gain the whole world and forfeit his life?" ~ Jesus

Commentary: If abundance comes, let it be a "perk of the job" so to speak, and then use it to further the work you are doing. The Course essentially is telling us to make the world and the things of the world nothing, because they are. If we are fervently seeking them and praying for them, then we are missing the point.

Gospel of Rock: http://www.youtube.com/watch?v=7tGuJ34062s

True Prayer Is Remembrance

("The only true prayer is for forgiveness.")

17) * *"The secret of true prayer is to forget the things you think you need."* *

"I once asked you to sell all you have and give to the poor and follow me. This is what I meant: If you have no investment in anything in this world, you can teach the poor where their treasure is. The poor are merely this who have invested wrongly, and they are poor indeed!" ~ ACIM

"Not my will, but Thy will." Not the ego's script, but the Holy Spirit's.

Commentary: In yoga, meditation is generally considered a more beneficial practice than prayer. There is a saying, "When you pray, you talk to God. When you meditate, God talks to you." Generally we only really pray unless we're in a crisis, or if we really need something. This type of prayer is coming from a place of fear, not love. Rather than speaking to God of our needs and wants (which is generally quite egoic), we would do better to learn to deeply listen to what is already right there in our heart. And when we do, we will remember that we already have and are everything.

Sex & Sense Pleasures Will Never Satisfy

18) * *"This course does not attempt to take from you the little that you have."*
*

"The special relationships of the world are destructive, selfish, and childishly egocentric. Yet, if given to the Holy Spirit, these relationships can become the holiest things on earth—the miracles that point the way to the return to Heaven.
The world uses its special relationships as a final weapon of exclusion and a demonstration of separateness.
The Holy Spirit transforms them into perfect lessons in forgiveness and in awakening from the dream.
Each one is an opportunity to let perceptions be healed and errors corrected. Each one is another chance to forgive oneself by forgiving the other. And each one becomes still another invitation to the Holy Spirit and to the remembrance of God." ~ ACIM

"A dream is nothing, and sex is nothing.
But I wouldn't recommend that you turn to your partner after making love and say, "That was nothing."
~ The Disappearance of the Universe

"Let not their form deceive you. Idols are but substitutes for your reality." ~ ACIM
First Commandment (Book of Exodus): *"I am the Lord thy God… Thou Shalt Have No Other Gods [Idols] Before Me."*
What other false idols do we have?
The Gospel of Rock: http://www.youtube.com/watch?v=fY9-98tkfvg

There Is No Death

19) * *"Death is the central dream from which all illusions stem."* *

"If death is real for anything, there is no life. Death denies life, but if there is reality in life, death is denied. No compromise in this is possible." ~ ACIM
"Death is the symbol of the fear of God." ~ ACIM
"God did not make death because He did not make fear. Both are equally meaningless to Him." ~ ACIM
"Are you afraid to find a loss of self in finding God?" ~ ACIM
"The reality of death is firmly rooted in the belief that God's Son [you] is a body." ~ ACIM
"Without the idea of death, there is no world. All dreams will end with this one." ~ ACIM
The Gospel of Rock: http://www.youtube.com/watch?v=mmASTC7wR6U

We Are Already Enlightened

20) * *"Enlightenment is but a recognition, not a change at all."* *

Commentary: Other names in the Course for Enlightenment are "Resurrection," "Salvation," "Atonement," "Awakening."
"Your resurrection is your reawakening."
"Before enlightenment – chop wood, carry water. After enlightenment – chop wood, carry water." ~ **Zen Saying**

Commentary: The "Son of God" which the Course so often mentions is none other than…You! You are the One you've been waiting for! You are Christ! (Or if you prefer, Mary!) And so is everyOne else, too! So…we are the One we've been waiting for! And this is a recognition or remembrance of what is and has always been the case, it's just that our mind has been clouded by guilt so we could not see the sun that is always shining.
The Gospel of Rock: http://www.youtube.com/watch?v=ELRBvDz6YgU

The Course In Miniature

21) "I must have decided wrongly, because I am not at peace.
I made the decision myself, but I can also decide otherwise.
I want to decide otherwise, because I want to be at peace.
I do not feel guilty, because the Holy Spirit
will undo all the consequences of my wrong decision if I will let Him.
I choose to let Him, by allowing Him to decide for God for me."
~ Text, Chapter 5

COMMENTARY: This passage is sometimes called "the Course in miniature." The point is that we only see what we want to see, and what we want to see – peace or conflict – depends on the degree to which we have taken the ego seriously or not. Trouble is, most of us are so much in the throes of the ego that we don't even realize that we always have a choice of what to see. This is why we generally need a compassionate guide (like Jesus in the Course) to point the way, to show us what our choices really are. And as we choose Spirit over the ego, we will see peace more and more and more, and we will gradually choose that and bear witness to that and understand that what we see is up to us.

The Gospel of Rock: **http://www.youtube.com/watch?v=piOlKl7hLhA**

APPENDICES

* God Is. *

22) "Life has no opposite, for it is God. "

"Life and death seem to be opposites because you have decided death ends life. Forgive the world, and you will understand that everything that God create cannot have an end, and nothing He did not create is real.
In this one sentence is our Course explained.
In this one sentence is our practicing given its one direction.
And in this one sentence is the Holy Spirit›s whole curriculum specified exactly as it is.» ~ *ACIM*
«We say ‹God is,› and then we cease to speak, for in that knowledge words are meaningless.
There are no lips to speak them, and no part of mind sufficiently distinct to feel that it is now aware of something not itself. It has united with its Source.
And like its Source Itself, it merely is." ~ *ACIM*
"You shall love the Lord your God with all your heart and with all your soul and with all your mind. This is the great and first commandment. And a second is like it: You shall love your neighbor as yourself. On these two commandments depend all the Law and the Prophets." ~ **Jesus**
Commentary: Funny how we need these big books to tell us "God Is" and all else, including all of the words, are ultimately meaningless. It's a work in process, the lifetime plan...
The Gospel of Rock: http://www.youtube.com/watch?v=KWhMyOs0pCQ

(22+ = 23) Come on, there had to be one more, the most important one!

Laughter!

* *"Into eternity, where all is one, there crept a tiny, mad idea,*

*at which the Son of God remembered not to laugh.
In his forgetting did the thought become a serious idea,
possible of both accomplishment and real effects."* *
[ACIM, T-27.VIII.6:2-3]
"Laugh at the ego and be free!"

COMMENTARY:
Trivia Question: Where does Jesus laugh in the Gospels?
I don't seem to recall Jesus ever laughing or smiling – let alone singing or dancing. Gotta watch the movie "Godspell" for that! But we do have Jesus crying as in the shortest verse in the Gospels: "Jesus Wept," which is just a little shorter perhaps than the saying of Jesus in the Gospel of Thomas (a non-canonical, Gnostic Gospel), "Be Passerby."
The point being that this "Cosmic Joke" happened (or seemed to happen) because the idea of separation was taken seriously rather than laughed at as just silly. So the way back must be through not taking anything seriously, but making light of everything.

The Gospel of Rock: http://www.youtube.com/watch?v=jHPOzQzk9Qo

More "Gospel" Music
CAN MUSIC SAVE YOUR MORTAL SOUL?
http://www.youtube.com/watch?v=uAsV5-Hv-7U
http://www.youtube.com/watch?v=i4s9wVRIXeU
http://www.youtube.com/watch?v=F6TFW1F6oY0
http://www.youtube.com/watch?v=V4SqDx1vi4c

"*This is all a dream we dreamed one afternoon long ago.*"
You Also Might be Interested in the "Gospel of Rock" (Ministry of Rock) blog I was doing for awhile…
http://ministryofrock.wordpress.com/2007/11/18/stairway-to-heaven-meaning/
(The above link to a piece on the deeper meaning of Stairway to Heaven was the most commented on.)

Appendix D

Awakening to Your Life's Purpose Conscious Intention Setting for Shamanic Journeying

My intention: to consciously hold space for your loving re-connection to and healing of body, mind and spirit. For this to be of most use to both of us, please be as honest and detailed as possible in your answers, *yet also please note that all questions are optional and your responses will be held in strict confidence.*

A little bit about my background & intentions in doing this work:

By this moment in time, I have had the opportunity to use the Amazonian plant spirit medicine known as ayahuasca many times.

Some of those times were very challenging for me, and others were not, but all were extremely insightful and powerful. I credit ayahuasca with some of the most profound awarenesses and experiences I have ever had in my life and spiritual quest.

Coming out of the study of religion and spirituality and general (I have a BA in Philosophy and an MA in Comparative Religion from the University of Pennsylvania), and the yoga tradition in particular, I was always a seeker after mystical experiences that could help me to better understand the nature of reality. Ayahuasca provided this for me, yet it in itself was not enough. I recognized that there still needed to be something to help me make sense of all that was coming through to me on the path of medicine work. What has helped me more than anything are the non-dual teachings of both the yoga tradition (advaita vedanta), and the teachings of A Course in Miracles.

So in a sense, the guidance I offer is more that of a yogi than a traditional shaman. Yes, we will make sure that we are safe and protected and not in any danger of malevolent entities of any kind, and at the same time we will be using the medicine to assist us in accessing our true Self, that which can never be hurt by anything. In other words, while acknowledging our fears, we will also be seeking to go beyond our fears to a space of pure love. We might just touch that placeless place together but for a moment, yet we will have touched it and that will make all the difference.

I have held ceremonial space on a number of occasions and there has never been an issue with any of the participants. You will be in good hands and there is nothing for which you need to be concerned. Please know that it is completely normal to feel some anxiety and nervousness about this experience; even people who have been doing this for some time still feel nervous!

Preparing for Ceremony

It is generally a good idea to prepare yourself physically, mentally, and spiritually for work with ayahuasca. On the physical level, getting enough rest, exercise, and pure, healthy food are highly recommended. General foods to avoid are excessive sugar, spices, meat, alcohol, drugs, and certain prescription medications. A vegetarian and possibly even vegan diet might be helpful. It is recommended to do this for at least 5 days before ceremony and 5 days after. There really are no hard and fast rules, just guidelines. In the end, you will receive whatever you need to from the experience.

On a mental level, keeping your mind free of worry, anxiety and stress and being focused on what you do want will be helpful. In general, observe your mind and replace negative thoughts and attitudes with positive ones. Remember that you are responsible for your peace of mind and that you can always choose to see things differently.

Spiritual practices can be very helpful at this time, too. These include avoiding company that can disturb your peace of mind, and this includes people, situations, and media. Maintaining silence and/or practicing meditation can also help. Deep breathing is especially helpful as it can also be a very powerful ally in ceremony. Yoga in general is recommended.

The questions provided below will also help you in getting into the proper frame of mind for this experience. Please consider this to be an important part of your preparation.

Basics

NAME _____
_____ DOB _____ / _____ / _____
EMAIL _____
PHONE _____
CITY _____
STATE _____
COUNTRY _____
GENDER _____
OCCUPATION _____
HEIGHT _____
WEIGHT _____
DOSHA (if known) _____
CITY OF BIRTH _____
EXACT TIME OF BIRTH _____
TODAY'S DATE _____

Conscious Intake Form

Questions to Assist You In Clarifying Your Intentions...

On a scale of 1-10, how much peace/ contentment do you experience in your life?
1 2 3 4 5 6 7 8 9 10

On a scale of 1-10, how much stress do you experience in your life?
1 2 3 4 5 6 7 8 9 10

How would you describe your current mental/ emotional state?

Are there any habitual emotional patterns or addictions that you currently struggle with?   (i.e. food binging, feelings of shame, drug or alcohol dependancy, toxic relationships, etc.)

Have you experienced any major traumatic events or accumulated stressors recently?

Do you experience any of the following? (Please circle or check.)
o Depression o Insomnia o Anxiety o Panic Attacks o Schizophrenia
o Eating Disorders o Other: _____

What medications, if any, do you currently use?

What are your greatest strengths?

What are your greatest challenges?

What's your story?

What was one of the happiest moments of your life?

What do you love? What are you most passionate about?

Have you ever used a psychoactive substance before? Please list and describe:

Have you ever used a psychoactive substance in a ceremonial or sacramental way before? If so, please describe. How did it help you? How was it not useful to you?

Have you ever used ayahuasca before? If so, when and in what context? Are you seeking to use it again because it did not have the expected/desired effect before, or because you just want to explore it more, or…

What do you currently know about ayahuasca? What is it for YOU? What are your sources of information about it (please be specific if possible)?

From what you know about ayahuasca, what do you hope that it will do for you? Please be as detailed and honest about this as you can.

Would you say that in general you have a high, medium, or low tolerance for "mind-altering" substances?

What are some of your greatest fears and/or phobias? What were some of your greatest fears as a child/young adult, and how did you overcome them? Or would you say you are still working on them?

What currently are you greatest sources of stress, worry, anxiety, and in general, dis-ease? How do you deal with them?

What physical ailments are you currently experiencing? Do you have any chronic pain or issues?

What psychological challenges do you currently deal with? Challenges such as obsessive-compulsiveness, depression, anxiety, etc. What are you doing to treat this?

What religion were you raised as, if any? What religion do you currently adhere to, if any? How did this affect your current understanding of life and spirituality?

What is the meaning of "spirituality" to you, and how would you define "Spirit"? Would you say that you are more spiritual than religious? If so, why? If not, why not?

Have you ever had any significant spiritual experiences? Please describe the most significant one or ones for you, plus how they altered your perception of things.

Do you believe in God or a higher power? What is your definition of God? What feelings do you associate with that word?

Do you currently practice yoga? If so, what does yoga do and mean for you? How would you define the term "yoga"? What do you most appreciate about yoga, and what are your greatest challenges? (Or: List and describe any other spiritual practices that you have engaged with that do not fall under the category "yoga.")

Although I do not view meditation as separate from yoga, let's pretend that it is for a moment. Do you practice meditation? Have you ever? What did you learn from meditating?

If pressed, what would you say happens after we die? If you were to die today, would you feel that you had lived a fulfilling life? Would you have regrets? Unfinished business? People with whom you still want to make amends?

What does the word "forgiveness" mean to you? How important is forgiveness for you? Who do you feel you still need to forgive? Do you find forgiveness challenging at times? Why?

Have you ever been exposed to a non-dual philosophy (the philosophy that there is only One reality) such as found in the Advaita Vedanta tradition of Hindusim and A Course in Miracles? What do these mean to you?

What does the concept of "Oneness" mean to you? What does it mean to say "we are all one"? Have you ever experienced this before? Another way of putting this: Have you ever experienced a state of unconditional love (joy, peace) before? If so, why do you feel it didn't last? How did it affect your life? How does it still affect your life?

Is there anything specific you wish to learn about in our time together?

Do you have any questions for me?

Are you prepared to submit yourself to what may be a challenging experience for you? In other words, are you ready? (You may sign your name to signify assent.)

[Please Note: This is an early intake/outtake form I wrote for a group ayahuasca journey I organized. Here I am answering my own questions...]

1) **Prior to the ceremony, had you ever used any plant medicine or psychedelic substance. If so, please briefly describe how the experience affected you, and whatever you wish to relate about it. How did that experience or experiences affect the approach you took to this experience? How were those experiences similar and how were they different from this one?**

Prior to age 36, I had not done any kind of drug other than MJ a few times. My one experience with that where I actually got off the ground was with a well known ex-DJ for a rock station in Philly. She was taking me to see the Dead at the Spectrum (this was in 2002, I believe), who at that time were calling themselves "The Other Ones." I took some very big hits of her doobie and then we started driving. She had a Kid Rock cd on, the one that begins with the song that goes "Who's in Da House?" Really scary-like. You can imagine what it sounded like stoned. I felt like I was right there in the music. I remember thinking this must have been what music used to sound like when I was younger. By the time we got to the Dead concert, I was getting more and more stoned. We were in these super box seats and at one point I just had to lie down on the floor because I could not sit up. I guess I realized at that point what it's like to be "wasted." I didn't have a very strong desire to do pot again after that, though as a musician I definitely appreciated how it could potentially help you to really focus on the music (there is a youtube video where George Harrison makes that very point.)

In the last few years, I've explored MDMA, San Pedro, mushrooms, and an Ayahuasca analogue known as "Jurema." The MDMA (Ecstasy) I did was a pure form of it, and it effectively took me into a place of what I would call "No Mind." It was pure feeling presence, pure loving presence. It's truly a beautiful, magical experience. I would definitely do it again in the right setting. The only thing about MDMA, which I experienced to some degree, is that the next day (and for some even the next few days), you definitely have a kind of hangover, and some people even get depressed. The reason is due to the fact that to some degree you have exhausted your supply of neurotransmitters. That's why it's good to take supplements with the E so that you can replace those neurotransmitters. I also felt like it really wouldn't be wise to do E too often, especially an older person, because you really do need to recover. All in all, E really taught me what a state of "Pure Presence" might feel like, and so I can kind of gauge my progress.

So after doing E a few times, I decided it might be good to do something natural that would have a similar effect. I had heard that the San Pedro cactus is very similar to E, though it does have a psychedelic component that is missing with E. San Pedro, like Peyote, contains mescaline which gives the visions, but unlike Peyote, San Pedro is legal to buy (just not to cook and ingest). So I ordered some and went about doing this long, somewhat elaborate process of cooking it in a crock pot. I got help from the internet, and from a guy who had done it already many times. When I finally did it, I was at first a bit disappointed because I was expecting more from it. The visions at first didn't mean much to me, and they were coming way too fast anyway. Once the SP really began to take effect, though, the visions became these incredible rainbow geometrical patterns that were absolutely stunning to behold (though of very brief duration). Better than anything I have yet experienced with Ayahuasca. I also experimented with listening to music with headphones on, and that was very much like my experience with MJ – I was right *in* the music. I also felt my entire body "Oming." I was literally vibrating and I heard the "Om" reverberating in my being. All in all, it felt very much like a "third eye" opening experience, and it also gave me insight into what it feels like to be fully present, fully "in the zone." I did it once more and had only the bodily experience without the visionary component. I did a lot of Oming that night and have some neat recordings of some very high powered chanting!

When it comes to ayahuasca, which is what I explored next, a paragraph really is not enough to tell the story. Suffice it to say, that I was so utterly blown away by my first ayahuasca experience that I committed myself to writing a book about it, with the thought that this might just be my life work (i.e., maybe I've finally figured out what I'm going to do be when I grow up :) So if you're really interested, you might just have to wait for the book, but to summarize: Ayahuasca was a shamanic/yoga initiation, the kind that I never had but always wanted. When I was initiated into Kundalini Yoga, I went with the hope that my kundalini would be awakened and I would have some kind of cosmic experience. I saw most everyone else around me having one, but not me. So with ayahuasca I finally had that cosmic experience, and then some. It was actually too much. It scared me. I was actually traumatized by it for at least a month afterwards. At the same time, it was the most incredible thing I had ever experienced. By the time the experience really took off (like the Starship Enterprise :), I felt like I was being hyperdriven through space at warp speed while my body exploded in rainbows of colors. As that was happening there was a part of me thinking that if I didn't understand Alex Grey's artwork before this, I truly did now! Good Lord! I joke about it, but it wasn't funny. It was like I was being reborn – like a death and rebirth experience. Don't ever let anyone tell you that psychedelics are the "easy" way or are "cheating" – it can be very very very challenging work, certainly much much more challenging than any yoga class you'll ever take, even if you were forced to do the Ashtanga 3rd series in a Bikram studio with the heat at 105 degrees :) with no water breaks! So needless to say, I finally had my cosmic experience. And after that, I really felt like: Okay, don't have to do that ever again!

But what's interesting is that I did do it again – 3 more times. Each time was just as cosmic, and with different lessons from each one. Each time I felt like I was dying, each time I felt like I had had enough…I'm not addicted, don't get me wrong; I think "fascinated" is more the word. Absolutely, terrifiably certifiably fascinated. So I went into the Ayahuasca session with PA with a certain sense that the session might be like that. I had not strictly followed a diet in my previous sessions, and this time I did, partly because I wanted to see if there was a difference, partly because I felt like maybe the previous aya sessions wouldn't have been quite so traumatic if I had followed a special diet. I actually still can't say for sure because even though the experience with PA was milder, it might have been due to the fact that we were given a different form of ayahuasca (and the kind I took is known for being one of the most powerful), and a lower dosage. In many ways I liked the fact that it was milder because it was less traumatic, felt better during and after (the other times, it took me a bit to fully recover), and I was actually able to sit still for most of it. On the other hand, I liked the others better because they were more cosmic. Probably closer to what smoking DMT is like, because that gives a very quick and powerful experience.

2) **How would you rate your diet, in general. Please be specific. To what degree did you stay on the suggested diet for this experience? Did you "cheat" a little? What foods were hardest to give up, besides chocolate ;) Did you think being on the diet or not affected this experience in any way?**

I was pretty disciplined about the diet, with a few minor backsliding moments. Definitely chocolate and sugar were the hardest to give up, but I'm really glad I did.

I do feel that chocolate, particularly dark chocolate, is itself a drug, and there's a time and place for it. For example, I've done some of my best yoga ever while "high" on dark chocolate. It's somewhat similar to E in that it brings me into a happy, loving, more sensual state. Yes, I do think that being on the diet this time most likely helped. I can't say how, really, because there are too many other factors involved. If I could do the exact same kind of Ayahuasca after not having kept the diet, maybe I would be able to get a better picture.

3) **Please talk a little bit about the purging. Did you purge, and how much? What did you purge? If you didn't vomit, did you nearly vomit, or have diarrhea? Did the medicine otherwise require you to use the restroom. Did you feel better after the purging? How much of a visionary experience did you have before the purging? How would you rate how strong your stomach is on a scale from**

one to ten, where 0 is never even feel nauseous, and 10 is vomit at the sight of something that looks nasty. If you did purge, did you feel that the purging was more than just a physical purging? Please explain.

I do not vomit easily. Even as a young boy, I hardly ever vomited. I recall getting extremely nauseous one night at an amusement park in Atlantic City (I must have been about 5 or 6), and recall how my mother sat with me out on a bench for a long time, comforting me and telling me to breathe deep. It eventually passed. I don't think I had much of a problem with nausea after that, maybe because I dreaded that feeling so much?

The closest I've ever gotten to vomiting with any of these substances was my first journey with Ayahuasca. It came up so quickly I ran to the toilet. It felt like it was going to come hurtling up, but then it didn't. I waited, but nothing. I would definitely like to explore the phenomenon of vomiting and purging more, because I would really like to know more about how doing it or not affects the experience, and why some people will purge almost immediately while others won't do it until 2 or 3 hours into it, etc.

I do sense that over the years I've built a much stronger constitution via physical activities like running, yoga, weight lifting, gymnastics, rebounding, etc.

4) **How did you relate to the shaman? How did you feel about him, and did you feel a strong connection to him? Did you trust him completely? Did he personally connect with you at any point during the ceremony? How were you affected by his icaros? How important did you feel the icaros were in the ceremony? Would you want to do a ceremony with PA again? Do you feel it would be possible for you or someone to do a productive session with ayahuasca without the guidance of a shaman? Why, or why not?**

As I wrote in my "Journey Report," I did trust PA implicitly initially, but there were moments during the session where I bumped up against some pockets of resistance – doubts, asleepness, other negativity. I can't say that I really felt much of a personal connection from PA at all, and perhaps that's as it should be – he wasn't there to socialize or stroke any egos, he was there just to do his job, and he did it very effectively and efficiently, without much fanfare or showmanship.

I feel that the icaros were very important, though I have a lot of questions about them, like if it matters really what is sung or played, just so long as there is music? Because not all of what PA did was the traditional icaros, some of them were Sanskrit chants (like the Mrtyunjaya mantra), and some were songs in English. R also said that he even once did "The Rainbow Connection" from the first Muppet Movie (!) So that makes me question how important the icaros themselves are to the whole process, whether they are truly essential, or whether it's just that there is music being performed by one who has taken the ayahuasca?

I would do a ceremony with PA again, definitely. In fact, during the ceremony, I was feeling like I wanted to go spend time down in Peru with PA for an extended retreat.

I did have some very amazing, transformational experiences using ayahuasca without the guidance of a shaman. Considering what PA did and didn't do (he didn't give much personal attention or insight into what we were experiencing), I would say that there's no reason why someone couldn't do a very meaningful, rewarding session at home with a friend and some cosmic music. But if there is the opportunity to do both, I would suggest doing both. I don't know that I would recommend doing ayahuasca completely alone, without any social support. Unless you don't mind the prospect of being traumatized for months, years, even lifetimes :) Some can do it, but for most – probably not such a wise idea.

5) **How did being in a large group affect you? Did you appreciate the group energy, or did you wish that there weren't so many people in such a small, enclosed space?**

I thought I would mind that there were so many people, but it really didn't matter because once my eyes were closed I was in my own internal world. Whenever I opened my eyes, it was nice to re-connect with the group energy, and towards the end we all shared some sweet laughs and smiles together. The only thing that concerned me early on was how my movements and "exposure" were being taken by those around me, but most of that was all in my head, lol :)

To someone who is concerned about being in a group, I would say "get over it." It can be looked at as yet another opportunity to humble the ego, to let go and let goddess :)

6) **Did you have difficulty sitting up for 6 hours? Do you think a backjack or something like it would have helped? What did you do when your back got tired? Did you do any yoga stretches? Headstands?**

Sitting that long was definitely a challenge. There were a number of times when I just wanted to get up and stretch my legs a bit. Instead, the most I did was to stretch my legs out on the floor for a stretch, then go back into lotus.

I didn't have my back propped up against anything, so keeping a good straight back sitting posture was another challenge. It always is for me as I tend to slump down (one reason for the "don't back down" message). To counter that, I will sometimes go into "*baddha padmasana*" or bound lotus, which really helps to keep the back straight, but the trade off is that it's difficult to actually meditate like that.

What I found this time, though, was that it got easier to sit as the night progressed. Towards the end, I even got off of the mat I was sitting on as I didn't feel I needed it any more. Being absorbed in the internal experience also certainly helped take my mind off my body, and sometimes it really took no effort to sit with my back straight in lotus. Before that I had been stretching out my legs every so often. It's actually a yogic *sadhana* (discipline) to stay in a given sitting posture like *padmasana* (lotus) or *siddhasana* (adept's pose) for a certain period of time without moving out of it. I found that using ayahuasca was a good way of practicing that.

7) **How did the ayahuasca feel in your body? Was there anything particularly striking about how your body was feeling? What did your head feel like? Have you ever had that feeling before?**

I had a hot/cold sensation in my body, particularly around my hands, which felt all tingly (like after doing the Transformational Breathwork – very similar sensation, might be connected). Some people felt a lot of heat, but I didn't experience that. In my previous experiences with ayahuasca, I had felt much more happening in my body, the most extreme being that I had the sensation that the top of my head was blasting off my body and that I was dying. One individual said she felt herself as if she was an old woman, and I also have had the experience of myself as a very old man on several occasions. I always half-expected to look at myself in the mirror the next day and see a very old man!

This ayahuasca was comparatively mild (or the dose was), and I really felt very little in my body except for the tingling, those internal sounds I would hear that were kind of like gurgling, and an overall sense of well-being, particularly in the second half of the evening, from around 11:30-1:30 am. On previous occasions with ayahuasca, it also took me some time to get back to "normal" afterwards – I felt like it had definitely taken its toll on my body, and I would need some time to rest, recuperate, replenish myself. This time, I actually felt awesome for the next few days, and everything seemed to go smoother and better. It made me feel as though I need to be doing this more often!

8) **Did you feel that this experience was healing for you? Howso? Did you have any physical ailments that are now gone as a result of the experience? Would you recommend this to others as a healing modality?**

I felt the experience was very healing, and not just physically. On a physical level, I felt very cleansed, purified afterward, and that feeling continued for the next several days. Mentally, my mind was clearer and more focused, and my meditations the next several days were much deeper and easier than normal. Some of the participants felt that they had been healed, at least partially. So yes, I would recommend this as a healing modality, both for physical ailments, and perhaps even more for mental dis-ease.

9) **What were the most important personal lessons you learned from this experience? What did the ayahuasca seem to be telling you? Did you receive any direct messages? Please describe in detail any spirit meetings or anything of that sort.**

It basically showed me all the things I need to work on, but it wasn't just destructive – it provided hope. It showed that there really is a clearer, brighter, purer world over the rainbow, beyond the vale/veil of tears & fears. This was a nice reminder of what I already knew. The beauty of the earth plane pales in comparison to the beauty and truth of these other realms of being. The reminder is also that if I could, I would more consciously inhabit these realms while in the body, and guide others to do the same.

No, I didn't meet any spirit beings or have any direct messages from "the beyond," beyond what I already said. The highlights of the whole thing in terms of personal experiences were: The fact that I was spontaneously having "kriyas" – unconscious movements of my body, and voice. This was something I have seen in the Kundalini Yoga group I was in , but never actually experienced myself. The experience is not at all challenging, but actually just blissful. There were also a few times when I spontaneously began to sing or chant. At one point, it seemed that I began to speak in tongues (sounded like Quechua, the Incan language PA was speaking in at points). That was totally cool, but it stopped as soon as I became conscious of it (as did all the other kriyas). From that little experience, I can totally understand how the phenomenon of "xenoglossy" works.

The other thing I will never forget were the moments when I felt like I was inhabiting this rainbow-hued universe where there was no time – it was eternity, no beginning and no end, and the whole of existence, including my individual existence, had always been right there all along. Hard to explain, especially writing this a couple of weeks later.

10) **How did you feel a day later (week, month, year later). Did the experience stay with you? Did it inform your view of yourself and your life and the world, or did it not have too much of an effect on your life? On a scale from 1 to 10… Did the experience inspire you**

to make certain changes in your life? Please explain. Were those changes permanent?

As already noted, I felt very very good for most of the experience, and for at least two days afterward. The experience did stay with me, but it's very subtle. Most people don't retain most of the experience, except as a pleasant memory. What does stay is whatever conscious changes you opt to make in your life, based on the experience.

The question always is: What do I need to do in order to embody this state more and more in my everyday life? Well, one easy way is yoga and meditation. It doesn't cost a lot, except your time and commitment. It's a slower path, but it will ultimately take you to a deeper understanding of consciousness and reality.

All in all, using psychedelics sacramentally, particularly ayahuasca, have without a doubt been one of the most important decisions of my life and has had a profound effect on me. Just as a deep encounter with yoga 12 years ago effected a radical transformation of my consciousness, so now have psychedelics. I would also say that the psychedelics have reminded me of states that I have already experienced in my yoga practice, though early on in my exploration of yoga.

11) **Would you participate in a ceremony like this again? Why, or why not? What would you tell someone who has never done something like this before, someone just like you were before your first ceremony?**

I would absolutely do this again. If I could, I would do it very regularly. But for someone who has not done this before, I would not necessarily recommend it very highly to them, it really would depend on the person. For someone who is on the fence about it, I would say how much it has helped me, and how positive most of the participants were about the experience.

A COURSE IN MIRACLES
....DATE....LESSON....TEXT....

JANUARY

1	1	HOW IT CAME
2	2	WHAT IT IS
3	3	WHAT IT SAYS
4	4	MIRACLES 1-25
5	5	26-50
6	6	7
7	7	8
8	8	11
9	9	12
10	10	13
11	11	15
12	12	17
13	13	19
14	14	21
15	15	23
16	16	24
17	17	27
18	18	28
19	19	31
20	20	33
21	21	36 M-1
22	22	38
23	23	40
24	24	41
25	25	44
26	26	46
27	27	49
28	28	52 M-2
29	29	53
30	30	56
31	31	60

FEBRUARY

1	32	62
2	33	65
3	34	67
4	35	69 M-3
5	36	72
6	37	73
7	38	75
8	39	78
9	40	81
10	41	83
11	42	86 M-4
12	43	88
13	44	91
14	45	91
15	46	96
16	47	99
17	48	100
18	49	103 M-5
19	50	104
20	51	106
21	52	108
22	53	112
23	54	114
24	55	116
25	56	117 M-6
26	57	119
27	58	123
28	59	127
29		

MARCH

1	60	129
2	61	132
3	62	133
4	63	136 M-7
5	64	138
6	65	139
7	66	141
8	67	143
9	68	146
10	69	148
11	70	151 M-8
12	71	155
13	72	157
14	73	160
15	74	163
16	75	166
17	76	168
18	77	171 M-9
19	78	173
20	79	175
21	80	177
22	81	181
23	82	182
24	83	183
25	84	184 M-10
26	85	187
27	86	189
28	87	193
29	88	194
30	89	197
31	90	198

APRIL

1	91	200 M-11
2	92	202
3	93	207
4	94	210
5	95	211
6	96	215
7	97	218
8	98	220 M-12
9	99	223
10	100	225
11	101	227
12	102	229
13	103	233
14	104	236
15	105	237 M-13
16	106	239
17	107	242
18	108	245
19	109	247
20	110	250
21	111	254
22	112	258 M-14
23	113	260
24	114	262
25	115	266
26	116	270
27	117	270
28	118	272
29	119	274 M-15
30	120	279

MAY

1	121	282
2	122	285
3	123	287
4	124	289
5	125	291
6	126	293 M-16
7	127	296
8	128	301
9	129	304
10	130	306
11	131	309
12	132	312
13	133	314 M-17
14	134	317
15	135	320
16	136	322
17	137	324
18	138	327
19	139	330
20	140	332 M-18
21	141	334
22	142	337
23	143	341
24	144	345
25	145	347
26	146	351
27	147	352 M-19
28	148	354
29	149	352
30	150	362
31	151	365

JUNE

1	152	367
2	153	370
3	154	372 M-20
4	155	375
5	156	378
6	157	360
7	158	382
8	159	364
9	160	388
10	161	390 M-21
11	162	393
12	163	398
13	164	402
14	165	404
15	166	406
16	167	407
17	168	412 M-22
18	169	416
19	170	420
20	171	425
21	172	426
22	173	429
23	174	432
24	175	434 M-23
25	176	436
26	177	439
27	178	441
28	179	445
29	180	445
30	181	448

APPENDICES

JULY
1	182	451 M-24
2	183	454
3	184	456
4	185	459
5	186	461
6	187	465
7	188	467
8	189	468 M-25
9	190	471
10	191	474
11	192	477
12	193	478
13	194	480
14	195	485
15	196	486 M-26
16	197	489
17	198	495
18	199	496
19	200	499
20	201	499
21	202	502
22	203	505 M-27
23	204	507
24	205	509
25	206	511
26	207	514
27	208	518
28	209	518
29	210	520 M-28
30	211	523
31	212	526

AUGUST
1	213	527
2	214	529
3	215	531
4	216	534
5	217	538 M-29
6	218	542
7	219	544
8	220	546
9	221	548
10	222	549
11	223	553
12	224	553 M-30
13	225	558
14	226	560
15	227	562
16	228	565
17	229	568
18	230	572
19	231	574 M-31
20	232	576
21	233	579
22	234	581
23	235	585
24	236	589
25	237	592
26	238	596 M-32
27	239	598
28	240	600
29	241	602
30	242	604
31	243	606

SEPTEMBER
1	244	608
2	245	611 M-33
3	246	612
4	247	614
5	248	615
6	249	617
7	250	619
8	251	622
9	252	625 M-34
10	253	629
11	254	630
12	255	633
13	256	635
14	257	638
15	258	640
16	259	642 M-35
17	260	645
18	261	648
19	262	651
20	263	653
21	264	656
22	265	660
23	266	662 M-36
24	267	656
25	268	1 MANUAL FOR TEACHERS
26	269	3 "
27	270	5 "
28	271	7 "
29	272	9 "
30	273	9 M-37 "

OCTOBER
1	274	10
2	275	11
3	276	12
4	277	12
5	278	13
6	279	14
7	280	14 M-38
8	281	15
9	282	15
10	283	16
11	284	17
12	285	17
13	286	17
14	287	19 M-39
15	288	20
16	289	22
17	290	24
18	291	26
19	292	27
20	293	29
21	294	31 M-40
22	295	33
23	296	36
24	297	38
25	298	40
26	299	44
27	300	47
28	301	49 M-41
29	302	51
30	303	53
31	304	55

NOVEMBER
1	305	58
2	306	60
3	307	62
4	308	64 M-42
5	309	66
6	310	68
7	311	70
8	312	77
9	313	79
10	314	81
11	315	83
12	316	85
13	317	87
14	318	89
15	319	91
16	320	15
17	321	33
18	322	49
19	323	69
20	324	88
21	325	108
22	326	136
23	327	157
24	328	177
25	329	189
26	330	211
27	331	233
28	332	266
29	333	296
30	334	327

DECEMBER
1	335	347
2	336	370 M-46
3	337	393
4	338	407
5	339	410
6	340	412
7	341	414
8	342	416
9	343	417 M-47
10	344	420
11	345	421
12	346	441
13	347	465
14	348	480
15	349	496
16	350	514 M-48
17	351	538
18	352	562
19	353	585
20	354	604
21	355	622
22	356	642
23	357	666 M-49
24	358	324
25	359	327
26	360	143
27	361	218
28	362	320
29	363	434
30	364	83 MANUAL M-50
31	365	91 MANUAL

Once upon a time... Nothing Happened.

THE   END

APPENDICES

In the end, only kindness matters

THE END

Made in the
USA
Middletown, DE